The Book That Breathes New Life

The Book That Breathes New Life

Scriptural Authority and Biblical Theology

Walter Brueggemann

Edited by Patrick D. Miller

Fortress Press
Minneapolis

Cover design: Kevin van der Leek Design Inc.
Interior design: Beth Wright

Library of Congress Cataloging-in-Publication Data
Brueggemann, Walter.
    The book that breathes new life : scriptural authority and biblical theology / Walter Brueggemann.
        p. cm.
    Includes bibliographical references and index.
    ISBN 0-8006-3667-8 (hc : alk. paper)
    1. Bible—Evidences, authority, etc. 2. Bible—Theology. I. Title.
    BS480.B739 2004
    220.1'3—dc22

                                    2004014293

The paper used in this publication meets the minimum requirements of American National Standard for Information Sciences—Permanence of Paper for Printed Library Materials, ANSI Z329.48-1984.

Manufactured in the U.S.A.
09   08   07   06   05   2   3   4   5   6   7   8   9   10

For Tim Simpson

Contents

Editor's Foreword

No person on the North American scene has contributed as much to the enterprise of Old Testament theology as has Walter Brueggemann. That is indicated foremost, of course, in his monumental work *Theology of the Old Testament: Testimony, Dispute, Advocacy*, surely the most creative and original theology of the Old Testament since the work of Gerhard von Rad over forty years ago. This deep commitment to a theological understanding of the Old Testament is not confined, however, to a single volume. It pervades his publications and in fact is never out of sight in his scholarly work. Most of his efforts are directed toward a constructive theological reading of the Old Testament, epitomized in the volume cited above but evident throughout his work. At the same time, he has sought to make his proposals about the Old Testament and how we are to read it and understand it in dialogue with and drawing upon the efforts of many other persons, especially those who have been most influential and constructive themselves. Once again, that is the starting point of his own Old Testament theology, whose first hundred pages review and engage with the history of Old Testament theology and the current scene.

The purpose of this collection of Brueggemann's essays is to bring to the fore a much more extensive critical engagement on his part with the current discussion about the Old Testament, its character, its authority, its theology, and especially its God. These essays have the further value of bringing us up-to-date on Brueggemann's thinking about the issues involved, most of the essays having been published after his *Theology of the Old Testament* and all but two of them within the last decade.

There are two large foci in the collection. One of them is the authority of Scripture, the subject of the first three essays. There Brueggemann comes at this important task with particular attention to the Old Testament but in full awareness that the question of authority is not finally a testamental issue. Nor is it one that is "settled." He comes at the issue from three angles. The first is a sweeping look at the Bible's authority in the postcritical modern world. While Brueggemann could well have provided a helpful overview of that question from a more historical perspective, incorporating early, medieval, and Reformation perspectives, it is not surprising that his focus is on the modern period. While he draws upon the tradition in doing his theological work, his perduring concern is for the contemporary world and how we are to understand it and ourselves in the light of Scripture and how it is that we can claim that the Bible makes sense—to use one of his book titles—in our world and our time. The third essay takes up the question of the authority of Scripture in the context of his own denominational location, sensing that the continuing liveliness of Scripture in the United Church of Christ is at stake. He sees a church that lives between the tendencies to be reductionistic or to be dismissive. Many of us in other denominations may see ourselves in this mirror that he has set before his own church.

Finally, Brueggemann's third angle of approach to the issue of scriptural authority is highly personal. I expect that this essay may capture readers more than any other single piece in this book. Here one learns more about this scholar's own personal theological journal than one can find in any other source. One should not anticipate, however, that the essay is simply a personal reminiscence. On the contrary, the personal reflection leads into several key issues of biblical interpretation and biblical authority. What is especially interesting about the essay may be missed by the casual reader: It was written for a conference on sexual concerns and how one reads Scripture to think about sexual matters. Part of the genius of the essay is the way in which that specific context is directly addressed in a manner that makes the essay of use in totally different contexts as well.

The second and third parts of this collection comprise essays that deal with Old Testament theology, more particularly Brueggemann's own theology and how it fits into the larger scene as well as how it has been received by others who have made large contributions to the field. One can find no better orientation to what has gone on in Old Testament theology for the last several decades than to read through these essays. The discussion reaches back into the critical rebirth of Old Testament theology in the twentieth century in the work of Walther Eichrodt and Gerhard von Rad, whose contributions Brueggemann describes in a highly appreciative manner—note especially his introduction to the most recent edition of von Rad's two-volume *Old Testament Theology*—while at the same time

delineating how the context that shaped their work led to various emphases and approaches that need rethinking in a different time and world. A
larger space is given to more recent endeavors on the part of such scholars
as Brevard Childs, James Barr, Bernhard Anderson, Jon Levenson, and
others. Most of these scholars have not only produced their own theological depictions of the Old Testament, but engaged Brueggemann himself,
sometimes in rather strong critique. In irenic tone, Brueggemann takes
up their critiques, often citing where he thinks they are on target but also
being straightforward when he believes that he has been misread or mis-
understood and, in so doing, clarifying his own theology and its particular
emphases.

The essays in these two parts of the volume return in various ways to
the same theologians, but they are not simply repetitive. In each instance
when Brueggemann takes up a figure he has treated in another context,
he brings a fresh look to the description and analysis that he proposes.
One will see him, in effect, coming back to some of the same persons he
has treated in an earlier essay, but not to say the same thing. Rather, each
look evokes a new discernment. Thus, while it is possible to take any one
of the essays in Part II, say, and find a fairly comprehensive treatment of
the major issues and personalities in the field of Old Testament theology,
it is only in reading from one essay to the other that one encounters the
depth and breadth of Brueggemann's understanding and approach. Part
III then offers a special gift to the reader as it provides a dialogue between
Brueggemann and other figures that has been largely confined to, need I
say hidden, in various journals of one sort or another.

Readers of these essays who think they may have grasped what Brueggemann has to say about the theology of the Old Testament from reading
his magnum opus will find that he is still thinking, still listening, and still
helping us understand the scriptures of Israel and the church at an ever
deeper level.

—Patrick D. Miller

Preface

The matter of biblical authority is ancient, endlessly vexed, and of immense importance in the church. The long history of interpretation is filled with the problematic of scripture, with ample evidence of skewed interpretation and imposed, interested readings, with here and there a glimpse of genuine, disciplined, and responsive listening. Karl Barth's famous phrase, "The strange new world within the Bible," stands as a stunning and remarkable summons to faithful, responsive interpretation, a summons that has echoed from Barth through the twentieth century.[1] But of course, alongside the summons of Barth, scripture interpretation in recent time has been largely enthralled by questions of history, a distinctly modernist agenda from which we are only now beginning to be free.

In Old Testament studies, critical work has aimed at situating texts in their contexts of origin and original meaning, but such critical work has become almost trivial in its determined reconstruction of context that pro tests too much that the text is *reportage* rather than *interpretation*. It is odd that the most conservative interpreters and the radical debunkers of the reliability of the text have made common cause around historical issues, commonly failing to recognize the power of interpretation that permeates the texts and that regularly transposes whatever may have been reportage into interpretation and often into confessional assertion. That the fixation on historical questions has largely overlooked the fingerprints of interpretation is one of the sad and defining issues of twentieth-century interpretation, a practice made even more sad by the collusion of conservative scholastics and erudite liberals, the latter expressed in current form by the so-called "minimalists" in Old Testament study and by the Jesus Seminar in New Testament studies.

Currently the issue of biblical authority, through the work of Brevard Childs, Ronald Clements, and James Sanders, is focused on the interface of *canon and criticism*.[2] Current interpretation has a long legacy of historical criticism that is rooted both in the Reformation perspective of Calvin and in the autonomous reason of the Enlightenment. There is no doubt that such critical perspective is urgent, a matter recognized by Roman Catholicism in 1943 in the papal encyclical, *Divino Afflante Spiritu*, that permitted Roman Catholic biblical scholars to engage in critical questions. It is evident that such critical study has helped to protect the practice of scripture in the church from reductionism of the Bible into church doctrine.

The recent recovery of canon as an interpretive reality has gone far to legitimate in a fresh way the theological intentionality of the text, an intentionality celebrated in a variety of faith communities both Jewish and Christian. Canonical approaches at the end of the twentieth century have revitalized scripture study, lessened the attention given to historical questions, and focused on the character and substance of the text as a voice *from* and voice *to* the community of faith.

Four convictions have grown within me as Old Testament interpretation has changed in recent decades:

1. While it is necessary that faith communities must have normative and more-or-less theoretical formulations of the authority of scripture, in fact such formulations do not carry us very far. Thus, we may have a very high view of scripture with claims of "inspiration" and/or "infallibility." But in truth such formulations are characteristically shaped with reference to particular issues or even with reference to particular texts. After one offers such a formulation that more often serves as a coercive instrument rather than a guideline, what finally counts is the practice of particular texts. And while there may often be agreement on "authority" in general, one is still left with all of the hard work and the tricky hermeneutical issues with reference to particular texts. It is odd and perhaps ironic that in current U.S. church circles, the question of "authority" is mostly prattled about with reference to the issues of sexuality, all the while, to some great extent, indifferent to a variety of other biblical attestations concerning economics, the idolatry of absolute power, the seductions of imperialism, the urging of neighborliness, and so on. Thus we must have and inevitably will have such broad formulations, but our judgment about such formulae will be held in abeyance until we see what happens in the details of textual reading and proclamation.

2. Canonical interpretation is a most important advance in current study. It is nevertheless an open question whether what is termed "canonical" is in fact read out of the textual tradition and the extent to which it is

imposed upon the tradition. It is widely recognized that "canonical" lives close to the "ideological."[3] The first important aspect is that, in current scholarly study, there is a great deal of attention given to ideology found in both the textual tradition itself and in the interpretive tradition that follows, with particular reference to patriarchal categories and sexism, but also tribal ethnicity and the excesses of colonial interpretation.[4]

The twin notions of *canon* and *ideology* of course never occur for the same scholar. On the one hand, those who take a high view of scripture tend to celebrate canon as a mode of true faith and do not ever ask about their own reading, whether it itself may be participation in an ideological venture. On the other hand, those who champion critique of ideology and practice reading "against the grain" of the text tend to regard "canonical" as an interpretive imposition that seeks to shut down inquiry and openness. It is not too much to say that *the appreciation of the text as canon* or *the critique of text as ideology* is in the eye of the beholder, or better, in the practice of the interpreting community, faith-based or aggressively critical. In either case, the status of the interpreter (or interpreting community) is now an important one. What one finds in scripture is to some (large?) extent determined by what one brings to the text, either a *fideistic* or *skeptical* inclination. "Canon" should get no free ride among us, for it has much for which to answer. But the critique of ideology also cannot be taken at face value, for it characteristically reflects a deeply felt interpretive passion that is most often rooted in a woundedness.

3. The purpose and effect of scripture in the Christian faith community is that it is "revelatory," that is, it is in its very character a "revelation." But of course the category of revelation is deeply problematic; some take it to mean the establishment and assertion of a package of propositional certitudes. But of course that is scarcely what is best meant by the Bible as revelation.[5] We are led in a very different direction by Barth's famous phrase, "The strange new world within the Bible." The Bible mediates a "world" by which Barth surely intends a network of relationships and signs that give order and form to lived reality.

The formation of a "world," in the phrasing of Barth, draws us close to current dimensions of imagination concerning the productive power of good rhetoric. Thus Amos Wilder can conclude:

> If we ask a prestigious body of modern critics about the relation of story-world to real world, they will reply that it is a false question. For

one thing the story goes its own way and takes us with it; the storyteller is inventing, not copying. He weaves his own web of happening and the meaning of every part and detail is determined by the whole sequence. We lose our place in the story if we stop to ask what this feature means or refers to outside it.

More important, these students of language will ask us what we mean by "real world." There is no "world" for us until we have named and languaged and storied whatever is. What we take to be the nature of things has been shaped by calling it so. This therefore is also a story-world. Here again we cannot move behind the story to what may be more "real." Our language-worlds are the only worlds we know![6]

Thus the text exhibits for us a "world" we may inhabit to which we had no access until the particular performance of the text. That "world," moreover, is in deep contestation with many other "worlds" that might be on offer from other textual traditions that may also pose as "canonical."

This generative capacity of the text means that words—the force of rhetoric—in the text are to be taken as enactments of fresh reality that are on offer nowhere else. Thus the recent appreciation of rhetoric in scripture is not simply an aesthetic concern, but a recognition that in a "theology of the Word" (which is what we have when we take scripture as revelatory because it is "only" words) utterance through the text gives new reality . . . and thus the "foolishness of preaching."[7]

4. Finally, I belong to a tradition of hermeneutics that eschews literalism. In the phrase often attributed to Reinhold Niebuhr, the perspective has been to "take the Bible seriously but not literally." Such a view, however, misunderstands the term "literal" that is most often taken to mean "historically reliable." The problem with the familiar mantra is that it leaves everything to the discretion of the interpreter, often with great liberties taken beyond the text. But in fact "literal" does not mean "historical." It means, rather, "according to the letter." Thus "serious but not literal" has resulted in an interpretive trajectory that trades on *themes*, *ideas*, and *concepts* within the Bible, but often without specific reference to the text itself.

The new emphasis upon "close reading," attentiveness to rhetorical criticism, and fresh appreciation of Jewish perspectives on interpretation permit a focus on the "literal" that thus invites immense imagination in connecting *the literal* to *the contemporaneity* of the faith community. In a social context of acute polarization, which we now inhabit, attention to the "literal" is one way in which communication across partisan lines is possible. To be sure, such a perspective does not leave unchallenged our most avid ideological commitments, but the foregoing of such passions for the sake of shared attentiveness to the text is surely a high priority in our current scene of interpretation. In the end, scripture is not a contest to see who can prevail in interpretation. It is, rather, an address that offers a "newness" and a "strangeness" that are out beyond all of our pet projects. It is urgent, even if difficult to remember that it is "The word of the Lord" and not our word. The "world" given us in the text, moreover, is not our world but God's new world into which we are ourselves invited as sojourners and eventually as citizens. The offer is a homefulness amid our deep, shared homesickness. It is, however, home on terms other than our own!

—WALTER BRUEGGEMANN

Acknowledgments

A book that consists in extant, older materials requires an important team effort. I am glad to thank Patrick D. Miller for his sustained editorial oversight of the volume, Hal Rast to seeing it through to publication, Tia Foley for bringing it all together in a credible way, and Davis Hankins for a lot of work including preparation of indices.

Over the period of these essays, Mary Miller Brueggemann has been an ongoing conversation partner, intuitively sensing where Calvinist issues are most urgent. I am glad to dedicate this book to Tim Simpson with thanks and deep respect. Tim, my former student and long-time companion in matters textual, has always understood about the authority of scripture. He has made his deep fundamentalist grounding into a crucial resource for his mature critical interpretation of scripture. This book is offered to Tim with thanks and good wishes.

Credits

1. "Biblical Authority in the Post-Critical Period," in *The Anchor Bible Dictionary* (New York: Doubleday, 1992), 5:1049–56. Used by permission.

2. "Biblical Authority: A Personal Reflection" is reproduced from *Struggling with Scripture* (Louisville: Westminster John Knox Press, 2002), 5–31 and is copyright © 2002 Walter Brueggemann. Used by permission.

3. "Biblical Authority and the Church's Task of Interpretation" was published first in *Prism* (1986): 12–21. Used by permission.

4. "Twentieth-Century Old Testament Studies: A Quick Survey" originally appeared in *Word &World* 20 (2000): 61–71. Reprinted by permission.

5. "Introduction" to Gerhard von Rad, *Old Testament Theology*, vol. 1: *The Theology of Israel's Historical Traditions* (Louisville: Westminster John Knox, 2001), ix–xxxi. Used by permission.

6. "The Loss and Recovery of Creation in Old Testament Theology," *Theology Today* 53 (1996): 177–90. Used by permission.

7. "The ABCs of Old Testament Theology in the U.S." Originally published in *Zeitschrift für alttestamentliche Wissenschaft* 114 (2002): 412–32. Used by permission of de Gruyter, Berlin.

8. "Contemporary Old Testament Theology: A Contextual Prospectus" was originally published in *Dialog* 38 (1999): 108–16. Used by permission.

9. "Biblical Theology Appropriately Postmodern" originally appeared in Alice Bellis and Joel Kaminsky, eds., *Jews, Christians, and the Theology of the Hebrew Scriptures* (Atlanta: SBL, 2000). Used by permission.

10. "Theology of the Old Testament: A Prompt Retrospect" was originally published in Tod Linafelt and Timothy K. Beal, eds., *God in the Fray: A Tribute to Walter Brueggemann* (Minneapolis: Fortress Press, 1998), 307–20.

11. "Israel's Creation Faith: A Response to J. Richard Middleton" was originally published in the *Harvard Theological Review* 87 (1994): 279–89. Used by permission.

12. "Against the Stream: Brevard Child's Biblical Theology," *Theology Today* 53 (2000): 228–38. Used by permission.

13. "Walter Brueggemann's *Theology of the Old Testament: Testimony, Dispute, Advocacy*" and "A Response to Professor Childs" were originally published in *The Scottish Journal of Theology* 53 (2000): 228–38. Used by permission.

I.
Biblical Authority

CHAPTER ONE

Biblical Authority in the Postcritical Period

Each generation of believers and scholars must answer its own particular form of the question of the authority of scripture, for the question is posed differently for different communities in different intellectual and cultural circumstances. The Jewish and Christian religious communities have characteristically accepted the scriptures as revelatory, but have been mostly unclear and largely uninterested in stating precisely in what ways this literature is authoritative. It has been enough to affirm that this literature provides norms and permits for the abundant life intended by God for the creation. Specificity beyond that affirmation has been only hard and tenuously won. The problem is that the articulation of any formal criteria concerning authority or revelation turns out to be in tension with the actual concrete practice of the communities affirming the authority.[1] In most circumstances, the actual concrete practice is to be taken more seriously than is the formal statement which tries to objectify and intellectualize that practice.

A. The Modern Discussion

The governing categories for the questions that have dominated the modern discussion of biblical authority for the last two centuries need to be assessed and appreciated in their own cultural context. The question of the authority of scripture as understood in the Euro-American context has been framed in response to the rise of science, the emergence of scientific method, and the dominance of historical-critical modes of handling literature.[2] Prior to this development in the seventeenth and eighteenth centuries, there was in the West a sufficient cultural consensus concerning the nature of scripture. Thus, even critical questions were set within the secure framework of well-established and widely held convictions about the religious authority of the Bible. Prior to the rise of scientific consciousness, questions of authority were indeed an enterprise of "faith seeking understanding."[3]

The above changed, however, with the introduction of new thought patterns that shattered the theological consensus and paved the way for the study of the Bible as an autonomous piece of literature—a literature that was increasingly understood in relativizing ways. This suggestion of relativity concerning the Bible in turn evoked an urgency with respect to its certitude and absoluteness, a phenomenon new to biblical studies. Thus the "Battle for the Bible"[4] forced extreme positions, radical and reactionary, concerning such matters as inspiration, revelation, inerrancy, and infallibility. It must be recognized that the very posing of the question in terms of revelation and scientific criticism is reflective of a cultural crisis that challenged every settled authority and defined the debate in terms of relativity and absoluteness. The above categories of discussion unfortunately skewed the matter in a number of ways. The controversial discussion from the eighteenth century until now (which is roughly coterminous with the practice of Enlightenment criticism) has a strange quality to it, in that the categories of the conversation have been more or less imposed from external sources such as scientific accuracy or historical precision—categories essentially alien to the material itself. This is just as true of radical views that jeopardized the authority of scripture as it is of reactionary views that submitted the claims of scripture to the canon of modern scientific certitude. On the one hand, radical criticism provided a sense of autonomy and freedom within the literature, that is, now the Bible need not be taken with such heavy authoritarianism when understood to be historically conditioned in all its parts. On the other hand, reactionary scholasticism provided a sense of intellectual control and technical assurance; the Bible was understood as a lone champion of unbending reality in a situation marked by "change and decay." "Change and decay" is one important perception of the rise of science, technology, secularization, and individual freedom, and its corollary, the demise of the old hegemony in its intellectual, moral, economic, and political dimension. "Change and decay" is one experience of the emergence of modernism. But neither such autonomy and freedom, nor such control and assurance, seems particularly germane to the biblical literature itself; nor are they finally satisfying as responses to the religious thirst for truth as mediated by the Bible. The Bible does not mediate the *kind* of certitude sought in these categories.

In retrospect, the recent controversial discussion, which opposed criticism and scholasticism, now appears to have been misguided. Since the controversy failed to mediate the faith-claims of the text itself, it proceeded on both sides in alien, inappropriate categories. That particular conversation has now become somewhat obsolete because our present-day culture no longer excessively trusts nor fears such scientific methods. These scientific-critical methods, whether willingly embraced or vigorously resisted, really do not touch the issue of the authority of scripture as a theological problem.

The modern polemical conversation concerning faith and criticism, now so well documented in the handbooks,[5] has distorted the character of the Bible. On the side of literalism, the truth of God's power was cast in Enlightenment categories of script, document, authorship, and historical accuracy of written reports. In response to this, on the side of liberalism, resistance was offered to such scribalism, which was viewed as authoritarian. Scholars distanced themselves from the religious claims of the text through an appeal to (1) personal experience that judged the text, (2) cultural values held over against the text, and (3) events that happened outside and behind the text. Neither literalism nor liberalism faced the theologically dangerous character of the text; that is, both articulations of authority became defenses against yielding to the potentially dangerous, upsetting, and subversive power of the text that speaks characteristically against our settled, constructed worlds on behalf of a world yet to come.

B. The Cultural Context for the Question of Authority

Ours is a religious and cultural situation in which the question of authority must be posed anew, because the categories of the conversation have shifted. Ours is a postmodern, post-scientific, post-Enlightenment, post-positivistic situation.[6] It will not do to frame the question of authority as a scholastic one of proof, or as a romantic one of experience, or as a probe into scientific categories. The question now becomes one of what it means to be a community of interpretation and action called into existence by a text that remains distant and of less utility in the pursuit of certitude. Thus it appears that the question has been wrongly cast as one of *authorship*, a question we might expect from a book-oriented society preoccupied with questions of copyrights, sources, documentation, and scientific facts. The Bible itself has almost no interest in such modern questions of authorship, which result in hopeless and misguided investigations of claims of inspiration and revelation.

Rather, authority has to do with *issues of authorization,* that is, how, in a pluralistic world like ours, concrete communities can be authorized to live, act, and hope in a manner that may at times oppose the accepted norm, a manner that can be justified neither scientifically nor experientially. It is this authorization of a community's obedience and praise that is the real issue in the question of the authority of scripture. In order to answer this question of authorization, we must attempt to free ourselves of the immobilizing influence of the Enlightenment categories of certitude. An increasing number of people draw the conclusion that communities created and authorized by these texts are summoned and permitted to live, act, and hope in different and dangerous ways, and authorized by a different "voice" that is heard in the text, even if that voice cannot easily be accommodated in the conventional categories of academic investigation. The "authorizing voice" of scripture "heard" in the community needs to be understood as a theological reality mediated through the biblical literature. That is, the authorizing voice heard in the text, albeit mediated through social institutions and more immediate experiences, is indeed the voice of the Holy God. That is the voice communities of faith heard in the text, a voice that authorizes in odd and unsettling ways.

Communities of faith around the world, and especially in the West, where the old "Battle for the Bible" has been largely conducted, are now in deep crisis. Questions of authority cannot be considered apart from this crisis that concerns believers and nonbelievers alike.

The overarching crisis of Western culture (within which the authority of scripture must be articulated) is that the values and institutions of society are mostly organized against the "prospect of humanness."[7] Two articulations of this crisis may be cited. Robert Bellah has characterized the mood of conventional modern life (largely shaped by the social sciences) by the terms "positivism, reductionism, relativism, and determinism."[8] Bellah further observes that such values are inherently antihuman. Moreover, the live alternative to this practice of society lies only with the religious community, which is authorized to preserve values and practices of humanness:

> To the extent, however, that real religious communities can retain or
> recover a sense of being in but not of this world, can live, at least to

some extent, in patterns of voluntary simplicity and mutual concern, then they may act as genuine alternatives to the prevailing current . . . it is more than ever necessary that there be demonstration communities where elementary decencies can be maintained and handed down, humanizing a bad situation as long as it exists, and providing seedbeds for larger amelioration when that becomes possible.[9]

In a more recent, extended treatment, Bellah and his colleagues have concluded that American society has lost or neglected those acts and gestures that make sustained human community possible.[10] They propose that the religious community has a responsibility and an opportunity to foster and encourage more fully human possibilities.

In a much more abrasive analysis, Richard Rubenstein has proposed a reading of the economic history of the West as a history of triage.[11] Legitimated practices of land management and use of money and power have as their social result the devaluation and elimination of marginal and useless people. Rubenstein proposes that only the biblically based religious community can hope to terminate such destructive values and practices; in other words, the social vision of the Bible is the only effective alternative to this triage:

> Only a religious faith radically polemic to magic and to belief in earth's indwelling spirits could have brought about the cultural revolution in which an entire civilization came to reject what men and women had revered as sacred from time immemorial. . . . Perhaps the most influential example of a congery of strangers forming a community by adopting a common faith is that of the Hebrews of Sinai. . . . Neither unending growth nor unending movement offers a solution. . . . That is why a religious transformation is crucial. . . . The call for religious transformation is in reality a call to conversion, a call to change ourselves. Our preachers have rightly told us that we must be converted, that we must be born again. Unfortunately, what has been understood as conversion has all too often been devoid of the inclusive social component our times demand. In truth, we must be born again as men and women blessed with the capacity to care for each other here and now.[12]

The question of biblical authority is too urgent to be reduced to a parlor game of conventional scholastic categories. It is not a mechanistic question of proof and certitude for intramural debate within the religious community. It is now a public question of energy, courage, and freedom to act. The larger question is, What will provide energy, courage, and legitimacy for action against the destructive tendencies embedded within our civilization?

C. Originary Power and Practice

Against such settlements that reflect the intellectual climate and needs of the modern world, it must be recognized that the biblical text is in an odd way "originary," that is, it has the capacity to generate real newness. This text contains the power to work a newness that is indeed an act *creatio ex nihilo,* to call into being that which does not exist until brought to speech (Rom. 4:17). This "originary" character of the texts means that the text cannot be shackled by theories of inspiration, cannot be domesticated by archaeological proofs, and cannot be assessed by religious antecedents drawn from surrounding cultures. This power to articulate newness shatters all our cherished presuppositions and in turn pushes the question of authority outside the realm of explanation, leading into the world of testimony.

It is necessary, for that reason, to find new modes of articulation of the matter of authority. It is clear that an Enlightenment notion of technical-scientific explanation (either of literalism or of critical scholarship) is irrelevant to this question. One recent attempt with much to commend it is a literary approach that draws attention to the artistic power of the text; that is, authority is located in the speech of the text itself and not in something behind the speech of the text. Such an artistic approach, however, fails to face the ethical demands imposed by the text. It tends, instead, to remain preoccupied with the aesthetic dimensions of the literature.

The authority of scripture must ultimately be articulated in confessional terms by communities that assert that they have discerned the truth of power and the power of truth precisely in this text. (In this shrewd analysis Bruce Chilton has argued that this is true for individuals in their experience as well as for communities.)[13]

This confessional claim is what is meant by the "self-authenticating authority of Scripture."[14] It is the readiness to act that keeps a confessional claim honest. This way of putting the matter is honest in not claiming that this authority can be objectively demonstrated, even though authority is claimed to be grounded objectively in the character of the classic. This way of making a claim is honest in asserting that there is a compelling power we have discerned and upon which we are prepared to act. Such a statement of authority will not claim less. But it will not claim more, as though the claim were objectively provable. Its only credible authentication is, finally, the readiness of a confessing community to stake its life on the summons of the text. But the church, with its excessive penchant for dogmatic certitude, and the academy, with its fascination with objective rationality, characteristically stop short of the evidence of communal obedience. The question of authority is and must be shaped around the issue of obedient practice at the end of the Enlightenment period.

D. Authority as "Classic"

David Tracy has offered a fresh perspective on scriptural authority centered around the theme of "classic."[15] In that term he proposes a category of authority that is not the special pleading of a partisan community, but a claim submitted to the criterion of public conversation. Tracy understands a text as a "classic" when

> its "excess of meaning" both demands constant interpretation and bears a certain kind of timelessness—namely the timeliness of a classic expression radically rooted in its own historical time and calling to my own historicity. . . . The classic text's real disclosure is its claim to attention on the ground that an event of understanding proper to finite human beings has here found expression. . . . Every classic lives as a classic only if it finds readers willing to be provoked by its claim to attention.[16]
> . . . If, even once, a person has experienced a text, a gesture, an image, an event, a person with the force of the recognition, "This is important! This does make and will demand a difference!" then one has experienced a candidate for classic status.[17]

It is the text and not the community of the text that has authority. Tracy nonetheless understands that the response of the community of the text is important in determining the classic character of a text.

> At the very least, we will be willing to listen to that wider community of enquirers and readers who have found and find this text a classic. We will listen to them and then return to our dialogue with the subject matter of this "formed" text. After that second exposure, we may still decide that the community of enquiry in this instance has been mistaken. . . . At that point, tentativeness must cease. For in those instances

where a matter of importance is at stake—and the assignment of the status "classic" to any text is a matter of singular importance—then we must insist. But where tentativeness ceases, listening never does. The wider community of readers, living and dead, must continue to be heard as all return to the struggle of finding some appropriate response (from some initial sense of import to a formed judgment) to this possibly classic text.[18]

For Jews and Christians this tentativeness has ceased concerning the Bible. The decision that the Bible is a classic that mediates power and truth is a settled question for those communities. The church and the synagogue have found here "a certain kind of timelessness" that "demands constant interpretation."

With this characterization, Tracy hopes to avoid the circular argument of establishing the authority of the text by quoting the document itself. This practice satisfies only those who are already predisposed to accept the internal testimony of the text. Tracy also avoids the claim to authority that appeals to inspiration, revelation, or the work of the Spirit. Claims of this type may be valid, and are not here denied, but they bear the marks of special pleading as traditionally formulated. Moreover, Tracy eschews any notion of authority imposed externally through declaration, promulgation, or canonization. Circular argument, special pleading, and external imposition are not finally persuasive in such an urgent matter. Rather, authority is recognized (not given) by a public judgment that this text bears authority in its powerful offer of truth, which has been recognized over time as having an inescapable claim upon us. The other dimension of Tracy's characterization is that, since the text is distant in time, it requires interpretation that both discloses and conceals, so that the affirmation of authority requires and invites interpretation rather than resisting it. Understood in this way, interpretation is not a threat to the initial claim of the text, but is appropriate to its character and intention.

E. Spheres of the Question of Authority

The power of the Bible as a classic as norm and authorizer is operative in three realms. In each of these we may observe the way in which the Bible authorizes.

1. *Church and Synagogue.* The classic is peculiarly linked to the synagogue and church out of whose memory the text has come. There is no

doubt that text and community are dialectically related, that is, that community forms text and text evokes community. The formal claim of canon asserts that this literature is normative, functioning as a form for life and faith. It functions in the church (in the language of Paul Ricoeur) to permit an imaginative rereading of reality, so that the believing communities can discern and respond to the world in ways different from those dominant responses described by Bellah and Rubenstein.[19] Indeed, this text mediates "truth" to these communities—truth about God, truth about self, truth about human history, and truth about the world as God's creation. Langdon Gilkey has summarized this "rereading of reality" in ways that show the distinctiveness of this mediation:

> In the Old Testament understanding of history there are three distinct moments or stages characterizing historical passages. . . . First of all, there was the divine constitution or "creation" of the people and their cultural life. . . . The second moment . . . is the appearance of estrangement or alienation, of the fallen character of even the life of a chosen people. . . . The final moment is also prophetic. . . . This is the promise of a new covenant beyond the destruction of the old . . . the promise of new possibilities in historical life. . . . [In the New Testament] divine constitution, divine judgment, and new creative acts become incarnation, atonement and resurrection/*parousia*, aspects of history, to be sure, but not of *ordinary history*.[20]

The problem with this classic in the religious communities is its possible subjugation to the "tyranny of the church," that is, it is made to conform to ideological claims of the religious community. Traditionally this tyranny has been especially evident when the Bible has been interpreted only as a reinforcement for patterns of dogmatic formulation. For a very long period the Bible was used in the Christian tradition primarily to support such creedal formulations and it was precisely the rise of historical-critical methods that rescued the Bible, so that it could have its own liberated way, apart from these dogmatic categories. Thus the truth of the Bible cannot in good faith be accommodated to such tyranny, nor can it legitimately be made to serve ideological, partisan, or sectarian ends. Moreover, the truth given in this classic does not concern every kind of question that might be asked—scientific, astronomical, psychological, biological—but it is truth of a theological kind having to do with God's sovereign graciousness and gracious sovereignty.

The urgency of the Bible as authorization for the community of faith is its potential to release from false notions of absoluteness and certitude, and to unite a community currently beset by partisan and divisive pluralism. In the latter regard, the classic would gather disparate communities of faith together around a truth that is larger and more majestic than any similar partisan "truth" claimed by a particular community.

2. *The Academy*. This classic is also historically and culturally linked to the academy. Ebeling has shown how the Bible has played a key role in the origin of the Western intellectual and educational tradition.[21] In the United States, the Bible has been crucial in forming the school tradition now so much taken for granted.[22] However, the posture of the academy toward the text differs greatly from that of the church.[23] Whereas the community of faith has characteristically bowed before the authority of the text, the academy has sought to analyze and understand the text, believing that clear understanding according to the best canon of reason poses no threat to biblical authority, but is a practice natural and congenial to the nature of the texts.

We can, however, speak of the "tyranny of the academy" over the voice of the Bible. The rise of historical criticism, which freed the Bible from tyranny of the church, has led in turn to an autonomous reason that fundamentally resists the claims of the text. In contrast to the older discussion of reason and revelation, the academy has taken up a form of reason not only in tension with revelation, but deeply hostile to the claims of the text. Analytic methods have been joined to rationalistic categories of interpretation so that dimensions of mystery, awe, and inscrutability have been denied the text. Scientific or pseudoscientific norms of knowledge have been imposed on the Bible, which have reduced it to an archaic book emptied of its power to transform or to authorize.

An example of the above tyranny is found in the well-articulated article of Smith, who candidly observes that the perceptual field of scholars is in contradiction to the claims of the text.[24] Smith fails to notice, however, that the problem does not lie with the claims of the classic, that is, the text, but with the methods and questions of the scholarly guild. This type of tyranny of reason has been dramatically identified by Walter Wink and more programmatically articulated by Brevard Childs.[25] The issue has yet to be connected, however, with the larger crisis of technical reason that largely dominates the conversation of the academy.[26]

The function of the classic, that is, the Bible, in the academy concerns epistemological questions and the nature of knowledge. The academy in the modern world practices a form of knowledge aimed at control and which characteristically tends to domination. Lamentably, too many discussions about biblical authority have assumed such theories of knowledge and technique. Against that, however, the Bible is concerned with modes of knowledge that are relational, covenantal, and interactional, believing that knowledge should not dominate, but should serve to liberate and transform communication.[27] Modes of knowledge that tend toward domination cannot offer genuinely "new truth"; that is, they cannot be revelatory, but can only rearrange old patterns of power. "New truth" comes where imagination challenges, where spirit blows against letter (2 Cor. 3:6), and where yielding replaces control.

3. *The Public Arena.* Lastly, the classic is culturally available in the public arena. It is a remarkable and enduring fact that the Bible has authority in the Western world far beyond the limits of its proper confessing communities. Indeed, the dominant images and metaphors still governing public life are largely and powerfully shaped by the Bible.[28] Bellah has shown that while civil religion in America may be distorted ideology, it nonetheless still partakes of echoes and sentiments derived from the Bible.[29]

To be sure, the Bible in our society has been utilized in coercive, oppressive, and ideological ways—for instance, as a law to keep minorities and women in their respective places, and as a lever against all sorts of "objectionable" people in the public arena (such as homosexuals). Nonetheless, it has been the Bible and its derivative traditions that have provided impetus and power for restorative notions of personal health and social humanness. Characteristically, liberation movements in our time have found their central images in the Bible.[30] A striking example is Martin Luther King Jr., a child of this text, who had the imagination and the ability eloquently to articulate the issues of racial discrimination through biblical metaphors that mobilized both public and secular responses.[31]

The key to public issues in our society, as in every society, concerns access to power and the processes of decision making. It is obvious that a monopoly of access exists and that many are voiceless and excluded from decision making. Access is characteristically arranged in the interest of certain notions of order and merit. In the public conversation, against such a destructive commitment to an order which opposes egalitarianism in politics and economics, the Bible powerfully insists that questions of justice, questions of abundant life for the marginal, and questions of social access, social goods, and social power cannot be silenced.

The issue of biblical authority in our time, then, may be understood as an issue of the juxtaposition of *the crisis of inhumanness*[32] and *the classic*[33] which has enduring authority. Without this classic, it is probable that the church and synagogue would settle for distortions of truth in partisan forms of absolutism or divisive forms of pluralism. The classic, however, summons the church to a *truth that liberates* us from our certitudes and *frees* us from our private and partisan commitments. Without this classic, it is probable that the academy would settle for distorted modes of knowledge, aiming at control and eventually leading to domination. This classic, however, invites the academy to practice *knowledge that heals, reconciles, and mobilizes power* in the service of human dignity, while simultaneously it provides a broad definition of what constitutes human dignity. Without this classic, it is probable the public domain would distort justice, pursue an oppressive order, and practice economic and political inequality. This classic urges those public practices of power to be *concerned with questions of justice,* so that marginal and powerless persons can be included in the formation of public policy. Thus the classic invites the church and synagogue to consider a truth that liberates, invites the academy to consider a knowledge that reconciles and heals, and invites the public arena to practice a form of justice that provides equal access to all, irrespective of privilege, power, or accomplishment.

The fact does, however, remain that some wield the authority of scripture as a sponsor of sectarian truth, of ideological knowledge, and of a social order indifferent to issues of justice. To such an alternative and distorted reading of the Bible, one may respond in two ways: First, that it is on the issues of truth, knowledge, and justice (in the ways here characterized) that the Bible has established its claim as a classic. The Bible would not anywhere, at any time, have arrived at the status of classic, if it had been a text characteristically in the service of oppressive truth, technical knowledge, of partisan injustice. It is the largeness of its vision and its promise of a viable alternative that determines its functional power. The Bible is recognized in its classic proportion because it attempts to mediate and make available that which we judge most definitional for human life.

Second, we insist that the question of authority should not concern authorship, but authorization. As soon as the question of authorization is posed, one must ask, Authorization to what? To what are the church and synagogue, the academy, and those in public life authorized? Within the scope of the biblical texts, the inescapable answer is the substantive disclosure of the Bible on all three counts, namely, there are (1) a God committed to liberation, unity, healing, knowledge, and justice; (2) an ongoing conflict within the course of public history precisely over these matters; and (3) a vision of the eventual triumph of these commitments of God.

F. Authorization and Communities of Praxis

The test of the authorizing power of the Bible is not, however, to be settled according to intellectual formulation. The test in this time of need for human possibility is in praxis, that is, in the emergence of communities that embody and implement the rereading of the world which is voiced in the text. These communities of obedience bear witness to the authorizing power of the book as well as to the spirit that blows through that book. The text gives them not only advice and guidance but also the energy and courage for a life of obedience. It is staggering evidence of the authority of scripture that even in the face of harsh, systemic brutality there have been and still are communities of faith who have demonstrated this alternative vision in the public arena. We may identify these communities under the rubric of those authorized by *biblical requirement* and those authorized by *biblical permit*.

1. *Biblical Authority as Requirement*. The Bible gives authorization to *communities of requirement* in its voice as the norm of commandment. The Bible, as the classic in which tentativeness is ended, is heard as the voice of summons and command, which can be answered only with obedience. There is a stringent insistence in the Bible concerning expectations and demand for the community that it authorizes. Such communities ask in the face of this text, "What is required?" (cf. Deut. 10:12; Mic. 6:8). The answer, given in a variety of ways, is justice and mercy.[34]

This authorization *as requirement* is evident especially in communities of radical obedience in contexts of affluence, satiation, and accommodation. This has been true through the history of the church and the synagogue. In such contexts, the biblical text authorizes communities of the faithful who, in obedience to the text, order their lives in ways distinct from the dominant value system so as to disengage from those practices of power and well-being advocated by the society in which they find themselves placed. Such communities of obedience are given over to acts of mercy, strategies of justice, and visions of peace peculiarly authorized by this text.

2. *Biblical Authority as Permit*. The Bible reciprocally gives authorization to *communities of permit* in its voice as the norm of deliverance.[35] In quite parallel fashion we may speak of "communities of permission." These

communities are located not in contexts of affluence but in contexts of oppression and marginality where people hear the voice of liberation and acceptance, a voice that can be answered only in energy, freedom, and trust.

These are communities of faithful individuals who are authorized and permitted by this text to stand against oppression and to refuse marginality in the name of justice and liberation. Such communities are characteristically found in so-called third-world situations where the dominant value structures preclude justice, legitimize marginality, and invite docility and passive acceptance of the status quo. Within such context, this text acts as an impetus to new life through the assertion of one's dignity, rights, worth, and power.[36]

These communities of requirement and permission clearly concern public values of justice and dignity. But these same communities also have an intense pastoral concern in that individual persons are called to be obedient and are invited to assert and enact their own dignity, worth, and self-respect.

The authority of scripture can be understood only in relation to and in terms of the communities it authorizes. The authorizing power of the text is evident through both its demand for obedience and its grant of permission to act in new ways against both accommodation and oppression.[37] The force of such authorization implies that the book and its authorized communities cannot wait for the resolution of scholastic arguments concerning inspiration or revelation, nor can they wait upon the academy to formulate properly its own intellectual stance on the matter. The authorizing power of the text is of another order.

In communities of requirement and permission, the Bible does not offer strategies or advice. What it does offer is energy, courage, vision, and hope. Historically, we have spoken of these matters in the text as "the inspiration of the Holy Spirit," and that is indeed what they are. But "Holy Spirit" needs to be understood apart from literary questions of authorship. Rather, the Spirit has to do with faith questions of authorization, imagination, and life. The power of the Spirit functions to permit communities to discern, imagine, and appropriate life differently, as it is mediated, remembered, and hoped in this text. The work of the Spirit is the liberation of the community's imagination mediated through the text. These communities of requirement and permission find such liberation mediated in these texts in ways that permit a new life in the world. The text is "in-spirited" in the sense that it is "peopled" with the force of God's power to permit new communities to emerge in the world. It is "infallible" in the sense that it authorizes a way of living and believing that without fail leads to the fruits of the Spirit (Gal. 5:22-24). It is "revelatory" in the sense that it discloses a new way of living in the world that was not previously known and that seemed heretofore prohibited by the structures of coercion and domination.

The central thrust of this classic that mediates new life is its offer of an alternative reality of governance that is sure but not dominating, producing new modes of certitude, power, and knowledge. The "otherness" of the text is the disclosure of a "secret" (cf. Luke 10:23-24). In the scripture of Israel, that "secret" is about a transcendent governance rendering all other imperial power inoperational (Exod. 8:18), confounding spear and sword with a power name (1 Sam. 17:45), and opening the world against might and power by the spirit (Zech. 4:6). In the New Testament that same secret concerns "the impossible" being made possible (Mark 10:27), weakness in obedience that turns out to be triumphant strength (cf. 2 Cor. 11:30; 12:5, 9).

G. Strange Authorization for Newness

Martin Buber, in a voice of faithful Judaism, and Karl Barth, in a voice of faithful Christianity, both understood that the Bible is a strange voice and a strange book that gives life. Buber writes:

> The modern person must read the Jewish Bible as though it were something entirely unfamiliar, as though it had not been set before him ready-made, as though he has not been confronted all his life with sham concepts and sham statements that cited the Bible as their authority. He must face the Book with a new attitude as something new. He must yield to it, withhold nothing of his being, and let whatever will occur between himself and it. He does not know which of its sayings and images will overwhelm him and mold him, from where the spirit will ferment and enter into him, to incorporate itself anew in his body. But he holds himself open. He does not believe anything a priori; he does not disbelieve anything a priori. He reads aloud the words written in the book in front of him; he hears the word he utters and it reaches him. Nothing is pre-judged. The current of time flows on, and the contemporary character of this man becomes itself a receiving vessel.

In order to understand the situation fully, we must picture to ourselves the complete chasm between the Scriptures and the man of today.[38]

Barth asserts in parallel fashion:

Within the Bible there is a strange, new world, the world of God. This answer is the same as that which came to the first martyr, Stephen: Behold, I see the heavens opened and the Son of man standing on the right hand of God. . . . We must openly confess that we are reaching beyond ourselves. But that is just the point: if we wish to come to grips with the contents of the Bible, we must dare to reach far beyond ourselves. The Book admits of nothing less. . . . A new world, the world of God.[39]

Once more we stand before this "other" new world which begins in the Bible. In it the chief consideration is not the doings of man but the doings of God—not the various ways which we may take if we are men of good will, but the power out of which good will must first be created.[40]

It is not the right human thoughts about God which form the content of the Bible, but the right divine thoughts about men. The Bible tells us not how we should talk with God, but what he says to us; not how we find the way to him, but how he has sought and found the way to us; not the right relation in which we must place ourselves to him, but the covenant which he has made with all who are Abraham's spiritual children and which he has sealed once and for all in Jesus Christ. It is this which is within the Bible. The word of God is within the Bible.[41]

The Bible is fundamentally alien to modernity, even as it is fundamentally alien to every dominating mode of rationality in every age of the synagogue and the church. It is for this reason that the Bible and its authority can never be articulated or summarized in dominant modes of rationality. The book can be received and its authority evidenced only in communities of obedience and praise which, with marvelous indifference to categories of explanation, act with power, courage, freedom, and energy toward a new world envisioned, imagined, and promised in this text. To try to reduce such liberated imagination either to the categories of literalism or to the more respectable but equally problematic categories of liberalism is a sorry, mistaken assessment of this book. The practice of literalism is to hope for a kind of control that this inspirited book will never countenance. To practice liberalism is to hope for a kind of benign distancing that this restless book will never tolerate. In the face of such ill-conceived control or distance, genuinely authorized communities regularly find the book more terrifying than that, and more dangerously healing. Any formulation of authority that alleviates the terror or domesticates the healing is inadequate for the book. Such a reduction in either direction is an attempt at domination, whereas the book insists upon yielding as the point of access to its truth and power. This yielding means that truth and power, with all their terror and healing, are yet to be granted in new forms. That is what the theories of *"Sensus Plenior,"*[42] "The New Hermeneutic,"[43] and "world-making speech"[44] have attempted to articulate. The authorized communities will continue in obedient interpretation. In the midst of interpretation and obedience, there is a waiting (Hab. 2:3) and a watching (Mark 13:37) for what will soon be given by God through this text.

CHAPTER TWO

Biblical Authority

A Personal Reflection

The issue of the authority of the Bible is a perennial and urgent one for those of us who claim and intend to stake our lives on its attestation. But for all of the perennial and urgent qualities of the question, the issue of biblical authority is bound, in any case, to remain endlessly unsettled and therefore, I believe, perpetually disputatious. It cannot be otherwise, and so we need not hope for a "settlement" of the issue. The unsettling and disputatious quality of the question is, I believe, given in the text itself, because the Bible is ever so endlessly "strange and new."[1] It always, inescapably, outdistances our categories of understanding and explanation, of interpretation and control. Because the Bible is, as we confess, "the live word of the living God," it will not submit in any compliant way to the accounts we prefer to give of it. There is something intrinsically unfamiliar about the book, and when we seek to override that unfamiliarity we are on the hazardous ground of idolatry.

Because I am not well schooled in the long, formal discussions and considerations concerning "the authority of scripture" (perhaps better left to theologians), I offer here a quite personal reflection on the authority of scripture, to consider how it is that I work with, relate to, and submit to the Bible. I do not suggest that my way is in any sense commendable or normative. Nor do I know if my ruminations will particularly serve the current crisis in the church, and I do not intend my statement to be particularly attentive to the "culture wars" in which we are engaged.

Thus, I offer a more or less innocent personal account, though of course none of our personal accounts is very innocent. Your invitation has provided an opportunity for me to think clearly about my own practice. In the process, moreover, I have become convinced that we will be well served if we can be in some way honest about the intimate foundations of our personal stance on these questions. Indeed, rather than loud, settled slogans about the Bible, we might do better to consider the odd and intimate ways in which we have each, alike and differently, been led to where we are about the Bible. In setting out such a statement, I say at the outset that you do me a great privilege by inviting me here, a non-Presbyterian, though I hope when I have finished you will judge me to be reliably, if not with excessive intensity, Reformed.

I begin by telling you about what I take to be the defining moment in my attachment to the Bible. In my German Evangelical upbringing, confirmation was a very big deal. In that act of confirmation, the pastor (in my case, my father) selected a "confirmation verse" for each confirmand, a verse to mark one's life—read while hands were laid on in confirmation, read at one's funeral, and read many times in between. My father, on that occasion of confirmation, read over me Psalm 119:105:

> Your word is a lamp to my feet
> and a light to my path.

He did, in that act, more than he knew. Providentially, I have no doubt, he marked my life by this book that would be lamp and light, to illumine a way to obedience, to mark a way to fullness, joy, and well-being. The more I reflect on that moment, the more I am sure that I have been bound more than I knew to this book.

Before that moment of confirmation in baptismal vows, in my nurture in the church, my church prepared me to attend to the Bible in a certain way. I am a child of the Prussian Union, a church body created in 1817, on the 300th anniversary of Luther's theses. The Prussian king was weary of Calvinists and Lutherans arguing about the Eucharist and so decreed an ecumenical church that was in its very founding to be ecumenical and not confessional, open to diversity, and aimed not at any agreement beyond a broad consensus of evangelical faith that intended to protect liberty of conscience. This is the church body that brought to the United States a deep German church slogan now taken over and claimed by many others:

> In essentials unity;
> in nonessentials liberty;
> in all things charity.[2]

In actuality, moreover, the last line, "in all things charity," became the working interpretive principle that produced a fundamentally irenic church.

The pastoral ambiance of that climate for Bible reading may be indicated by two examples. First, the quarrels over historical-critical reading of the Bible, faced by every church soon or late, were firmly settled as long ago as 1870, when one seminary teacher was forced out of teaching but quickly restored to a pastoral position of esteem, so the issue did not again cause trouble. Second, in its only seminary, Eden Seminary, there was no systematic theologian on the faculty until 1946, and things were managed well enough in a mood of trustful piety that produced not hard-nosed certitude, but rather an irenic charity of liberated generosity. All of that was before my moment of confirmation, in which I became an heir to that tradition, with its trustful engagement with the book as "lamp" and "light."

After my confirmation came a series of teachers who shaped me in faith, after my father, my first and best teacher, who taught me the artistry as well as the authority of scripture. In college my first Bible teacher was a beloved man still at work in the church, still my friend. He mostly confused me about JEDP, perhaps because he did not understand very well himself, being a theologian and not an exegete.

In seminary I had an astonishing gift of Bible teachers, none of whom published, as perhaps the best teachers do not. Allen Wehrli had studied under Hermann Gunkel in Halle and taught us the vast density of artistry of the Bible, with attention to the form of the text. His pedagogy, for which he was renowned in our circle, was imaginative storytelling; he understood that the Bible is narrative, long before G. Ernest Wright or Fred Craddock. Lionel Whiston introduced us in 1959 to the first traces of Gerhard von Rad that reached English readers. Von Rad showed that the practice of biblical faith is first of all recital, and I have devoured his work ever since.[3] I learned from Wehrli and Whiston that the Bible is essentially an open, artistic, imaginative narrative of God's staggering care for the world, a narrative that will feed and nurture into obedience, that builds community precisely by respect for the liberty of the Christian man or woman.[4]

After seminary, purely by accident, at Union Seminary in New York, I stumbled on to James Muilenburg (arguably the most compelling Old Testament teacher of his generation), who taught us that the Bible will have its authoritative, noncoercive way if we but attend with educated alertness to the cadences and sounds of the text as given in all its detail.

And, since graduate school, I have been blessed by a continuing host of insistent teachers—seminarians who would not settle easily, church people who asked new and probing questions—and I have even read other Bible teachers, to mixed advantage. But mostly my continuing education has been from the writing and witness of people whose faith is powered by the text to live lives of courage, suffering, and sacrifice. In noncoercive ways and seemingly without effort at forcing anyone else, they have found this book a wind and source and energy for the fullness of the true life lived unafraid.

When I think about that moment of confirmation in 1947, seeing it better now than I did then, I have come to see that gathered all that day was my church tradition of simple, irenic piety from the past, and gathered all that day was this succession of teachers still to come who would let me see how broad and deep and demanding and generous is this text, how utterly beyond me in its richness, and yet, held concretely in my hands, offering to me and to those around me unprecedented generativity. "A lamp to my feet and a light to my path." How remarkable a gift that my father knew all that and willed all of that and gathered all of that for me on that incidental day in 1947 at St. Paul's Church in Saline County.

I take so much time with my particular history not because you are concerned with it, or because the story has any great merit, but perhaps as nothing more than the pondering of an aging Bible man. I tell you in order to attest that how we read the Bible, each of us, is partly a plot of family, neighbors, and friends (a socialization process) and partly the God-given accident of long-term development in faith. From that come two lessons:

1. The real issues of biblical authority and interpretation are not likely to be settled by erudite cognitive formulation or by appeal to classic settlements, but live beneath such contention in often unrecognized and uncriticized ways that are deeply powerful, especially if rooted (as they may be for most of us) amid hurt, anger, or anxiety.

2. Real decisions about biblical meanings are mostly not decided on the spot but are long-term growths of habit and conviction that emerge, function, and shape, often long before they are recognized. And if that is so, then the disputes require not frontal arguments that are mostly exercises in self-entertainment but long-term pastoral attentiveness to each other in good faith.

If that is true, a church in dispute will require great self-knowing candor and a generous openness to allow the legitimacy of long-term nurture that gifts others. Such attentiveness may be so generous as to entertain the thought that the story of someone else's long-term nurture could be a gift not only for that person but could be, once removed, a transformative gift to me when I read the text through their nurture that is marked, as are we all, by joy, doubt, fear, and hurt.

With this perhaps too long personal reflection, I will now identify six facets of biblical interpretation about which I know something that I believe are likely to be operative among us all.

Inherency

The Bible is inherently the live Word of God that addresses us concerning the character and will of the gospel-giving God, empowering us to an alternative life in the world. I say "inherently" because we can affirm that it is in itself intrinsically so. While I give great credence to "reader response" (how can one not?) and while I believe in the indeterminacy of the text to some large extent, finally the Bible is forceful and consistent in its main theological claim. That claim concerns the conviction that the God who creates the world in love redeems the world in suffering and will consummate the world in joyous well-being. That flow of conviction about the self-disclosure of God in the Bible is surely the main claim of apostolic faith upon which the church is fundamentally agreed. That fundamental agreement about main claims is, of course, the beginning of the conversation and not its conclusion, but it is a deep and important beginning point for which I use the term *inherent*.

From that four things follow:

1. Because this is the foundation of apostolic faith to which we all give attestation, it means that all of us in the church are bound together, as my tradition affirms, "in essentials unity." It also means, moreover, that in disputes about biblical authority nobody has high ground morally or hermeneutically. We share a common commitment about the truth of the book that makes us equal before the book as it does around the table.

2. The inherency of evangelical truth in the Bible is focused on its main claims. From that it follows that there is much in the text that is "lesser," not a main claim, but a lesser voice that probes and attempts, over the generations, to carry the main claims to specificity, characteristically informed by particular circumstance and characteristically in the text open to variation, nuance, and even contradiction. It is a primal Reformation principle,

given main claims and lesser voices in the text, that our faith is evangelical, linked to the news and not biblicism, thus recognizing the potential tension or distinction between good news and lesser claims. That particular tension and distinction is, of course, the arena of much dispute in the church just now, and it is important at the outset to make the distinction, so that we can see the true subject of the dispute.

3. The inherent Word of God in the biblical text is, of course, refracted through many authors who were not disembodied voices of revealed truth. They were, rather, circumstance-situated men and women of faith (as are we all) who said what their circumstance permitted and required them to speak, as they were able, of that which is truly inherent. It is this human refraction, of course, that makes inescapable the hard work of critical study, so that every text is invited to a suspicious scrutiny whereby we may consider the ways in which bodied humanness has succeeded or not succeeded in being truthful and faithful witness. Each of us, moreover, would concede that some bodied human witnesses in the text were more successful and effective than some others.

4. Given both inherency and circumstance-situated human refraction, the Bible is endlessly a surprise beyond us that Karl Barth famously and rightly termed "strange and new." The Bible is not a fixed, frozen, readily exhausted read; it is rather a "script," always reread, through which the Spirit makes new. When the church adjudicates the inherent and the circumstance-situated, the church of whatever ilk is sore tempted to settle, close, and idolize. And therefore inherency of an evangelical kind demands a constant resistance to familiarity. Nobody makes the final read; nobody's read is final or inerrant, precisely because the Key Character in the book who creates, redeems, and consummates is always beyond us in holy hiddenness.[5] When we push boldly through the hiddenness, wanting to know more clearly, what we thought was holy ground turns out to be a playground for idolatry. Our reading of inherency, then, is inescapably provisional reading. It is rightly done with the modesty that belongs to those who are yet to be surprised always again by what is "strange and new."

Interpretation

The claim of biblical authority is not difficult as it pertains to the main affirmations of apostolic faith. But from that baseline, the hard, disputatious work is interpretation that needs to be recognized precisely for what it is: nothing other than interpretation. The Bible, our mothers and fathers have always known, is not self-evident and self-interpreting, and the Reformers did not mean that at all when they escaped the church's magisterium.[6] Rather, the Bible requires and insists upon human interpretation that is inescapably subjective, necessarily provisional, and, as you are living witnesses, inevitably disputatious.

I propose as an interpretive rule that all of our subjective, provisional, disputatious interpretation be taken, at the most, with quite tentative authority, in order that we may (1) make our best, most insistent claims, but then, with some regularity, we may (2) relinquish our pet interpretations and, together with our partners in dispute, fall back in joy into the inherent apostolic claims that outdistance all our too familiar and too partisan interpretations. We may learn from the rabbis the marvelous rhythm of deep interpretive dispute and profound common yielding in joy and affectionate well-being.[7] The sometimes characteristic and demonic mode of Reformed interpretation is not tentativeness and relinquishment but tentativeness that is readily hardened into absoluteness, whether of the right or of the left, of exclusive or of inclusive, a sleight-of-hand act of substituting our interpretive preference for the inherency of apostolic claims.

The process of interpretation that precludes final settlement on all questions is self-evident in the Bible itself. As Gerhard von Rad spent his life making clear, Deuteronomy is the model and engine of an ongoing interpretive dynamic in the Old Testament. Moses becomes the cipher for all those interpreters yet to come who dispute with the text of Moses, so that what we have in the text is Moses *contra* Moses.[8] We can see this dynamic in the text itself, for even Deuteronomy acknowledges that its own tradition is not from Sinai but is a derivative form and an extrapolation as a "second" (*deuteros*) reading for a new time and place (Deut. 17:18). Thus Moses enunciates the required interpretive principle:

> Not with our ancestors did the Lord make this covenant, but with us, who are all of us here alive today. (Deut. 5:3)

After the reiterated Decalogue of chapter 5, the tradition of Deuteronomy proceeds to extrapolate from Sinai for many chapters at the Jordan for a new circumstance. A stunning case in point is the Mosaic teaching in Deuteronomy 23:1-8 that bans from the community all those with distorted sexuality and all those who are foreigners. In Isaiah 56:3-8, this

Mosaic teaching is frontally overturned in the Bible itself, offering what Herbert Donner terms an intentional "abrogation" of Mosaic law in new teaching.[9] The old, no doubt circumstance-driven exclusion in the mouth of Moses in Deuteronomy 23 is answered by a circumstance-driven inclusiveness in Isaiah 56.

To cite another example, in Deuteronomy 24:1-5, Moses teaches that marriages broken in infidelity cannot be restored, even if both parties want to get back together. But in Jeremiah 3, in a shocking reversal given in a pathos-filled poem, God's own voice indicates a readiness to violate that Torah teaching for the sake of restored marriage to Israel.[10] The old teaching is seen to be problematic even for God. The later text shows God prepared to move beyond the old prohibition in order that the inherent evangelical claims of God's graciousness may be fully available even to recalcitrant Israel. In at least embarrassment and perhaps in humiliation, the God of the poem in Jeremiah willfully overrides the old text in a new circumstance of pathos. It becomes clear that the interpretive project that constitutes the final form of the text is itself profoundly polyvalent, yielding no single exegetical outcome, but allowing layers and layers of fresh reading in which God's own life and character are deeply engaged and put at risk.

As we observe the open dynamic of interpretation in the text itself, moreover, we ourselves are able to see that same dynamic operative in our own time and place. It is self-evident that new circumstances of reading permit us to see what we have not seen in the text heretofore. A clear case in point is that the ecological crisis now evokes awareness on our part that the Bible does indeed address the issues of a distorted, polluted creation, though in past "faithful" reading we missed all of that because we read in a specific time and place.[11] Interpretive humility invites us to recognize that reading in a particular time, place, and circumstance can never be absolute but is more than likely to be displaced by yet another reading in another time and place, a reading that may depart from or even judge the older reading or even the older text, as in these two cases from Deuteronomy.

The Spirit meets us always afresh in our faithful reading, in each new time, place, and circumstance. Anyone who imagines that reading is settled and eternal simply does not pay attention to the process in which we are all engaged, liberals and conservatives. Following George Steiner, I suspect that interpretation—albeit subjective, provisional, and disputatious—is a God-given resistance to monologue.[12] There is not simply one voice in scripture, and to give any one voice in scripture or in tradition authority to silence other voices surely distorts the text and misconstrues the liveliness that the text itself engenders in the interpretive community.

Imagination

Responsible interpretation requires and inevitably engages in imagination. Imagination makes us serious Calvinists nervous, because it smacks of subjective freedom to carry the text in undeveloped directions and to engage in fantasy. Apart from such a fear, I would insist that (1) imagination is in any case inevitable in the interpretive process if it is ever anything more than simple reiteration and that (2) faithful imagination is characteristically not autonomous fantasy but good-faith extrapolation.

I understand imagination to be the capacity to entertain images of meaning and reality that are out beyond the evident givens of observable experience.[13] That is, imagination is the hosting of "otherwise," and I submit that every serious teacher or preacher invites to "otherwise" beyond the evident givens, or we have nothing to say.[14] When we do such hosting of "otherwise," however, we must, of course, take risks and act daringly to push beyond what is known to that which is hoped and trusted but not yet in hand.

Interpretation is not the reiteration of the text. It is rather the movement of the text beyond itself in fresh ways, often ways never offered until this moment of utterance. A primal example, of course, is constituted by Jesus' parables, which open the listening community to possible futures.[15] Beyond parabolic teaching, however, there was in ancient Israel and in the early church observed wonder.[16] As eyewitnesses created texts out of observed and remembered miracles, there is no doubt that these texted miracles in turn became materials for imagination that pushed well beyond what is given or intended even in the text. This is an inescapable process for those of us who insist that this old text is a contemporary word to us. We transport ourselves out of the twenty-first century back to that ancient world or, conversely, we transpose ancient voices into contemporary voices of authority. We do it all the time:

> Those of us who think critically do not believe that the Old Testament was talking about Jesus, and yet we make the linkages.
>
> Surely Paul was not thinking of the crisis of sixteenth-century indulgences when he wrote about "faith alone."
>
> Surely Isaiah was not thinking, in writing Isaiah 65, of Martin Luther King Jr. having a dream of a new earth.

We make such leaps all the time:

> What a huge leap to imagine that the primal commission to "till" and "keep" the earth (Gen. 2:15) is really about environmental issues and the chemicals used by Iowa farmers. But we do it.

> What a huge leap to imagine that the ancient provision for jubilee in Leviticus 25 in fact concerns cancellation of third-world debts, with an implied critique of global capitalism. But we do it.

> What a huge leap to imagine that an ancient purity code in Leviticus 18 bears upon consenting gays and lesbians in the twenty-first century and is concerned with ordination. But we do it.

We do it, and we are commonly, all of us, committed to the high practice of subjective extrapolations, because we commonly have figured out that a cold, reiterative objectivity has no missional energy or moral force. We do it, and we will not stop doing it. But it is surely healing and humbling for us, all of us, to be self-knowing enough to concede that what we are doing in imaginative interpretation is not "inherent" but is subjective extrapolation that will not carry the freight of absoluteness.

No doubt Karl Barth, that great father of us all, understood this when he imagined for an instant that Romans 13 pertained to Christian obedience in Communist Hungary. Indeed, of imagination Barth himself could write:

> We must dismiss and resist to the very last any idea of the inferiority or untrustworthiness or even worthlessness of a "non-historical" depiction and narration of history. This is in fact only a ridiculous and middle-class habit of the modern Western mind which is supremely phantastic in its chronic lack of imaginative phantasy, and hopes to rid itself of its complexes through suppression. This habit has really no claim to the dignity and validity which it pretends. . . . But human possibility of knowing is not exhausted by the ability to perceive and comprehend. Imagination, too, belongs no less legitimately in its way to the human possibility of knowing. A man without imagination is more of an invalid than one who lacks a leg. But fortunately each of us is gifted somewhere and somehow with imagination, however, starved this gift may be in some or misused by others.[17]

If we grant that interpretation is our bounden duty, then it follows, inescapably, I believe, that imagination is the vehicle for interpretation. This is what Moses was doing at the Jordan in Deuteronomy; this is what Jesus was doing in his rabbinic way, "You have heard it said of old." And this is what the church always does when it risks moving the text to its own time and place. Imagination can indeed be a gift of the Spirit, but it is a gift used with immense subjective freedom, which we would do better to concede even if that concession makes unmistakably clear that our imaginative interpretations cannot claim the shrillness of certainly but only the tentativeness of our best extrapolations. After our imaginative interpretations are made with vigor in dispute with others in the church, I submit that we must regularly, gracefully, and with modesty fall back from our best extrapolations to the sure apostolic claims that lie behind our extremities of imagination, liberal or conservative.

Ideology

A consideration of ideology is difficult among us, precisely because U.S. church people are largely innocent about our own interpretive work, and not often aware of or honest about the ways in which our own work is shot through with distorting vested interest.[18] But it is so, even if we are innocent about it. There is no interpretation of scripture (or interpretation of anything else, for that matter) that is unaffected by the passions, convictions, and perceptions of the interpreter. Ideology is the self-deceiving practice of taking a part for the whole, of taking "my truth" for *the* truth, of running truth through a prism of the particular and palming off the particular as a universal.[19] It is so already in the text of scripture itself, as current scholarship makes clear, because the Spirit-given text is given us by and through human authors.[20] It is so because Spirit-filled interpretation is given us by and through bodied authors who must make their way in the world, and in making our way, we do not see so clearly or love so dearly or follow so nearly as we might imagine.

There are endless examples of ideology at work in interpretation:

The practice of historical criticism is no innocent practice, for it intends to fend off church authority and protect freedom for the autonomous interpreter.

The practice of so-called canonical criticism is no innocent practice, for it intends to maintain old coherences of truth against the perceived threat of more recent fragmentation.

The practice of high moralism is no innocent practice, even if it sounds disciplined and noble, for much of that high-grounded moralism comes from fear and is a strategy to fend off anxiety.

The practice of communitarian inclusiveness is an interpretive posture
that is no innocent practice, because it reflects a reaction against
exclusivism and so is readily given to a kind of reactive carelessness.
There is enough of truth in every such interpretive posture and strategy—
historical criticism, canonism, moralism, communitarianism, and a hundred others we might name—to make the posture credible and to gather
a mass of constituency in order to maintain a sustained voice. But it is
not, for reasons of ideology, innocent, and if not innocent, then it has no
absolute claim.

In a disputatious church, a healthy practice might be to reflect upon
the ideological passion, not of others, but of self and cohorts who agree. I
believe that such reflection would invariably indicate:[21]

That every passionate interpretive voice is shot through with vested
interest, sometimes barely hidden, so shot through that it is completely predictable that interpreters who are restrictive about gays
and lesbians will characteristically advocate high capitalism and a
strong national defense; conversely, those who are "open and affirming" will characteristically maintain a critique of consumer capitalism and a whole cluster of issues along with it. One can argue in
each case, of course, that such a package is only a theological-ethical
coherence. Perhaps, but in no case, I should argue, is the package
innocent, precisely because given the package, we incline to make
the next decision without any critical reflection but only in order to
sustain the package.

That every vested interest has working in it, if it is passionate, a high
measure of anxiety about deep threats, perhaps perceived, perhaps
imagined, and anxiety has a forceful passion to it that permits us to
deal in wholesale categories without the nuance of the particular.[22]
A judgment grounded in anxiety, anywhere on the theological spectrum, wants not to be disturbed or informed by the detail of facts
on the ground.

That every vested interest shaped by anxiety has near its source old fears
that are deep and hidden, but for all of that authoritative.

That every vested interest informed by anxiety and infused with fear has
at its very bottom hurt, old hurt, new hurt, hurt for ourselves, for
those remembered, for those we love; the pain, lingering, unhealed
pain, becomes a hermeneutical principle out of which we will not
be talked.

We can see such ideology in the text itself that surely reflects vested interest, anxiety, fear, and hurt. In Deuteronomy, as Carolyn Pressler has shown, the marriage laws are deeply patriarchal, perhaps echoed in some corrected form by Paul.[23] We can see it in Hananiah, who picked up the buoyant Zionism of Isaiah and, a century later, against Jeremiah turned it into an absolute principle that blinded him to lived reality.[24] We can see it in Ezra, who not only fathered Judaism but fended off other Judaisms in an exercise of complete domination and hegemony.

Every such ideological passion, liberal or conservative, may be encased in scripture itself or enshrined in long-standing interpretation until it is absolute and trusted as decisive authority. And where ideology becomes loud and destructive in the interpretive community, we may be sure that the doses of anxiety, fear, and hurt within it are huge and finally irrepressible.

I am not suggesting that no distinctions can be made or that it is so dark that all cats are gray. And certainly, given our ideological passions, we must go on and interpret in any case. But I do say that in our best judgments concerning scripture, we might be aware enough of our propensity to distort in the service of vested interest, anxiety, fear, and hurt that we would recognize that our best interpretation might be not only the vehicle but also the block and distortion of the crucified truth of the gospel. If interpretation is unavoidable, as I think it is, whereby old text is made new, and if imagination is an inescapable practice, as it surely is, it is clear that interpretation and imagination are immensely open to traffic in our penultimate passions that seem to us so ultimate.

I have come belatedly to see, in my own case, that my hermeneutical passion is largely propelled by the fact that my father was a pastor economically abused by the church he served, economically abused as a means of control. I cannot measure the ways in which that felt awareness determines how I work, how I interpret, whom I read, whom I trust as a reliable voice. The wound is deep enough to pervade everything; I suspect, moreover, that I am not the only one. It could be that we turn our anxieties, fears, and hurts to good advantage as vehicles for obedience. But even in so doing, we are put on notice. We cannot escape, I believe, from such passions, but we can submit them to brothers and sisters whose own history of distortion is very different from our own and as powerful in its defining force.

Inspiration

It is traditional to speak of scripture as "inspired." There is a long history of unhelpful formulations of what that notion might mean. Without appealing to classical attempts at formulation that characteristically have more to do with "testing" the Spirit (1 John 4:1) than with "not quenching" the Spirit (1 Thess. 5:19), we may affirm that the force of God's purpose, will, and capacity for liberation, reconciliation, and new life is everywhere around this text. In such an affirmation, of course, we say more than we can understand, for the claim is precisely an acknowledgment that in and through this text, God's wind blows through and blows past all our critical and confessional categories of reading and understanding. That blowing force that powers and enlivens, moreover, pertains not simply to the origin of the text but to its transmission and interpretation among us. The Spirit will not be regimented, and therefore none of our reading is guaranteed to be inspired. But it does happen—on occasion.

It does happen that we are blown in and through the text beyond ourselves. It does happen—on occasion—that through the text the Spirit teaches and guides and heals so that the text yields something other than an echo of ourselves. It does happen in prayer and study that believers are led to what is "strange and new." It does happen that preachers in sermon preparation and in utterance are led to utter beyond what they set out to do.

It does happen that churches in council, sessions, and other courts are led beyond themselves, powered beyond prejudice, liberated beyond convention, overwhelmed by the capacity for new risks.

It does happen; it happens among faithful charismatics who frighten us Calvinists but who are led to newness. It has happened in Rome, with a push toward "separated brothers and sisters," including Jews, in ways we have not. I have seen it happen in a Bible study led by an Aboriginal woman in the Australian outback who in ways primitive to me saw clearly about the gospel. And even among Calvinists, so well defended against the Spirit, it happens in leaps over old barriers and tall buildings, in acts of generosity that defy capitalist parsimony, in reconciliation across lines of repugnance and abhorrence, in acts of forgiveness of unfathomable hate and resentment.

Such newness might have happened without the text, of course, because the wind blows where it will. But it does happen in and through the text—new resolve, new vision, new assurance, new summons. And we say, "I don't know what came over us." It is the wind in the words that comes over us, not one more grudging echo of us, but a word from out beyond, and the world begins again, "very good" indeed. We find, on such strange occasions, that not all of our historical criticism or all of our canonical reductionism, not all our moral pretense or all of our careless receptivity, not all of that or any of that can withstand the force. Because we are not speaking here of reasoned categories, but of the holy Wind that blows and destroys and makes new. The script of the book is a host and launching pad for the wind among us that the world cannot evoke and the church cannot resist.

Important

Biblical interpretation, done with imagination, willing to risk ideological distortion, open to the inspiring Spirit, is important. I would say "urgent," except that I am seeking to maintain the symmetry of the "I" terms. The importance of biblical interpretation, however, is not primarily in order to seize control of the church. It is rather that the world may have access to the good truth of the God who creates, redeems, and consummates. Of course, that missional intention is important (urgent) in every circumstance and season, and so the church at its most faithful has always understood that reading scripture is for the sake of the missional testimony of the church to the news for the world.

But we may say more particularly and more precisely that the reading of the Bible, in all its truthfulness, is now urgent because our society is sore tempted to reduce the human project to commodity, to the making of money, to the reduction of persons to objects, to the thinning of human communications to electronic icons. The threat is technique, whether "ten ways to wealth" or "six ways to sex" or whatever. Technique, in all its military modes and derivatively in every other mode, is aimed at control, the fencing out of death, the fencing out of gift, and eventually the fencing out of humanness.

Nonetheless, we dare affirm, all of us in the church together, that this lively Word is the primal antidote to technique, the primal news that fends off trivialization. Entertain the notion of thinning to control and trivialization to evade ambiguity as the major goals of our culture. Then consider that the church in its disputatious anxiety is sorely tempted to join the choice for technique, to thin the Bible and make it one dimensional, deeply tempted to trivialization by acting as though the Bible is important because it may resolve some disruptive social inconvenience. The dispute tends to reduce what is rich and dangerous in the book to knowable technique, and what is urgent and immense to what is exhaustible trivia.

Well, it's too important for that because the dangers of the world are too great and the expectations of God are too large. What if liberals and conservatives in the church, for all their disagreement, would agree and put their energies to the main truth against the main threat? This is not to sneak in a victory about gays and lesbians for anybody, but to say that the issues before God's creation (of which we are stewards) are immense; those issues shame us in the church when our energy is deployed only to settle our anxieties. Shame, shame! Take a look at the real issues. We all know the list. What this script does is to insist that the world is not without God, not without the holy gift of life rooted in love. And yet we, in the meantime, twitter!

Conclusion

My verse goes like this:

> . . . A lamp to my feet . . .
> a light to my path.

It is a lamp and light to fend off the darkness. It is for feet and path, on the way in venture. The darkness is real, and the light is for walking boldly, faithfully in the dark we do not and cannot control.

In this crisis, the church will usefully consider what it is that is entrusted peculiarly to us with the book. If we renege on this trust, we may find that

instead of apostolic inherency, we settle for what is familiar;
instead of interpretation, we reduce to monologue;
instead of imagination, we have private fantasy;
instead of facing ideology, we absolutize our anxiety;
instead of inspiration, we win control;
instead of importance, we end with trivialization.

There are important decisions to be made that are not partisan or sectarian, not liberal or conservative, but profoundly evangelical, and so to be made in freedom and joy.

Consider this voice from German piety outside Presbyterianism:

> In essentials, unity.
> It is not in doubt among us concerning the God who creates, redeems,
>   and consummates—good news indeed!
> In nonessentials, liberty.
> Nonessentials, matters never settled by the apostles, or by councils.
> In all things—in things essential and things nonessential—charity.
>
> Love is patient and kind, love is not envious or boastful, or arrogant or
> rude. It does not insist on its own way; it is not irritable or resentful.
> . . . Love bears all things, believes all things, hopes all things, endures
> all things. . . . And now abide faith, hope, and love, these three, and the
> greatest of these is love. (1 Cor. 13:4-5a, 7, 13)

In all things charity.

Recently, an Israeli journalist in Jerusalem commented on the fracturing dispute in Israel over who constitutes a real Jew—orthodox, conservative, or reformed. And said he about the dispute, "If any Jew wins, all Jews lose." Think about it: "If any Presbyterian wins, all Presbyterians lose."

In all things charity.

CHAPTER THREE

Biblical Authority and the Church's Task of Interpretation

I

The church's discussion about the authority of scripture takes place between the factors of *normativeness* and the *problematic*.

1. The matter of the authority of scripture is normatively settled in the church, and at the same time endlessly problematic. It is *normatively settled* because we are agreed that the Bible is indeed God's live word which addresses us as the only rule for life and faith. We will use various languages about inspiration and revelation and "Word of God," but all this language intends to attest to that decision about the normative character of scripture. Without that consensus it is not likely that the church will have either unity or fidelity to its mission. Some may not attest to that claim, but my judgment is that such voices are definitionally precluded from this particular conversation.

That normative claim, however, is *endlessly problematic* because every generation in the church (including our own) has found it difficult to agree on what is heard in the Bible as God's live word, or how indeed it is to be heard. It is problematic because we are dealing with a very ancient document that did not have in mind our particular set of issues, nor the linguistic and epistemological modes in which our issues are presented to us. But the problematic is not only because of antiquity. It is also because we do not agree among ourselves on our context and our situation in which we seek to receive, hear, and respond to the word of scripture. Our discernment of our life-world causes us to hear and discern the voice of the text differently.

2. It is self-evident that interpretation of scripture is unavoidable. David Tracy has nicely said that in order for a classic document that is timeless

to be timely, it must be interpreted.[1] It is for that reason that a claim about the authority of scripture is not the end of our trouble, but only the beginning. When we have accepted the Bible as normative, then we must ask how, in what way, to what end, for what claim. To answer those questions, we must interpret. When we interpret we render judgments, and those judgments rarely claim universal assent. (To be sure, in the church's long history of interpretation there are interpretations, as in the great creeds, which claim such assent. But the problem is that even the creeds about which there is general consensus are remote from us and in turn require interpretation.) Any serious engagement with scripture requires interpretation. And interpretation is always advocacy about which there is dispute. The interpretation may be as explicit as exegesis and proclamation, or it may be as seemingly innocent as the selection of one text and not another (as with a lectionary committee), or a public reading that intones, inflects, and accents certain ways. The fact of interpretation means that the Bible never fully has its own say, but is always in part acted upon by the interpreter. The Bible in practice is therefore open to various significations.

3. Interpretation is never objective but is always mediated through the voice, perceptions, hopes, fears, interest, and hurts of the interpreter. If interpretation is not objective, it is likely to be less than fully adequate, however well intended and true it may be. Every interpretation then must be kept open to the review of the whole church, which is bound to listen as a whole community to what God seems to be saying in scripture.

We are mostly clear that advocates of a liberation hermeneutic, that is, the interpretive voices of the third world, are advocates who speak from and for a certain context and interest. They are voices of the poor and oppressed who read scripture in terms of a "preferential option for the poor."[2] These interpreters themselves readily acknowledge their contextualization and how it governs their interpretation.

We are now coming to see that Euro-American theology done in classic historical-critical ways, done in the academy, done by white, established males is also contextualized and speaks from and for a certain context and interest.[3] This is true for those who speak through scientific methods and for those who speak primarily out of a dogmatic tradition. This does not mean that these interpretations are wrong or easily to be dismissed. It means that they must be taken for what they are, as statements of advocacy. They have no interpretive privilege, but must be held along with other readings in a church that seeks to be faithful and obedient.

The problem for any church, and especially a church that claims to be as genuinely diversified and open as the United Church of Christ, is how to practice the normativeness of scripture in a way that lets all interpretations be taken seriously, so that all interpreters listen and submit their readings to the judgment of the whole church, without imagining ahead of time that the truth has been spoken by any single interpretive voice.

Two implications flow from this problematic. First, we cannot be a faithful church if private, isolated communities of interpretation simply insist on reiterating their interpretations without the discipline and impingement of the whole church, and especially without counter-interpretations that are wrought in good faith. Second, if scripture is normative, as the main body of the church attests, then it is likely that the United Church of Christ has as a single national body no more important work to do than serious scripture interpretation. It behooves the governing officers and bodies of the church to provide sustained means whereby the church can do scripture interpretation that is not simply ad hoc, that is not undisciplined "ferment," and that is not simply private communities who congratulate themselves on their own interpretation. The United Church of Christ, to be genuinely ecumenical, is required to listen to widely different voices of interpretation, thereby necessitating the modification of our own best, preferred interpretive judgment.

II

In what follows I will comment on three sets of matters that function in the United Church of Christ in its interpretation of scripture. First, the history of biblical interpretation is beset by *two tyrannies,* both of which still have considerable force.

1. Because the Bible is peculiarly the church's book, the Bible came to function in the service of the church's faith. The Bible for a long period of church history was understood to be simply the material available for the dogmatic decisions of the church. Over time the Bible came to be reduced so that it was subservient to the church's dogmatic position. This may be called the "tyranny of the church" over the Bible, in which the Bible was required to agree with the dogmatic consensus of the church.

We may identify two effective voices in freeing the Bible of that tyranny. First, in foundational ways the Reformation of the sixteenth century was an argument for the freedom of scripture from the interpretive monopoly of the church. It was argued either that the Bible is its own interpreter, or that every person is capable of interpretation. What was noticed is that there is much in scripture that is not credited in or contained by the church's settled consensus. We in the United Church of Christ are children of that liberated recognition that the Bible must have its own say, even when it abrasively rubs against the church's settled judgment.

Second, the emergence of historical-critical scholarship was an attempt to find methods that respected the distinct character of the biblical text, without submission to formal church opinion. This liberated effort was largely an academic one, which insisted that scripture must be handled with the canon of criticism and reason like any other book.

By and large our tradition of interpretation is not greatly troubled by the tyranny of the church. However, in times of stress and anxiety one may detect those who want to reduce scripture to make the fit between church and Bible. This may happen by insisting on the classic monopoly of interpretation,[4] or it may happen by a sectarian ideology that forces all scripture through its prism. Newer methods of interpretation, for instance, sociological and literary, may serve precisely to guard against this reductionist tyranny.

2. The second tyranny is what I call the "tyranny of the academy." This is less noticed but very powerful. I refer to the long academic tradition of interpretation that is committed to historical-critical study. These methods were fashioned, as just indicated, to resist church tyranny. But they themselves have become a new tyranny. The danger in this direction is that the text is rationally explained so that its serious faith claims are relativized and nothing is left but a historical memory and a positive ethic. Gone then is the intellectual scandal, the abrasion to our reason, the stunning energy of God's miraculous presence and an ethic that subverts all our attempts to control, manage, and explain the world. In this tyranny the Bible ends up being congenial to "the cultural despisers of religion" but without the evangelical impetus to subvert the modern world.

This danger is likely more prevalent in our church context, because seminary instruction has been completely committed to historical-critical interpretation. Much of that study has relativized the Bible so that it is rendered innocuous. We are still finding our way out of this trouble, which is a part of a very large cultural commitment to Enlightenment modes of knowledge and power.[5] Oddly, those Enlightenment modes beset "liberal" critical interpreters as well as the literalist reaction. Both tend to be attempts at rational control which diminish the dynamic of the text. Post-critical interpretation probes for ways in which, utilizing our best learning, we may still discern an authority other than our own. It may be that interpretation in the presence of third-world voices is the best check on our propensity for liberal rationality that is dismissive of the text.

In the United Church of Christ we live between the tendencies to be reductionist or to be dismissive. Both tyrannies pretend to know in advance what the text as live word will say.

III

Second, I suggest we find in the church *two temptations* as we engage in the difficult but necessary task of finding an interpretive frame. Every interpretation I know about inclines to a frame of interpretation, so that there is a coherence and a certain predictability about the outcome of interpretation. The temptations that I think are evident are tendencies to *privatization* and *politicization*. Either temptation can easily become ideological, denying to the text the power to have its own surprising say among us.

1. The *temptation to privatization* reflects the fact that we have become largely a therapeutic community designed to deal with the psychic world of self.[6] The Bible then is read as a resource for one's growth, maturation, and well-being. One form of this temptation is to submit the Bible to the mode of one's favorite psychological theorist, whether Freud, Jung, Rogers, Maslow, or whomever.

But privatization, as I use the term, may also refer to treating the Bible according to the so-called social agenda of the right, so that the Bible is read around the issues that surface in relation to domestic, interpersonal life to the neglect of public issues. Such an inclination guilelessly misreads the public character of biblical faith and ends up handling the Bible to serve a reactionary agenda. Reading the Bible in this way tends to disregard the transcendent power of God and the urgency of God's purpose and will concerning the great public questions.

2. The alternative temptation among us is the *temptation to politicization*. Such an interpretive posture is inclined to see everything in scripture as a legitimation or even a strategy for social action and social transformation. It cannot be denied that the Bible is mightily concerned with questions of justice and peace, but to press the text always in this one direction puts the text to bad use in two recurring ways. First, the Bible is too easily "applied"

to contemporary situations, whether this be taken with reference to disarmament and welfare, or to abortion and homosexuality. Such moves to contemporaneity, whether the moves are made by radicals or reactionaries, disregard the differences in the ambience of ethical issues, choices, and strategies related to the Word in the ancient world and in the contemporary world.

Second, politicization runs the risk of denying the eschatological claim of the text. That is, the "kingdom of God" as a concrete metaphor in biblical faith cannot be completely identified with any social construct we may contrive. There are, to be sure, examples in the Bible of such ideological identification but these identifications are regularly under harsh critique.

It is important in the United Church of Christ that we review and understand these inclinations toward privatization and politicization. For myself, I believe that the political tendency more closely honors the text, but we need to recognize that every such judgment (including this one) emerges from a particular context and needs to be submitted to the judgment of the whole church.

IV

Finally, in our interpretive practice, we can identify in the church *two practical tendencies* that live in profound tension, the tendencies toward *equilibrium* and *transformation*. The Bible is the story of the ways in which God has broken things in the world open for newness, and the ways in which God has legitimized and established new constructs of order in the church and in the world.[7] These two tendencies are present in the liberating tradition of Moses and the power-arranging tendency of David.[8] More closely they are present in the transformative narrative of Exodus and in the ordering Torah of the Sinai covenant. In the New Testament one may find a stress on disruption in Mark, revolutionary propensity in Luke, and discipline in Matthew. These are not stark contrasts, but they are tendencies of interpretation that are very clear in various interpretive communities in the early church.

These tendencies show up in our interpretation so starkly that one would not conclude we are all reading the same Bible. The practical tendency to equilibrium places emphasis on biblical teaching about order, respect for authority, discipline, and purity. The practical tendency to transformation places accent on liberation, inversion of power arrangements, and the gift of freedom. On the one hand there are those who greatly appreciate the disciplined teaching of the Bible on sexual conduct, while on the other hand there are those who resonate with God's permission to be new creatures, unfettered by old restrictive practice. The problem, of course, is that both tendencies are biblical. Clearly the difficulty is how to adjudicate such tendencies, and that can only be done by paying attention to context: the context of the text itself and the context of the interpreter.

I suggest that matters of equilibrium and transformation be understood in terms of the discernment that "Everyone to whom much is given, of him much will be required" (Luke 12:48). A counterstatement that seems congenial to the witness of Jesus might be, "to everyone who has little, much will be permitted." That is, the "haves" of the world have heavier requirements from the summons of the gospel to more stringent obedience, whereas the "have-nots" are peculiar objects of God's liberating news. I believe this is the claim of the parable of Luke 16:19-31.

No single text can be understood as absolutely appropriate, for ethical decision making is always contextual. Such a principle of interpretation has important implications in the handling of biblical requirements with reference to many social and moral issues. The main point is that we must (and I believe inevitably do) make contextual differentiations in thinking of the Bible in terms of equilibrium and transformation. We do not consistently practice "law and order," nor do we consistently practice toleration and forgiveness. But we might be more intentional in our differentiations as we struggle with "splinters and beams" (Matt. 7:3-5)—and perhaps more honest in our adjudication of these two tendencies.

The need for contextual adjudication between equilibrium and transformation can be helpfully illustrated by two concrete contemporary ethical issues. I suggest that the Bible knows that the two great ethical issues about which we are most vexed and from which we hope the most are *sexuality* and *money*. I submit that the Bible affirms: (*a*) sexuality and money are the two great human issues; (*b*) both issues must be submitted to God's sovereign, gracious rule; and (*c*) the two issues are inextricably related to each other and cannot be understood apart from each other. Sexuality and money are of a piece in terms of human possibility, domination, and brutality. For evidence of their interrelatedness, I see them linked as the primary points of righteousness in Ezekiel 18:6-8, and Job 31:1, 9, 16, 24.

As a starting point for thinking about the authority of scripture in which the critical practice of the church is concerned, I urge that the inextricable relation of sexuality and money requires new clarity and fresh decisions. Such a beginning point may suggest that the church should never speak on one of these issues without a complementary statement on the other, so that conservatives do not make sexuality their issue and liberals do not make economics their issue, but that all of us together must submit our propensities and fears to the rule of God.

V

In my judgment the interpretive issues I have articulated show that interpretation is exceedingly problematic. I have identified three ways of thinking about the problem of interpretation:

1. The tyranny of reductionism (in the *church*) and of dismissiveness (in the *academy*).
2. The temptation to *privatization* and to *politicization*, when we know what the text will say before we listen.
3. The practical tendencies to *equilibrium* and to *transformation*, without making necessary and appropriate differentiations in context.

I am aware that my topic is *authority* and my discussion thus far has been preoccupied with *interpretation*. But it is precisely the relation of authority and interpretation that is our problem.[9] On the one hand, an authoritative Bible without interpretation has little pertinence or power. On the other hand, as soon as one interprets, we want our interpretation to be included in the scope of the authority we assign to the Bible, so that we imagine we possess an "authorized" interpretation.

Because of its openness and diversity the United Church of Christ has a chance to probe in fresh ways the juxtaposition of authority and interpretation. But that new probe cannot happen by competing "proposals of absoluteness." It can only be done if interpretations are offered to the church that are submitted provisionally and in vulnerability, so that our interpretations listen to other voices in the church and "look not only to our own interests, but the interests of others" (Phil. 2:4). Where shall we do interpretation that is obedient, so that our own ideological presuppositions stand under the judgment of God? *Formally,* our interpretation is to be done in the presence of Jesus Christ who is crucified and risen, who had nowhere to lay his head (Matt. 8:20), who was friend of publicans and sinners (Luke 7:34), who became poor that by becoming poor he might make us rich (2 Cor. 8:9). I submit that what we know of Jesus is a clue about interpretation. Our interpretation (which is our real practice of authority) is to be crucified and risen to new truthfulness. Our interpretation is not to be done in our comfortable established posture, but as exiles on the way. Our interpretation is to be amenable to the poor and marginal for whom our controlled epistemology, our assured affluence, and our certain morality lack complete credibility. Our interpretation is an act of our poverty and not of our fullness, so that it might enrich others. The Bible, its authority and our interpretation, is a scandal. The scandal is not that we have certitude but that we have been given power for life.

Functionally, our interpretation is to be done, I propose, gathered around the Eucharistic table which anticipates our gathering around the throne. In our interpretative act we are not the host, but the invited guest. As we watch the bread broken and given to all, we are invited to see that our interpretation does not speak the truth unless it is broken truth. As we watch the wine poured out, we know our lives must be poured out, or our interpretation is a lie.

The language spoken at the table is the peculiar language of evangelical faith. This language is not our language, whether our language be that of certain scholasticism, partisan moralism, or strident revolution. Only certain words bespeak God's word in ways that can claim the church. We will not claim again the authority of scripture unless we recover its language, which is the language of trust and amazement, of gratitude and obedience.

II.

Old Testament Theology in the Twentieth Century

Twentieth-Century Old Testament Studies

A Quick Survey

The contours of Western cultural history through the twentieth century are in large sweep identifiable: an initial moment of innocence until 1914, the willful barbarism of the two wars (1914–1945), the long tense stand-off of the cold war (1945–1989), and a final decade of localism in the presence of "the last superpower" (1989–2000). I do not suggest that the story of critical Old Testament study is dictated or controlled by the forces of public history. But neither does this particular tale of scholarship exist in a vacuum, without reference to context. In reviewing and assessing such scholarship, it is important to remember that scholarship is conducted by real people who live in the real world with its immense gifts and dangers.

I

Old Testament studies at the outset of the twentieth century were completely dominated by the historical methods and synthesis of the nineteenth century. Julius Wellhausen's great book of synthesis was at the turn of the century only twenty years old, and it largely carried the field.[1] Indeed, the force of nineteenth-century scholarship continued well into the mid-twentieth century, and it continues to exercise important influence even now. That nineteenth-century synthesis had, of course, reached certain "consensus" conclusions on substantive issues, most notably the "documentary hypothesis" concerning the formation of the Pentateuch.

The defining power of that scholarship, however, is not so much in the substantive conclusions it reached, but in the way in which it legitimated the asking of certain questions. Nineteenth-century scholarship, in almost every intellectual discipline, had come to regard historical issues as primary; not surprisingly, Old Testament study was at the time largely a historical enterprise, asking not only "What happened?" but "When was it written?" The governing assumption was that historical context would decisively illuminate the intent of the text.

Two subpoints need to be noticed under the unchallenged dominance of a historical perspective. First, nineteenth-century history was premised on an assumption of *progressive, unilateral evolution* within the dynamic interpretive categories of Hegel, Marx, Darwin, and Freud. That is, everything was understood to develop from the simple to the complex, from the primitive to the sophisticated. It was no stretch then for the religion of ancient Israel to be understood as a movement from the "mythical" to the "ethical," reflected in the "development of God" and the presentation of God from J through E to DP. Second, such a developmental approach, shared by almost all critical scholars, had the effect of making every religious claim relative to context and sure to be superseded by the next new development. This perspective dissolved all normative claims of the text, and rendered normative theological reflection almost impossible. Indeed, this phase of scholarship is completely lacking in what has since come to be seen as *theology* of the Old Testament.

II

It is impossible to overstate the importance of Karl Barth for the altered shape of Old Testament studies in the mid-twentieth century. As is well known, Barth, in the context of World War I, published his radical summons to theological reflection and theological obedience in his Romans commentary of 1919.[2] It was Barth's insistence that scholarly interpretation must break from liberal relativism and must voice normative theological claims that provide a theological place to stand against the emerging barbarism of Europe. Barth's urgency in the wake of World War I was only made more urgent by the rise of National Socialism in Germany in the 1930s, against which Barth stood immovably.

Barth had no particular interest in Old Testament studies *per se,* but he did trenchantly observe that historical-evolutionary interpretation and the niceties of critical scholarship must not stand as an impediment to decisions about the theological claims of the Bible made for the God who is offered in the testimony of ancient Israel and in the confession of the early church. Barth's daring challenge became a decisive turning point for Old Testament studies. He attracted to his urgent theological enterprise a great company of those who would become the most influential and defining Old Testament scholars in the next generation, since until midcentury Old Testament studies of a critical kind were largely a German enterprise. For some, of course, Barth's break with nineteenth-century evolutionary thought was too radical, too theological, too authoritarian. He was emphatically not followed by all scholars. Those who did not follow his daring challenge by and large continued the evolutionary-historical scholarship of the previous century.

III

We may observe that the 1930s, the time of Barth's most spectacular theological thought, was a period of uncommon generativity in Old Testament studies, a generativity that was to govern the next decades in the discipline.[3] We may identify two developments that lived in considerable tension with each other.

First, Barth's influence evoked and legitimated important efforts at "Old Testament theology," attempts at stating the God-claims of the Old Testament in some coherent fashion. Two scholarly efforts have been most influential. Walther Eichrodt, a Calvinist scholar and colleague of Barth at Basel, published a three-volume theology of the Old Testament.[4] This effort was an immense breakthrough against the dominance of evolutionary relativity. While Eichrodt paid attention to "developmental" matters, he was concerned to identify the abiding "constancies" of faith that endure in flexible and resilient ways through every stage of religious development. He found these constancies under the rubric of "covenant," that is, the durable God–Israel, God–world relationship that is definitional for the faith of Israel in the Old Testament. Eichrodt made use of old and proven Calvinist categories.[5] In the 1950s, under the impetus of George Mendenhall and Klaus Baltzer, the idea of covenant came to a dominant position in much critical Old Testament interpretation.[6]

The second and more influential effort at Old Testament theology was by Gerhard von Rad, who wrote two volumes in the 1950s on the basis of essays he had written already in the 1930s.[7] Just prior to his death in 1971, von Rad published *Wisdom in Israel*, a book that constituted something of a third volume to his theology.[8] In his first and most important volume, von

Rad proposed that Old Testament theology consists in the endless, ongoing recital of "God's mighty deeds in history." By this formulation, von Rad was able to focus theology on a distinct inventory of God's "miracles" in the life of Israel, and was able to attend to the "historical" issues related to those "historical miracles." In this way he made room for the dynamic processes in the continuing development of the classic and stylized recital on the lips of Israel.

It is impossible to overstate the emancipatory power of von Rad's work, which exercised immense impact in the United States as well as in Europe. It was only later noticed that von Rad had not at all resolved the vexed relationship between the relativity of history and the normativeness of theological claim. In dealing with that issue, he averred:

> Historical investigation searches for a critically assured minimum—the kerygmatic picture tends towards a theological maximum.[9]

Indeed, it is not clear that a resolution of the issue identified by Lessing is possible. This lack of resolution was to continue to haunt Old Testament interpretive work with its legacy of nineteenth-century historicism.

IV

While the theological proposals of Eichrodt and von Rad are the most noticed and enduring German-Swiss contributions, and while conventional historical-critical work continued, a very different enterprise emerged in the United States under the leadership of William Foxwell Albright. This brilliant researcher at Johns Hopkins University almost single-handedly fashioned archaeology to be a credible scientific way to investigate the historical antecedents of the Old Testament.[10] By his excavations in Palestine in the 1930s, his creative powers matched to his vast learning, Albright formulated methods of research that could be replicated in various digs and assessed on common ground by other scholars. His methods came to be shared by a number of scholars, most especially his brilliant cadre of students who came to dominate Old Testament studies in the United States for over a generation.

The product of Albright's work, summarized and popularized by John Bright in his much-used *A History of Israel,* was a consensus presentation of Israelite history that in large measure showed the biblical record to be historically reliable.[11] In retrospect, subsequent scholars have been able to see that Albright's work proceeded too much on the grounds of historical positivism to be well connected to theological claim. There is, moreover, the current suggestion that Albright set out to "prove" the Bible in a way that undermines claims to historical objectivity.[12] Be that as it may, the methods of archaeology at midcentury dominated much U.S. scholarship and offered assurance of the historical reliability of the biblical account of Israel's past. While Albright broke decisively with the evolutionary assumptions of the nineteenth century, he continued to be focused primarily upon issues of historicity.

V

These twin developments in the 1930s—post-Barthian articulations of *normative theological claims* and Albrightian claims of *historical reliability*—dominated the field of Old Testament studies. It may be observed that there was a good deal of tension between these two enterprises; while that tension was voiced and noticed (especially from the Albrightian side), it is now clear that both approaches were deeply concerned with the normative authority of the Bible that was to be established by insisting upon its early dating of historical traditions. Neither approach could break with *historical* bases for *theological* claims.

The key figure in U.S. Old Testament studies at midcentury was George Ernest Wright, a Presbyterian teacher who established the premier Old Testament program in the United States at Harvard in the 1950s. Wright was a foremost student of Albright, and he himself led important excavations and wrote extensively on archaeological matters.[13] At the same time, Wright emerged as a foremost theological interpreter of the Bible. He published a series of monographs that exercised immense influence, most notably *God Who Acts* and *The Old Testament against Its Environment.*[14] Wright's primary theological point was to insist upon the profound and intentional *distinctiveness* of YHWH as the God of Israel, and derivatively to show that Israel, as the people of God, lived in the world with a distinct identity and a distinct ethic that we may at every point contrast with "Canaanite religion." It is evident that Wright's account of Israel's faith stands in important continuity with Barth's rejection of "religion," even as Wright polemicized against "Canaanite religion."

In retrospect one may see some irony in Wright's work, for his archaeological leaning appealed to the evidence of borrowings from context, but his theological work in every way possible contrasted Israel with context.

In any case, Wright's great synthetic work, scientifically informed and theologically propelled, came to dominate the scholarly enterprise and to exercise immense influence more popularly in the life of the church in the United States that flourished in the 1950s. (I should note that after the papal encyclical of 1943, granting freedom to engage in critical scholarship, Roman Catholic scholars began also to participate in the critical enterprise.[15] Given the differences due to confessional awareness, it is fair to say that Roman Catholic scholars participated in the same scholarly work that had heretofore been the domain of Protestants.)

The main lines of influence, in terms of assumptions and methods, that emerged in the 1930s—theological and archaeological—continued to dominate the field through the 1960s. The scholarly synthesis that arose out of these twin perspectives resulted in a great revival of interest in biblical study in seminaries and in graduate programs, a revival in the churches, and the beginning of a new season of publication, most of which sought to move from *evolutionary* historical concerns to the *normative* theological claims now celebrated from the text. The decades of the 1950s and 1960s were a time of stability, confidence, and positive energy in the field.

VI

The end of the 1960s and the decade of the 1970s were, of course, a time of great upheaval in the United States and in western Europe. This was the time of the civil rights movement, the Vietnam War, and the Watergate hearings. Perhaps the pivotal symbolic moment was the student revolts in Paris in 1968, matched in this country by the disastrous Democratic convention in Chicago in the same year. Many things came to a decisive and brutal ending in these years, most especially a widespread readiness to accept old certitudes and authorities.

It is fair to say, in my judgment, that Old Testament studies participated in the wider cultural exercise of rejecting long-settled certitudes. The 1960s, it is clear in retrospect, was a period of great scholarly ferment that was not much noticed until later. What began to happen were the challenging, questioning, and break-up of the dominant patterns of the long-standing theological-archaeological-historical settlement. It had long been held that the foremost revelatory claims of the Old Testament were about "God acting in history." All three terms in this formula are important, and now all three terms were made deeply problematic, so that the familiar formulations of von Rad, Albright, and Wright were now less compelling. Among the contributing factors in the demise of the midcentury consensus the following are most important:

- James Barr published a staggeringly important book suggesting that old habits of "word study," upon which a great deal of interpretation had been staked, were methodologically indefensible.[16]
- Brevard Childs began a series of books that repeatedly made the case that reliance on "history" behind the Bible in order to make theological claims for the Bible is an impossible and untenable appeal.[17]
- John Van Seters and Thomas L. Thompson initiated a trajectory of scholarship, later to be joined by many other scholars, making a case that archaeology did not and could not yield the kinds of historical certitudes on which the field had come to count for a very long time.[18]

The entire category of "history" was seen to be profoundly problematic, this especially in a much-noted essay by Langdon Gilkey.[19]

It became apparent that the nearly triumphant, midcentury consensus of Old Testament studies had relied upon a finally untenable combination of Barthian *normativeness* and nineteenth-century *historicism*, a combination that under scrutiny could not be sustained. This collage of scholarly critiques brought to an end the dominance of the practices, assumptions, and claims that had governed the field at midcentury. The immediate result was confusion and disarray in the field. The longer-term prospect was to open the field to fresh initiatives. The most obvious outcome of the upheavals of this period has been the serious *deprivileging* of history, its claims and method. While historical criticism continues as an important work, it is no longer the defining method of the field.

In the face of that displacement, the field of Old Testament studies is opened to a *new pluralism* in methods, perspectives, and constituencies. Here I will mention three facets of that new pluralism.

1. As recently as the 1960s, Old Testament scholarship was largely a contained affair, with agreed-upon issues and methods, identifiable journals, and readily identifiable leaders who defined the field. Since about 1970 or so, the field has been opened to many new practices and perspectives. Particularly significant has been the entry of many new students and scholars who have not subscribed to the old models of white, male, Western hegemonic thinking. The entry of many women into the field with various

forms of feminist perspective, the emergence of liberation hermeneutics of various kinds, and fresh interpretive trajectories from Central America, Africa, and Asia all attest that there is no one right way to do responsible interpretation. This has led, in turn, to the founding of new journals in the field, so that scholars with different methods and perspectives can have a more formal, formidable say about matters. Among the more important of these is *Biblical Interpretation,* a journal committed to new perspectives and to the continued deprivileging of historical questions.

2. Among the more important emerging methods that now stand to challenge historical criticism is *sociological criticism.* This approach, perhaps most decisively championed by Norman Gottwald, has sought to consider texts along with their social power and social advocacy, and to see that texts may indeed be "functions" of material forces and interests.[20] While one does not need to subscribe to a Marxian vision of "text as power," a Marxian social analysis of the ways in which texts are instruments of power is now an important staple of textual study. Among other things, such a perspective reminds us endlessly that texts are not innocent, nor are our interpretive acts. As long as there was only one dominant interpretive trajectory with a relatively homogeneous community of interpreters, we had not noticed the immense power intrinsic to the act of interpretation. The newer methods permit no such lack of awareness.

3. Along with sociological awareness, *literary, rhetorical study* now pays close attention to the actual workings of texts as an intentional system of signs. The point of such work is to see that the text is not simply "report" or "history," but a characteristic act of generative imagination that conjures an alternative world well beyond what is taken to be a given. Derivative from the initiatory work of my own teacher, James Muilenburg, it is now a principal work of scholarship to notice what texts do, how they function, and how they form worlds that are outside and alternative to our taken-for-granted systems of power and meaning.[21]

It is impossible to overstate the energy and interpretive richness that has been unleashed into the discipline with the deprivileging of historical methods and questions and the fashioning of alternative approaches.

VII

The general disarray of the field by 1970 had begun to take a new, clear shape by 1990. In conclusion, I want to identify three issues that have more recently emerged in the field that will continue to warrant great energy and attention.

1. By 1990 there had come a renewed interest and vitality in the work of *Old Testament theology*. Given the disarray of 1970, it had been widely thought that one could no longer take up such a theological task, but now there is important energy in the enterprise. At the beginning of a new century a great deal of attention is once again given to interpretation that is unabashedly interested in theological questions and that seeks to articulate larger patterns of coherence in the faith of Israel as it is pertinent to the church and the synagogue.

The principal figure in this recovery is Brevard Childs, who culminated a steady stream of books with his programmatic statement in 1993.[22] This remarkable book is distinguished in many ways that are representative of Childs's program. Here I will mention only two. First, Childs is clear that he is doing *Christian* interpretation for the sake of the church. Such a claim means that Childs refuses the critical restraints and assumptions of the academy and that, from the start, he eschews any attention to Jewish interpretation with his explicit christological interest.

Second and equally important, Childs distances theological claims he finds in the text from any judgment about history that may be "behind the text." His powerful alternative to "history" is "canon," that is, the larger shape and theological claim of scripture in which any particular text is located. The enduring importance of Childs's work is his effort to interrupt and reverse the long-standing dominance of historical-critical study that has sapped the vitality and courage of theological interpretation. His effort has reasserted the legitimacy of such confessional study; evidence of that legitimation is a sudden flow of new books on the subject. Attention will usefully be paid to the recent work of Rolf Knierim, Bernhard Anderson, James Barr, and Rolf Rendtorff, among the most formidable and senior members of the discipline.[23]

2. A counterposition to theological interpretation must be noted as a major facet of study at the end of the century, namely, *ideology critique*. Without a very stable or clear understanding of "ideology," a number of scholars are attentive to ideological dimensions of the text, by which is meant special advocacy in the guise of either historical reportage or of disinterested theological claim. This propensity in recent scholarship, informed by a general Marxian analysis of ideology and particularly by Michel Foucault's recognition that discourse is an act of power, takes two

distinct forms. Scholars interested in "historical" questions are concerned to establish that the text rather regularly lacks historical reliability.[24] Other scholars are more attentive to theological claims that are in fact acts of social power.[25] These twin approaches stand in some continuity with the older historical criticism, but they stand against an older historical positivism as well as a less suspicious theological perspective.

My impression is that this approach is essentially reactive. That is, the higher the claims made by other scholars (historical or theological) from and for the text, the more vigorous is this critical response. Such scholars regard high claims (historical or theological) as fundamentally dishonest (thus, as deceptive "ideology"), and exposure of such dishonest claims is regarded as a moral responsibility. In the end, I suspect, it will be important, in a dialectical way, to show that such exponents of ideology criticism are themselves propelled by a value assumption that has most in common with the illusions of nineteenth-century objectivity.

3. A third issue emerging at the end of the century, important for students of this text, is how *Jewish reading* toward the synagogue and *Christian reading* for the church are to be related to each other, if at all. Through the twentieth century, two unfortunate tendencies are clear. First, in the interest of "objectivity," both Jewish and Christian scholars of a critical kind bracketed out any confessional commitment, sharing a critical project devoid of theological passion.[26] Second, Christian scholars who dominated the critical enterprise proceeded as if Jewish interpretive work did not exist, assuming a monopoly of interpretation that predictably carried with it nuances of supersessionism and anti-Semitism.

At the beginning of the twenty-first century, it is clear that neither "objective" interpretation nor Christian monopoly of interpretation is viable. This awareness arises partly on academic grounds with the growing recognition that these texts evoke and permit more than one lively interpretive trajectory, that is, that the text is polyvalent. Partly the awareness arises on moral grounds with the recognition that monopolistic interpretive practices lie in the background of the barbarism of the holocaust. It is not easy, however, to find fresh ways of interpretation that are responsible, honest, and open. Here I may mention three factors that will need to be considered in future work.

First, while there have always been prominent Jewish interpreters of the Hebrew Bible, those best known to Christian scholars have largely confined themselves to critical questions that did not pose strong confessional claims. Now attention must be paid to emerging Jewish interpreters of prominence—best known are Michael Fishbane and Jon D. Levenson who work from a clear Jewish perspective of interpretation.[27] As attention is paid to such interpretive work, Christian interpreters will need to proceed differently, not least to unlearn monopolistic assumptions. Second, important scholars—Childs as a Christian and Levenson as a Jew—strongly insist that Jewish and Christian interpreters have quite distinct responsibilities and cannot in fact cooperate without unbearable compromise of confessional convictions.[28] But third, at the end of the century with its immense record of hate and violence, there are scholars who suggest that Christians must rethink and reformulate in deeply different ways the assumptions of Christian interpretation in the presence of Jewish interpretation.[29] The work of this latter inclination, in contrast to the positions of Childs and Levenson, suggests that much of the polemical distinction between Jews and Christians is not in fact about truth claims but about the long-standing power of domination. All of that remains to be sorted out.

These three emergences that were hardly on the horizon at the turn of the discipline in the 1970s—fresh impetus in Old Testament theology, ideology critique, Jewish-Christian interfaces—indicate how deeply the field has changed, and how much fresh vitality and energy are present in the field at the beginning of the century. It is clear that the turn in Western culture, with its failed barbarism, and the emerging interpretive pluralism have impacted and changed the discipline in ways that could not have been anticipated in the simpler, more confident mood of the midcentury. The great contributions of the midcentury, still in the grip of nineteenth-century historicism, are not to be scuttled, but become durable resources and reference points out of which the field will continue to change in response to a cultural environment now vigorously pluralistic and deeply at risk.

CHAPTER FIVE

Biblical Faith as Narrative, Recital, Confession

An Introduction to von Rad's *Old Testament Theology*

The reissue of Gerhard von Rad's *Old Testament Theology* is a most welcome event, as welcome as it is important to us. It is clear that von Rad (1901–1971), long-time professor in the University of Heidelberg, is the defining and preeminent interpreter of the Christian Old Testament in the twentieth century, and that this two-volume work is the definitive publication of his long, prolific scholarly career. Von Rad's work occupies such a dominant place in twentieth-century theological exposition that it is possible and useful to trace theological interpretation in the twentieth century in terms of periods "pre-von Rad, von Rad, and post-von Rad." While that sequence has already become "history" for us at the outset of the twenty-first century, it is clear that the turn von Rad has wrought in expository method and horizon continues to inform our work in decisive ways and will continue to do so for years to come.

I

No scholar, not even one as brilliant as von Rad, operates in a vacuum or contributes to our learning *de novo*. Even the most innovative scholar stands in the midst of an interpretive tradition and works with the shape of questions and the horizon of possibilities that are already extant, even determinative, in prior work, before new work can begin.[1] Thus it is important to situate von Rad in his field of study and to discern, as best we can, the working assumptions and questions to which he was an heir. We may consider in turn the *critical* and the *kerygmatic* legacies to which von Rad was a worthy and imaginative heir.

Von Rad was of course well educated in the best historical-critical traditions of nineteenth-century Germany. This refers to the entire sequence of "assured results" that culminated in the great synthesis of Julius Wellhausen, whose book is commonly regarded as the great crowning achievement of the scholarship of two centuries.[2] It is common to judge that the trajectory culminating in Wellhausen received its clear manifesto in a lecture by Philip Gabler in 1787; Gabler asserted that the proper task of Old Testament scholarship is historical and not theological.[3] The negation that Gabler sought to establish was that scholarship should no longer operate within the categories of ecclesial church tradition or be subject to its theological requirements. That is, Gabler articulated the emancipation of critical scholarship from the dogmatic requirements that had emerged in the seventeenth century. Positively, Gabler's categories legitimated for scholarship the task of historical recovery of "what happened," a task that necessitated reading texts in their presumed contexts of origin.

Because the Old Testament is so complex and multilayered, the historical question turned out to be no simple one. It required great attention to the delineation of literary sources out of which "history" could be read; the delineation of sources led in turn to the identification of different "religious" pictures and assumptions reflective of different sources produced in different times and circumstances and from different perspectives. Out of such long-term scholarly problems concerning the historical and therefore the religious complexity of the Old Testament, there emerged a powerful and eventually dominant hypothesis of "developmentalism" that was profoundly different from any interpretation given according to ecclesial categories. The thesis of religious developmentalism—from simple to complex, from polytheism to monotheism, from cult and magic to ethics—was matched by a literary hypothesis that came to be termed "the Documentary Hypothesis."

By the end of the nineteenth century, and fully dominant by the time of von Rad, there was scholarly agreement about the sequence of sources to be found in the literature (JEDP). There was, moreover, agreement about the developmental course of Israelite religion as it culminated in the twin trajectories of Deuteronomic-prophetic ethics (regarded by German Protestant scholars as the highest development) and the Priestly tradition that eventuated in aspects of Judaism most disdained by the typical rational German scholar who had little appreciation for the function or intention of these materials.

The interpretive outcome of such long-term scholarly work is the awareness that there are multiple religious advocacies in the text, no one of which is ultimately dominant in the final form of the text. There is a dynamic development as one moves from one source to another and from one advocacy to another, so that no single religious affirmation may be taken as normative. The outcome of the whole is to see that the text offers a multiplicity of claims that are offered with a convinced relativism, every advocacy thus lacking in the kind of authority that ecclesial practices tend to require.

One other outcome of this critical venture may be noted. It was commonly recognized that as the "religion of Israel" developed, one may identify a major divide in practice and assumption in the fifth century as one distinguishes between the old traditions of Israel and the emergent claims of Judaism. Thus it became a truism of scholarship that the interrelatedness of "Israelite religion" and "emergent Judaism" is complex, featuring continuity between the two as well as discontinuity. All of this forms a background for von Rad's work.

Alongside that critical consensus, however, we must consider the kerygmatic impetus behind von Rad's effort at theological interpretation. The historical dynamic expressed as "religious developmentalism" resulted in an interpretive relativism. A sharp-edged authority for the theological claims of the text was absent in such scholarship. Its absence in the nineteenth century, moreover, was not accidental, but a deliberate outcome of critical work outside of and perforce against ecclesial authority. The scholarly outcome was the abandonment of any effort at "Old Testament theology" and a much-practiced "history of Israelite religion" that denied every authoritative theological claim.

The story is much told and well known that such relativism outside ecclesial authority—the prevailing mood of scholarly interpretation of the Bible at the turn of the twentieth century—proved to be theologically inadequate for the vast European crisis of World War I. It is well known that the "point person" for articulating the problem as "crisis" was Karl Barth, who dramatically and radically called into question the entire program of relativism and developmentalism in his Romans commentary of 1919.[4] Barth insisted that, and showed how, the theological claims of the Bible (including the Old Testament) must and can be taken as normative for the faith and ethics of the church, and not thinned away from this normative function. Barth's concern was practical, pastoral, and pragmatic; he sought a theological ground from which to act alternatively in the world, and he concluded that only scripture could provide the platform for such daring risk in the world.

In this way Barth stands in the line of the great Reformers with his appeal to scripture against anemic or distorted theological interpretation. Like von Rad after him, Barth was schooled in the best of German historical criticism. In the urgency of his pastoral task, however, he concluded that such scholarship was at best penultimate, and that in fact it trivialized the great truth of scripture that he showed to be compelling. In an act of great theological nerve, Barth simply read past the complexities that funded developmentalism and insisted that in their main claims all of the "sources" in scripture are agreed on what is said (revealed) of God and God's way in, and will for, the world. Barth refused the niceties of developmental distinctions, because the real issue, said he, is not in the specificities of textual detail, but rather in the witness of the text, which provides an adequate theological ground for courageous resistance and nervy alternative action in a dangerous world.

It is well known that Barth went on, not only to produce the great Protestant theological synthesis of the century, but also, and for our purposes more important, to recover the theological nerve of German Protestantism in its great "church struggle" with National Socialism. Derivatively, his work stiffened the theological spine of the church in many places in the world right through the twentieth century. Barth's frontal challenge to developmental relativism is the great story of twentieth-century biblical theology among Protestants.

As a young pastor scholar, von Rad was formed and shaped by the force, vitality, and liveliness of the work of Barth. Most specifically the German church struggle, with its theological culmination in 1934 in the Barmen Declaration, surely provided the matrix for von Rad's initial theological work.[5] Because of the force of the developmental hypothesis, there had been no serious effort at Old Testament theology in a very long time, that is, no attempt to formulate any normative theological-ethical claims out of the text for the sake of an ecclesial tradition. It was Barth's work that provided the impetus for fresh attempts at theological interpretation. The two preeminent attempts in response to the theological crisis that Barth identified were that of Walther Eichrodt, Barth's colleague in Basel, and that of von Rad, which reached its full expression only in the 1950s.[6]

It is clear, as we consider von Rad's work, that the two background features of *critical developmentalism* and *kerygmatic normativeness* were both exceedingly important to von Rad's theological exposition. It is equally clear that these two background features were in deep tension with each other, if not in the end mutually exclusive. Von Rad's work is a remarkable attempt to keep in play the important learnings and requirements of both. It was a question of how to retain the developmental multiplicity of religious claims in the text alive without detracting from the normative force of a theological claim that could be clear, deep, and durable enough to renew the courage of the church. It is a measure of von Rad's daring and brilliance that he would attempt such a task, indeed that he would accomplish the task with considerable and abiding success.

It is fair to say that von Rad dominated and shaped Old Testament theology at midcentury and continued to be a defining force, even after serious doubts had been raised about his assumptions and categories. The mid-twentieth-century period—under the impetus of Barth and before the questions of secularism, pluralism, and postmodernism took on such force—was a time of great energy, imagination, and excitement in the discipline. Largely because of von Rad's imaginative impetus, a whole generation of younger scholars was drawn into Old Testament studies. As a consequence, the discipline received a revitalization in universities and seminaries. The entire process generated by von Rad came to be termed pejoratively by its critics "the biblical theology movement."

Alongside the Lutheran effort of von Rad came the Reformed contributions of Walther Eichrodt and George Ernest Wright, the latter of whom had much in common with von Rad. This was also the time of the new stirring in Roman Catholic scholarship in the wake of the papal encyclical of 1943, *Divino Afflante Spiritu,* which opened the way for critical Catholic scholarship. This new impetus was especially represented by John McKenzie, Dennis McCarthy, Bruce Vawter, and Carroll Stuhlmueller. As in the academy, so in the church in the United States, attentiveness to a theology of "God's Mighty Deeds in History" proved to be a formulation to which laypeople could well relate. While many factors converged to make such a remarkable interpretive moment possible, there is no doubt that the key factor was von Rad's own work.

II

In good German fashion, von Rad published a number of important articles prior to his theology that voice crucial theses that became decisive for his theology. I will mention two of these. First, in 1936 he published

"The Theological Problem of the Old Testament Doctrine of Creation."[7] This essay proved decisive for his later work, and we may say fateful for Old Testament theology through the twentieth century. In this paper his thesis is that the focus of the Old Testament is on what God does in *history*, as distinct from what God may do in *nature*. This distinction, which exercised great subsequent influence, became the reference point for the programmatic slogan "God's Mighty Deeds in History," which dominated midcentury interpretation and was taken up in the United States, especially in the important work of G. Ernest Wright.[8] This formulation permitted the claim that the Old Testament is a recital of and testimony to the miraculous turns of affairs in public history wrought by the initiative of God, for which the test case in ancient Israel is the exodus event.

What is important in the article of 1936, however, is von Rad's exclusion of "nature" as a central arena of God's concern and governance. Here as much as anywhere we are able to see von Rad as a "contextual" theologian. He understood Israelite "historical" faith as a contrast to "Canaanite fertility religion," which focused on the cyclical rhythms of nature. In context, however, it is clear that the polemic against "Canaanite fertility religion" is, in von Rad's horizon, a polemic against National Socialism with its focus on "Blood and Soil" that led to a self-assured racism that was preoccupied with the generative power of nature. As "Canaanite fertility religion" became a surrogate for National Socialism, it is easy to conclude that "Israel" formed in "God's historical deeds" turns out, in context, to be the Confessing Church that resisted the "revelation" of "Blood and Soil" that in von Rad's own time turned to genocide. Von Rad's motives for such a decisive interpretive judgment are clear enough. It happened, unfortunately, that von Rad's decisive elimination of "creation" as a category for theology, perhaps derived from his Lutheranism, continued to be replicated by interpreters who were remote from the concrete context that required his dictum.[9]

This governing interpretive judgment of 1936 was matched in 1938 by what must surely be von Rad's most decisive essay and, arguable, the most definitive piece of Old Testament theology in all of the twentieth century, "The Form-Critical Problem of the Hexateuch."[10] In this article, which became the epitome for his Old Testament theology, von Rad identified what he judged to be the earliest "credo recitals" of Israelite faith that contained *in nuce* all that Israel was to confess theologically. In an act of stunning brilliance, von Rad identified the text in Deuteronomy 6:20-24;

26:5-6; and Joshua 24:1-13 as the core confessions that provided an outline of the primal "historical miracles" to which Israel normatively—in every time, place, and circumstance—gives assent. The simplest form of the confession is (a) the promise to the ancestors, (b) the deliverance from Egypt, and (c) the entry into the promised land. These affirmations become decisive, in von Rad's judgment, for all that follows in Old Testament theology. Von Rad then proposes a rather complex history of traditions in the two shrines of Gilgal and Shechem. (This proposed history of traditions via shrines has turned out to carry little conviction for subsequent scholarship.) Out of that complex history has come (a) the addition (*der Vorbau*) of materials concerning creation, (b) the expansion (*der Ausbau*) of ancestral materials, and (c) the insertion (*der Einbau*) of Sinai materials—a process that eventuated in the complete form of what became the Pentateuchal-Hexateuchal tradition. Thus the large literary unit we have in scripture eventuated from a long developmental process of recital, repetition of recital, expansion of recital, and adjustment to particular circumstances.

As preparation for the theology to come, what may interest us in this essay is that the core material that became the normative assertion of the Old Testament is a *confessed credo*, a bold assertion of faith in a cultural context where the recital of YHWH's deeds would have been new, unknown, and surely unwelcome. Von Rad does not say much about the context of confession, except that the texts themselves indicate in turn that the confession is for the sake of the children (Deut. 6:20-24), the presentation of an offering in order to assert that the land belongs to YHWH and to none other (Deut. 26:5-9), and that the God of the credo is contrasted with "other gods beyond the river" (Josh. 24:1-13). That is, the credo is an assertion of truth or countertruth—in either case normative truth—in the face of rival and contested truth claims.

Aside from the *substance* of credo that became Old Testament faith, and aside from the *process* of educating the children or challenging neighboring claims, we may particularly notice the organizing idea of *credo*—that is, bold, public, verbal self-announcement of faith that puts the speaking community at risk. It cannot be unimportant that Barth, a powerful force on the horizon of von Rad, exegeted the Apostles' Creed in 1935 under the title *Credo*, a usage that suggests the church before "the authorities" (see Luke 21:12-19).[11] In his essay published in 1938, von Rad's use of "credo" must surely relate to the Barmen Declaration of 1934 when the Confessing Church boldly asserted its faith in defiance of National Socialism. This essay in 1938 indicates that the immediate impetus for von Rad's interpretive project is to fund the ongoing life of the Confessing Church; he does so by showing that ancient Israel, from the inception of its faith, was a counter-community that voiced its daring challenge to dominant religious culture as a narrative that was an alternative claim from the bottom up.

We may notice three defining features to his initial characterization of Old Testament theology that are derived from Barth's radical turn of interpretation and that will shape von Rad's forthcoming theology.

1. The primal mode of theological articulation is *narrative*. The credo is essentially a narrative account of what is remembered in Israel as having "happened." Narrative is a form of articulation that begs the measure of conventional rationality and that focuses, without embarrassment, on the particular and the peculiar. And so von Rad sees Israel's core articulations as resisting any conventional rationality and celebrating the particular, which in this case is transformative miracle. Von Rad of course did this before the popular exposition of "narrative theology," for he found the form to be definitional for the text itself.[12] There are those, moreover, who suggest that there is a narrative structure to human reality and human self-awareness.[13] Von Rad of course would not venture into such a judgment, but had no doubt that there is an elemental, nonnegotiable narrative structure to the faith of Israel.

2. Von Rad understood that this material that lies behind the Hexateuch and that became the Hexateuch is not simply narrative.[14] It is narrative that is active, out-loud, public utterance whereby Israel makes its faith claim in an *either/or* mode of presentation that vigorously counters other religious claims, uttered by those who dare to put themselves at risk in utterance. The credo is not a document, but it is real recital.[15] Thus von Rad gives body to Barth's elemental category of testimony.[16] This is utterance in dispute, a recital that makes a claim and that polemicizes against other claims when truth is contested. Von Rad sees that the genre of testimony, uttered by witnesses, also protects against any biblicism with a scholastic view of faith, for narrative is clearly human utterance attesting to what is seen, known, remembered, and trusted; it is not, however, in the first instance that which is seen and known. That is, the "happening" of the exodus or any other "mighty deed" is not immediately available in the text, but is necessarily mediated by the witnesses. Subsequent generations have access not to the "mighty deed," but to the *attestation* of the "mighty deed." It is very well, subsequently, to take the canonical form of recital as

"revelation," but it is always revelation-as-testimony. The point is funda-mental to von Rad.

3. The courageous articulation of this recital as countertruth against the claims of "Canaanite religion," for example, indicates that von Rad understood the text and its function in what has come to be called a non-foundational or antifoundational way.[17] Congruent with Barth, von Rad's credo hypothesis appeals to no universal claim of religion and submits to the test of no generic rationality. Part of the splendor of von Rad's work, following Barth, is that he broke decisively with the older criticism that appealed to the norms of "universal reason" in the form of historical criti-cism. That refusal of universal reason in Israel's own confession is taken over by von Rad in his own exposition. It is that refusal that marked von Rad as a confessing, believing theologian and made him suspect to a great body of subsequent scholars who, following the trajectory from Gabler to Wellhausen, believe that interpreters have no business in "confession." Von Rad of course would insist that he is observing and reporting upon the confession of ancient Israel that is indisputably there in the text. But of course it is unmistakable that von Rad reports on that confession of ancient Israel in a posture of his own confessional readiness. The "confess-ing situation" of the Barmen Church in the 1930s, when von Rad wrote this essay, surely makes such a confessing perspective inescapable for him. Von Rad thus needs to be read and understood in light of the emergency that was his particular context.

When we approach von Rad's theology, we read the testimony of a con-fessor who stakes everything on the originary quality of the narrative tes-timony in the text, but who at the same time continues to value some of the results of historical criticism, namely, the multiplicity and dynamism, and some aspects of its relativism. It is part of his greatness that von Rad managed to hold together, albeit in a delicate, tentative way, the freedom of historical criticism and the gravitas of narrative confession. It is this com-bination that he accomplished with his magisterial poetic capacity. It is this capacity that makes his work monumental and defining for the field.

III

The *Old Testament Theology* itself went through a series of editions in which von Rad continued to revise and emend. Of these several editions, only the present one, the second edition, was rendered into English, and so our account concerns that presentation. (We may note in passing that as von Rad understood "credo" to be endlessly open and reiterated in always-changing form, so von Rad's own theology is itself endlessly open and reiterated in the form of new editions, his work in this way imitating what he understood the canonical process to be.)

The great structural divide of his theology is of course the presentation in two volumes. It is clear, moreover, that his energy, imagination, and decisive impact are all linked to the first volume, with the second being clearly derivative and less extraordinary. We may consider the relation of the two volumes to each other under two rubrics, even though neither quite fits. If we think in terms of *canonical* literature, it is clear that the first volume is preoccupied with the Torah (even though his governing hypothesis concerns the Hexateuch), and the second volume focuses on the prophetic canon, though the actual division of the volumes is not as clear as that. Or conversely, if we think *historically*, the two volumes reflect the great divide of "ancient Israel" and "emerging Judaism."

The opening citation of the second volume is indeed telling:

> Remember not the former things nor consider the things of old. For behold, I purpose to do a new thing. (Isaiah xIiii. 18f.)

The "former things" here refers to the early traditions of the Hexateuch. The "new things" refers to the prophetic recasting of "early traditions." Thus von Rad proceeds, along with his generation of theological interpreters, against the older critical judgment. It had been assumed that the prophets are primarily innovators. Against that von Rad treats them as imaginative users of old "canonical" traditions that they reshape in new form for new circumstances:

> For the prophets were never as original, or as individualistic, or in such direct communion with God and no one else, as they were believed to be.[18]

The play on "former things" and "new things" is not unlike that of Brevard Childs in his presentation of the book of Isaiah, wherein the two phrases refer to the judgment upon Israel voiced in "First Isaiah" and the hope given Israel in "Second Isaiah."[19] Thus it is possible to suggest that von Rad's own corpus, in like fashion, enacts a convergence of "old/new" as a theological but also a literary reality. The delineation of the two volumes in relation to each other is not, in any categorization, neat and simple. It is nonetheless important to notice that the two-volume arrangement is not just a happenstance, a case of material, too much for one volume, that simply needed to be divided. The two-volume structure constitutes, in a rough way, an important hermeneutical discernment about the "use" and "imaginative reuse" of tradition, "use and reuse" with continuity and dis-continuity being the dynamic pattern wherein old tradition moves afresh in the interpretive process.

This understanding of the interpretive process is fundamental to von Rad and, I suggest, it is the way in which he carefully appropriates the older theory of developmentalism that he had learned from the school of Wellhausen. Of course his notion of "developing tradition" is not unilateral or evolutionary, as the older scholarship had supposed. But it is surely a dynamism that holds together truth *old and new* as a central hermeneutical conviction for von Rad that he found in the text itself. Thus he manages, in the arrangement of the two volumes, to voice a dynamism that partakes of something *developmental,* but at the same time the dynamism has an ongoing *normative authority* for the community that the older develop-mentalism would eschew.

IV

In the first volume, von Rad does the most to make a fresh contribution to Old Testament theology and to establish himself as the premier inter-preter of his period. It is evident that the task of Old Testament theology is at least twofold: to propose a large "scheme" that suggests how texts are related to each other, and then within such a frame of reference to read specific texts with discernment. There is no doubt that von Rad is an acute reader of specific texts. What is noteworthy, however, is his frame of refer-ence, whereby he has made room for the pluralism and dynamism of the tradition by refusing to identify any single "center" for theological inter-pretation, as has been the practice in much of the discipline.[20]

The first volume begins with a relatively brief "historical" introduction in which von Rad follows the conventions of the discipline by paying atten-tion to the "crises" that constitute the generative context for the texts.[21] For von Rad these generative contexts include the conquest, the formation of the state, and the formation of the postexile cult, that is, emerging Judaism. The latter of course inescapably implies an allusion to the exile as context as well. Of particular interest in this section are delineations of the tradition of Deuteronomy and the Priestly tradition as "endeavors to restore the past."[22] By this rubric von Rad establishes a central category of his understanding: Tradition is endlessly recited and reiterated in new circumstances and contexts that require and generate radically new formulations.

The main body of the volume is "The Theology of Israel's Historical Traditions," wherein von Rad exposits at considerable length the six dominant "themes" of the Hexateuchal tradition (plus a special section on "The Conception of Moses and His Office").[23] This material constitutes the core of von Rad's theology and is, in fact, an implementation of the programmatic essay of 1938, "The Form-Critical Problem of the Hexateuch." He has taken up each of the themes of his credo hypothesis, including that which is "added, expanded, and inserted," and has shown how, with full literary elaboration, they offer a full account of Israel's faith. This material has its roots in brief cultic recital, but over time it has received multiple layers of elaboration. This elaboration permits von Rad at the same time to focus on each theme as a constant of faith and on the older source analysis as a way in which the constancy of themes received variation, pluriformity, and dynamic adjustment to different circumstances and perspectives.

By far the longest section, appropriately enough, is "The Divine Revelation at Sinai."[24] Von Rad pays particular attention to the first two commandments of the Decalogue,[25] and then gives focal attention to Deuteronomy (which has endlessly occupied him) and to the Priestly tradition, with its ritual proposals for reconciliation. In this extended presentation, which still has the cadences of credo recital to it, von Rad has broken decisively with the conventional Christian pattern of organizing Old Testament theology around core Christian doctrines and has sought to follow the contours of tradition given in the text itself.

Beyond the credo recital, von Rad adds a remarkable discussion on David, kingship, and the rootage of messianic faith.[26] This section of his exposition is marked by the recognition of the remarkable fact that "royal theology" and messianism come late to Israel and stand outside the horizon of Israel's credo. Von Rad pays special attention to the "Deuteronomic History" wherein the interface of credo and royal theology is definitional for the literature.[27]

The first volume concludes with a section that is, again, quite unusual for a book on Old Testament theology, "Israel before Jahweh (Israel's Answer)."[28] Von Rad offers a discussion of the Psalms and wisdom materials.

It is self-evident that the rubric of "Israel's Answer" does not really work, because the Psalms and the Wisdom literature make their own statement and do not in any direct or sustained way "answer" the "historical traditions." The section is not for that reason to be dismissed, however. In looking for a satisfactory rubric (which he does not in fact find), von Rad seeks a place for materials in an Old Testament theology, a notorious problem to which in times past no one had found a resolution.[29] Nonetheless, von Rad offers some of his most profound exposition in these sections. First he deals with the Psalter and seeks to identify the "kerygmatic" intention of the Psalter by an appreciation of praise as "man's most characteristic mode of existence."[30] This accent on praise is matched by an acute discussion of theodicy under the rubric of "The righteousness of Jahweh and Israel." He understands that "the question 'Why?' . . . acquired a new ring when posed on the basis of a definite skepticism and religious detachment."[31] But he will in the end insist, through such a discussion, that "this *sedaqah* bestowed on Israel is always a saving gift."[32]

After the dialectic of praise and questioning, the second "answer" is an amazing discussion of wisdom, which he understands as "faith seeking understanding":

> For wisdom, questions of faith entered in only on the periphery of its field. It works with reason, in its simplest form as sound common sense: it is reason, and not faith, that must verify and admit that pride goes before a fall, that a dish of herbs where there is love is better than an ox where there is hatred, that bread which is got in an underhand way turns to gravel in the mouth, etc.[33]

When seen in context it must be remembered that von Rad's exquisite interpretation of sapiential tradition was set forth well before wisdom had become a scholarly fad, as it was soon to do, indeed almost before it had anywhere else been regarded as a serious datum for theological reflection. Though the rubric under which he discusses wisdom is difficult, von Rad's peculiar theological sensitivity is evident here, matched by a boldness in finding fresh categories for reading. It was not noticed in this publication, and only later came to recognition, that in expositing wisdom, von Rad had taken a decisive step away from or beyond the "historical" that he had so much championed. This interpretive venture came to fruition in his last book, *Wisdom in Israel,* which functions almost as a third volume to his theology; in it von Rad works from the materials of volume I and further develops those insights.[34] It is as though late in his life von Rad had begun to come to terms with his own awareness that the "historical" categories that had preoccupied him for so long were no longer adequate or at least did not command the entire field of Old Testament theology. Von Rad's capacity to face in this new direction anticipated the fact that, in the 1970s and 1980s, scholars would begin to move away from the "historical." It is a mark of von Rad's courage and greatness that he himself provided the impetus for moving beyond the "historical" analysis that he had made dominant in the first part of volume one. He provides a harbinger of the way in which the first part of the volume would stand under serious critique in time soon to come.

V

Von Rad's second volume is more complex and has more at stake hermeneutically. He opens one carefully articulated issue of the second volume in this way:

> If I view the Old Testament "genetically," i.e., as a comprehensive process of religious and spiritual evolution, I can view it as, to some extent, a self-contained entity. But if what I principally see in it is the ceaseless saving movement of promise and fulfillment, then it becomes apparent how the expectations it contains fan out ever wider, then it is no self-contained entity, then it is absolutely open, and the question of its relationship to the New Testament becomes the question *par excellence.*[35]

Quite clearly von Rad here means to distance his work from any evolutionary scheme and the developmentalism of the nineteenth century, a major move indeed. He had already argued, in his discussion of the Hexateuch, that the text had in it the "ceaseless saving movement of promise and fulfillment." Now he considers that "ceaseless saving movement" first with reference to the prophets that he considers in this volume and then, at the end of the volume, the same "ceaseless saving movement" beyond the Old Testament and into the New.

In the Hexateuch he had considered the movement from the promise of Genesis 12:1-3 to the fulfillment in Joshua 21:34-44. He understood that that fulfillment is decisive; but it is not final. The promise of God continues to surge into the future, into many futures, to always new fulfillments.[36] It is this rubric that permits in this second volume a discussion of two futures to Israel's old memory, the prophets beyond the old credo traditions and the New Testament beyond the Old.[37] It is, in retrospect, self-evident that these two "futures" are of a very different order and constitute very different issues. Von Rad himself was of course aware of this, but nonetheless proceeded in this way.

The volume opens with a careful statement preparing for a study of the prophets.[38] Here von Rad takes on very difficult subjects and in some ways reflects the shape of the conversation in his time, when a contrast of Greek and Hebrew notions of time and language was operative for many scholars. Were he to write now, likely he would instead speak of "performative speech." In any case, he seeks to assert that the prophetic thrust toward the future is decisively related to Israel's old traditions (as in volume one). Thus the prophets

were "in greater or lesser degree conditioned by old traditions which they reinterpreted and claimed for their own time";

were engaged in "a great continuing dialogue: with that tradition";

but in the end they "expelled Israel from the safety of the old saving actions and suddenly shifted the basis of salvation to a future action of God."[39]

Within this dialectic of "old and new," von Rad takes up the "classical prophets" and shows how each draws from particular parts of the old tradition and makes a new statement out of the tradition in order to show a new historical circumstance as an arena for God's new utterance and new transformative action.[40] The boldness of this argument can only be fully appreciated when it is seen as a frontal assault on the old developmental hypothesis that treated the prophets as innovators not linked to Torah (which critically was taken in any case to be subsequent to the prophets).

In this core section of the book it is especially worth nothing that von Rad considered "the new elements" in exile and postexilic prophets that represented a fresh openness to the future that God would enact.[41]

This central section of the book, on the classical prophets, concludes with a brief discussion of apocalyptic wherein von Rad, almost alone against a scholarly consensus, sees apocalyptic as an outgrowth of wisdom and not, as the scholarly consensus held and holds, of prophecy:[42]

> Once it is realized, however, that knowledge is thus the nerve-center of apocalyptic literature, knowledge based on a universal Jahwism, surprisingly divorced from the saving story, it should not be difficult to

determine the real matrix from which apocalyptic literature originates. This is Wisdom, in which, as we already noted in Vol. I, exactly the same characteristic appears.[43]

This is one of the few places in which von Rad has not been followed generally by scholarship. But perhaps more important than the proposed (and largely rejected) rootage in wisdom is his sense of a deep openness to the future in apocalyptic, so that what he says about apocalyptic in fact fits with and advances the argument of the entire second volume about being "expelled from the safety of the old traditions."

In the final section of the book, von Rad takes his defining dynamic of "old and new" in a very different direction, this time with particular reference to the New Testament.[44] Indeed, he has signaled that agenda at the outset (already cited), and has already indicated the nature of his own answer: "The question of its relationship to the New Testament becomes the question *par excellence.*"[45]

This difficult and far from satisfactory section of the book suggests to me these observations:

1. Already in 1938 von Rad had proposed the governing rubric of promise and fulfillment, and had seen that the fulfillments of God characteristically outrun the promises. That is, the promise drives to the future but the fulfillment leaps beyond promise in a genuine *novum:*

> All presentation of history in the Old Testament is in one form or another inherently open to a future. "Radical openness for the future" has been rightly called the characteristic of the understanding of existence in the Old and New Testaments alike [a reference to Bultmann]; in this connexion "future" is always a future to be released by God. . . . Their intrinsic openness to a future actually needed such fresh interpretations on the part of later ages; and for the latter it was essential to their life to take up tradition in this way and give it a new meaning.
>
> Are these traditions in saga or short-story form solely shaped by past experiences? In answering this question, we should start from a characteristic trait of "Biblical" narration whose significance has only recently been appreciated—its openness to the future. . . . The words, "openness to the future," do not, of course, mean the truism that history continues on its course and that the events narrated will be overtaken by fresh events. It means something very different: it means the

conviction that there is an event still to come, from which, and from which alone, the event narrated is to receive its final illumination.[46]

Indeed, von Rad observes that "the reinterpretation of an older text by a later is often a violent one," indicating daring and deep discontinuity. This difficult dialectic of old and new is surely correct.[47]

2. This shrewdly discerned hermeneutical dynamic that saturates von Rad's interpretive angle, however, is given theological substance in a way that now seems deeply problematic.[48] It is one thing to talk about "old and new." It is a very different matter, is it not, to reduce those large, dynamic categories to the concrete claim of closure that the "old" is Israel's faith and the "new" is the Christian gospel. This reduction of a hermeneutical dynamic to a specific linkage to the New Testament is not a necessary one, but it is one that von Rad makes without reservation, even though he recognizes that

> we must be quite open about it and admit that much of the interpreta-
> tion of scripture practiced by the New Testament surely is conditioned
> by its own generation, and that we can no longer concur in it.[49]

Indeed, von Rad variously recognizes the following (with reference to Matt. 12:42):

> Here again there is an element of supersession, since the prediction dif-
> fers somewhat from the fulfillment and the type is less important than
> the antitype to which it points.
>   In the New Testament this phenomenon of ever more powerfully
> concentrated expectation appears in a new light; for there, following
> upon the numerous earlier new saving beginnings, it reaches its last
> hermeneutic modification and its full and final interpretation. . . . [We]
> see that the way in which the Old Testament was cited and interpreted
> and made to supply proofs was entirely proper. Such a transformation
> of the traditional material in the light of a new saving event was as
> proper for early Christians as were many other transformations which
> had already taken place in the Old Testament itself.[50]

It is worth noticing that in this statement von Rad refers to "a new saving event," and not "the" new saving event; he seems here to treat the move to the New Testament as not final and preemptive but as one such move to the future like many others.

The entire paragraph suggests von Rad's ambiguity over the issue.

> The question therefore is whether the reinterpretation of Old Tes-
> tament traditions in light of Christ's appearance on earth is not also
> hermeneutically perfectly permissible.[51]

Von Rad of course implies that the answer is "yes, permissible." It is, however, one thing to claim that it is "permissible," another to claim that it is
necessary and exclusionary. Von Rad seems to vacillate, sometimes asserting finality and sometimes treating it as an example of such a dynamic.

> All we have tried to do was to shed some light . . . on the sometimes
> tacit and sometimes openly expressed thesis that the Old Testament is
> "incomplete"; for when the Old Testament and the New are contrasted
> with each other in the way in which they are to-day, it certainly looks as
> though the divisions we draw are much too rigid.[52]

There is present in von Rad's discussion something of the old conviction
of Bultmann that the Old Testament, from a Christian perspective, is a
"failure" that awaits the New.[53] Von Rad has a larger view and will not be
so blatant. But the implication is the same in some of his statements, even
if not in all.

3. In retrospect, von Rad offers a "soft form" of supersessionism. One
cannot explain away such a judgment; but perhaps two points of qualifica-
tion are worth noting. First, von Rad connects the processive dynamic of
promise and fulfillment to Jesus Christ.[54] That linkage is not a necessary
one, but is a possibly "permissible" one that was inescapable in a practice
of Christian interpretation that did not have on its horizon the continuing
vitality and legitimacy of Judaism as a community of faith.[55] At points von
Rad seems to be interested in the ultimate linkage of the Old Testament
to the Christian gospel; at other points he is interested in the recurring
dynamic of promise and fulfillment, in which the Christian claim is one
case among many. The connection to the New did not need to be made
as he had done, but surely reflects the way in which von Rad received the
question in his own context; for all his daring he stayed with these categories when his own sense of the dynamic of "old and new" invited him to
say otherwise.

Second, von Rad is perhaps fighting against a Marcionism in his own
day, and he is working to secure a linkage of Old and New in which there

was much at stake in the face of National Socialism and its sociopolitical residue.[56] Without justifying or seeking to justify his argument that the Old Testament must lead inescapably to the Christian gospel, von Rad, like every interpreter, needs to be allowed his own historical circumstance. He does show that the New Testament has no chance of being understood apart from the Old. This book in that regard reflects what would now seem to be a consistent insensitivity of interpreters that indirectly supported the great harm of "Christian culture."[57]

The critique of von Rad on this point, however, should not blind us to the remarkable dynamic that he found and articulated. His major contribution in this second volume is to see the strange reality of continuity and discontinuity that redefines what we may mean by "history" and that allows the *Novum* of God as the defining agency in this view of history. That Agency in a mix of continuity and discontinuity surely echoes the insistence of Barmen that "history" is indeed wrested from human management to a fresh and ultimate openness, never subject to human management, not even by the sure and certain administration of the older traditions. This remarkable dynamism that allows for the Agency of God of course violates modern technological sensitivities. Given the revolutionary dimension of contemporary global existence, we may expect that such an openness to divine Agency resonates most with the excluded, least with those who are politically and economically tenured in the present age.

VI

In retrospect it is not difficult to mount a critique of von Rad's work, as can be done with any scholarly work that inescapably reflects the context of the scholar.

1. The particular critical assumptions from which von Rad worked are not sustainable. That is, his appeal to "old formulations of the credo" is impossible, because the texts on which he relied are now taken to be later. It may be that an *unfolding recital of testimony* is a valid way to proceed; but it would need now to be articulated quite differently, with many hedges that recognize the problematic of the claim.

2. Much more important is the recognition that the programmatic notion of "God's Saving Deeds in History" is difficult, if not a flat-out mystification. Of course von Rad's great claim is to bring together the future-generating capacity of God with lived human historical events. The

critique of this is now quite old and has often been repeated, initially by Langdon Gilkey, and has been exposited in a more general way by Brevard Childs and James Barr.[58]

More recently, we may notice the reiteration of the critique by the two current titans in the field of Old Testament theology. Childs more recently opines:

> Von Rad begins his theology by separating off the "real history" of Israel, reconstructed much after the fashion of M. Noth, from his own kerygmatic approach (3–102). He then confesses his inability to reconcile Israel's "confessional history" with that reconstructed by modern critical scholarship (107), which is at least a frank, if inadequate, statement of the problem. . . . The subtle dialectal relation between Israel's inner and outer history which at places is so stunningly espoused, is seriously undercut.[59]

James Barr makes a like point:

> The cleft between history as it really happened (if we may be permitted that phrase!) and the history as it is told in the Old Testament is probably a matter of importance for any Old Testament theology; but for one who insists on history as a central guiding category, and at the same time insists on the re-telling of the history as Israel itself told it, the problem becomes extremely severe. And it is this point more than any other that has suffered criticism from von Rad's critics.[60]

The point about "history" made by Childs and by Barr is well taken, and was acknowledged by von Rad himself. It does seem to me, however, that von Rad is not as defenseless in the matter as is supposed, and that his critics operate with an astonishingly "scientific" notion of history that von Rad did not intend, even as Barr concedes that von Rad is "much more romantic and poetic."[61]

In acknowledging the unsolved problem, von Rad observes,

> The other activity is confessional and personally involved in the events to the point of fervour. Did Israel ever speak of her history other than with the emotion of glorification or regret? Historical investigation searches for a critically assured minimum—the kerygmatic picture tends toward a theological maximum. The fact that these two views of Israel's history are so divergent is one of the most serious burdens

imposed today upon Biblical scholarship. No doubt historical investigation has a great deal that is true to say about the growth of this picture of the history which the faith of Israel painted: but the phenomenon of faith itself, which speaks now of salvation, now of judgment, is beyond its power to explain.

But our final comment on it should not be that it is obviously an "unhistorical" picture, because what is in question here is a picture fashioned throughout by faith. Unlike any ordinary historical document, it does not have its centre in itself; it is intended to tell the beholder about Jahweh, that is, how Jahweh led his people and got himself glory. In Jahweh's eyes Israel is always a unity: his control of history was no improvisation made up of disconnected events: in the saving history he always deals with all Israel. . . . Faith had so mastered the material that the history could be seen from within, from the angle of faith. What supports and shapes this late picture of Israel's taking possession of the land is a mighty zeal for and glorification of the acts of Jahweh.[62]

Von Rad is not free of nineteenth-century positivism, to be sure. But his argument is of another sort, interested not in verifiable facticity, but in the power of generative imagination to think and utter "outside the box."

Such generative imagination, of course, has a hard time with modernists.[63] It does seem clear, however, that were von Rad's intention transposed into the categories of our own time, he would have a large company of allies in his claim for understanding "history" differently.

Moreover, it is not unimportant that, from the same period as his own writing, he could claim powerful support from Karl Barth, who struggles with the same matter of verifiable history and another mode of testimony:

We must dismiss and resist to the very last any idea of the inferiority or untrustworthiness or even worthlessness of a "non-historical" depiction and narration of history. This is in fact only a ridiculous and middle-class habit of the modern Western mind which is supremely phantastic in its chronic lack of imaginative phantasy, and hopes to rid itself of its complexes through suppression. . . . In addition to the "historical" there has always been a legitimate "non-historical" and pre-historical view of history, and its "non-historical" and pre-historical depiction in the form of saga. . . . Both Liberalism and orthodoxy are children of the same insipid spirit, and it is useless to follow them. For after all, there seems no good reason why the Bible as the true witness of the Word of God should always have to speak "historically" and not be allowed also to speak in the form of saga.[64]

To be sure, Barth is concerned in these references only with creation and the resurrection of Jesus. But von Rad's case might be that while these "occurrences" baffle modernity, in fact the other "historical events" of Israel's confession are more like them than not.[65] In any case, von Rad's appeal to "history" cannot be forced into a straitjacket of positivistic history; it must allow for the generative power of imagination in the telling of an evangelical account of the world.[66] This of course will not meet von Rad's more "scientific" critics, but perhaps it shows how the critique is rather beside the point, given von Rad's intent.

3. I have already noted von Rad's gentle supersessionism. Jon Levenson makes the point:

> The other great exemplar of Old Testament theology in our century, Gerhard von Rad, was more gentle in spirit. Rather than flaying Judaism [as per Eichrodt], he generally pretended that it did not exist. In fact, his theology was, to a certain degree, implicitly predicated on the disappearance of Old Testament tradition after the death of Jesus.[67]

I do not think that von Rad can be excused or defended on this point. Without doubt he belongs to a long line of scholars who simply did not acknowledge the existence of vibrant contemporary Jewish faith communities. The remarkable thing about von Rad on this issue is that his program did not require the argument of New Testament closure to the traditions of Israel that he offered. He would have lost nothing in his argument about the "future" generated by God by recognizing that both Judaism and Christianity are "fulfillments" beyond promises. But of course he did not put it so! And therefore the final section of his second volume needs to be read with a reservation and perhaps with enough imagination to transpose the argument away from the poison of supersessionism in its articulation. What is to be valued is the sense of dynamism about God's futures given in the world that run beyond promises, of which the New Testament is one case in point. Whether that insight can be fully appreciated, given its rendering in soft supersessionism, remains for the reader to determine.

4. It is often remarked, as with Barr, that von Rad found no adequate place for wisdom in his presentation.[68] In the first place, that is only to recognize that von Rad worked in his time and place. The accent upon "historical acts" precluded appreciation of wisdom. But, second, I believe this point can be rethought if it is recognized that the link he proposed

between wisdom and apocalyptic is not simply a late judgment, about apocalyptic; rather, it is germane to the shape of his larger argument. That is, *wisdom* in the first volume linked to *apocalyptic* in the second volume in the same way, *mutates mutandis,* that *credo confessions* link to the *prophets.* In both cases, there is a promise and a fulfillment. I think this latter point has not been noticed or appreciated in seeing the wholeness of his argument.

It is evident that von Rad is very much a child of his own time—no surprise there! This is especially true on two points noted above:

- The whole matter of an exclusionary Christian claim
- The inability to escape positivistic notions of history, with perhaps some continuing developmentalism

These two volumes, however, are reissued in the conviction that, after these matters are fully acknowledged, there is a great deal yet to be learned from von Rad. What is to be learned includes at least:

- That the God of Israel is rendered narratively and in utterance;
- That the God of Israel keeps opening futures and "expels from the safety of old saving traditions";
- That the dynamic of "old and new" is defining for biblical faith.

This matter is surely so for Christians; but it is so also for Jews. It is, moreover, a deeply important dialectic just now in communities of faith, for the capacity to "treasure and relinquish" old tradition is deeply poignant in many contested arenas of church life. Beyond communities of faith, moreover, it seems clear that the revolutionary juices turned loose in the world that bring an end to the "old order" may indeed be understood as the juices of God's revolutionary commitment to the future whereby God is bringing to fruition very old promises but in shapes never before entertained. If it turns out that von Rad's entire program is an exposition of Isaiah 43:18-19, as seems likely, then *relinquishment* of what is old and treasured and *reception* of what is new and unwelcome is the work at hand. As von Rad understood so clearly and stated so majestically, the drama of relinquishment and reception is only possible by the tricky but inescapable dialectic of remembering into new futures—something about keeping by losing.

CHAPTER SIX

The Loss and Recovery of Creation in Old Testament Theology

There is no doubt that Old Testament theology, like every critical discipline, is organized around major, shaping models of interpretation.[1] And there is no doubt that such major, shaping models arise out of and in response to the social-political-cultural context in which scholarship is undertaken. In the present essay, I will explore the way in which a dominant paradigm has dictated the terms of Old Testament theology in the twentieth century, and the ways in which Old Testament theology is undergoing a major transformation at the end of the twentieth century.

The Marginalization of Creation in Theology

It is widely recognized that Karl Barth's commentary on Romans, published in Germany in 1919, constituted a decisive challenge to the theological liberalism of the nineteenth century. In his early writing, Barth posited a radical discontinuity and contradiction between "faith," as it is articulated in the gospel of Jesus Christ, and all forms of "religion" that are rooted in cultural assumptions and practices. There can be no doubt that Barth's program sought to provide, and in fact did provide, standing ground for the church in Germany, as it distinguished itself from the "Blood and Soil" religion of National Socialism. Practically, that conflict pitted the Confessing Church against the "German Christians." This conflict was especially dramatized in the life and work of Dietrich Bonhoeffer, whose program of "religionless Christianity" surely reflects in a practical way the governing antithesis of Barth. Barth's opposition to cultural religion came to be expressed as resistance to natural religion, that is, the claim that in the l processes of life, there is disclosure of God, God's will, and God's

What interests us in that development of theology, is that the enduring paradigm of theology articulated by Barth arose out of and in response to the social-political-cultural context of crisis in which Barth did his early work. The Barthian formulation of faith constitutes the beginning point and shaping influence for Old Testament theology in the twentieth century, with its antagonism between faith and religion, which is to be understood practically and concretely in terms of the expressions of the church struggle in Germany.

That model of antagonism, articulated sharply in the Barmen Declaration, became a rallying point in 1934. Two years later, Gerhard von Rad gave the continuing expression to the Barthian program, as it pertains to Old Testament theology, in his essay "The Theological Problem of the Old Testament Doctrine of Creation."[2] It was in this article (which adumbrated aspects of his epoch-making 1938 article "The Form-Critical Problem of The Hexateuch")[3] that von Rad asserted that "the doctrine of creation" was peripheral to the Old Testament, and that the Old Testament was not, at least until very late, at all interested in creation per se. There is no doubt that von Rad's reflection upon "creation" is to be understood within the context of the German church struggle.

Von Rad's framing of the problem transposed the opposition of Baal versus Yahweh, Israelite faith versus Canaanite religion, into the church struggle in which the opposing religion came to be regarded as natural religion.[4] This transposition alerts us to the likelihood that from the outset, von Rad's understanding of creation in the Old Testament was shaped by the German church struggle. Von Rad's cultural context caused him to pose the question as he did, because Canaanite Baal religion with its accent on fertility was easily paralleled with "Blood and Soil" religion in Germany. In so doing, he made creation a quite marginal matter in Old Testament theology, and his decision had far-reaching consequences.

In the United States, this same contrast between Canaanite religion and Israelite faith was championed by G. Ernest Wright, surely the most influential theological interpreter of the Old Testament in the U.S.A. in this period. In three books, Wright articulated what came to be the standard categories for Old Testament theology "as recital."[5] While Wright did not make the connection explicit, there is little doubt that he was pursuing the line of faith versus religion, as we know it in the program of Barth. Wright took aim against nineteenth-century developmentalism, which assumed that Yahweh evolved out of and so stood in continuity with ancient Near Eastern religion and its gods.[6] Wright's main insistence was that Yahweh is *sui generis* and has nothing in common with those gods.

In his assault on the religion of Israel's Canaanite environment, Wright was especially concerned with *polytheism*, which issues in gods who are *male and female* and are articulated in *myths*. This triad of polytheism, divine reproduction, and myth is characteristic of Wright's sustained polemic. By contrast, Israel's faith is historical, has no mythology, and comes to be expressed as covenant. The contrast between the two is total, between polytheism, which supports the status quo, and Yahwism, which maintains a critical perspective on the social status quo: "But Israel was little interested in nature, except as God used it together with his historical acts to reveal himself and to accomplish his purpose."[7]

The work of Gerhard von Rad and G. Ernest Wright, taken up, advanced, and echoed by numerous scholars, articulated a radical either/or of history versus nature, monotheism versus polytheism, and ethical versus cultic categories. It is my judgment that this entire enterprise came out of Barth's assault on liberalism and, more specifically, was shaped by the German church struggle. In the end, I submit, as with any such program that remained largely uncriticized, this model of Old Testament theology came to be rather an exercise in sloganeering, in which large, sweeping antitheses were traded upon, and in which the Canaanite enterprise, although obscure and variegated, came to be reified and demonized.

Wright's statement "Israel was little interested in nature" seems to yield a form of faith that is removed from human birth, suffering, and dying—bodily and communal processes in which the mystery of human life is lodged. Such a perspective intended to resist the reduction of the divine to the natural. But what it did, in effect, was to reiterate the Cartesian dualism that served masculine logic while not appreciating the feminine-maternal hosting of the mystery of God-given life as an important theological datum.

Emerging Criticism of the Model

The critique of and departure from this model of interpretation was not an abrupt one. Two mediating figures provided a way out of the reification of this model, without rejecting its theological intention. Claus Westermann

Rad's close associate in Heidelberg for many years. It is strik-
enormously important for our purposes that Westermann, in the
ndertook a quite new task that moved, in effect, against the faith-
versus-religion model that von Rad had established as normative.

In an extraordinary essay published in 1971, Westermann offered in
outline form an argument for the crucial place of creation in Old Testament theology.[8] He fully accepted von Rad's judgment that creation lies
at the edge of the Old Testament, but he proceeded to show that creation
is integral to and decisive for Israel's faith: "Israel in this regard saw no
alternative: not to believe in the creator or creation was impossible. . . .
Because God's acting for his people and God's acting in history are bound
together, the Old Testament does not know a one-track, all-encompass-
ing concept of history."[9] Westermann then proposed a new model for Old
Testament theology, one that departs from the over-againstness of von Rad
and Wright and sees creation and history in tension but together. "The
acting of God in creation and his action in history stand in relation to one
another in the Old Testament; the one is not without the other. . . . Creation and history arise out of the same origin and move toward the same
goal."[10] But the major gain in Westermann's work, one he has elaborated
in a variety of forms, is the accent upon blessing:

> The Old Testament knows a wholly different kind of divine acting not
> manifested in history; a constant acting not manifested in momen-
> tary events, namely, God's work of blessing. Blessing really means the
> power of fertility. God's blessing causes a developing and growing, a
> ripening and fruit-bearing, a silent advance of the power for life in all
> realms.[11]

Westermann offers an alternative scenario of Old Testament theology
that has undermined, in my judgment irreversibly, the radical and simple
either/or that has dominated scholarship. One notes in the perspective of
Westermann: (1) an absence of polemic against Israel's religious environment, allowing that Yahweh participates in functions otherwise attributed
to Baal; (2) an absence of the ominous construct of "Canaanite fertility
religion," which has been demonized; (3) a readiness to take seriously all of
the texts of the Old Testament, including those that do not fit the regnant
construct; and (4) a willingness to be genuinely dialectical about deliverance and blessing. The gain in this changed model is that the contextual,
dailiness of life is to be taken as a positive theological datum. It is not

unimportant that this crucial shift also represents a break with the extreme masculinization of biblical faith. While the continuing advocates of the either/or model claim to put God beyond sexuality, in fact, the action celebrated in Yahweh is that of a macho, intrusive God.

Frank Moore Cross's influential book *Canaanite Myth and Hebrew Epic* articulates the primary challenge to Wright (and to the larger either/or of the German church struggle) in the United States.[12] The title of Cross's book is voiced in the familiar either/or contrast of Canaanite myth and Hebrew epic. The force of the book, however, is exactly the opposite. Cross aims to show that the modes of thought and speech and the ways of imagining the world expressed in the religious documents of Canaan thoroughly saturate Israel's text. The appeal to the evidence of Canaanite myth as a way of understanding the Old Testament frontally assaults the neat distinction between myth and history upon which the older model relied.

In his study of the Song of the Sea (Exod. 15:1-18), Cross shows that the imagery of exodus is informed by and closely parallels the Baal and 'Anat texts of Canaanite mythology.[13] Moreover, the fight against "the waters," Cross suggests, was not, in the first instance, a fight against the historical waters of the Sea of Reeds but against the primordial waters of the god of chaos, Yam. Thus, Israel's telling of its primal "mighty act" of exodus depends completely upon mythic categories that are clearly and unmistakably Canaanite. And in the end, one cannot distinguish between the battle for creation against chaotic waters and the battle for exodus against historical waters. While Cross concedes that Israel did have a distinctive historical consciousness, he insists, "It is equally unsatisfactory to posit a radical break between Israel's mythological and cultic past and the historical cultus of the league. The power of the mythic pattern was enormous. The Song of the Sea reveals this power as mythological themes shape its mode of presenting epic memories."[14]

It is instructive that Westermann's work was published at the end of the 1960s and Cross's book in 1973. We may suggest that it was in the period of the 1960s and 1970s that a shift in models was occurring in Old Testament study. It is worth remembering that there was enormous political and cultural upheaval in this period in Europe (for example, the Paris revolt of 1968) and, especially, in the United States (for example, civil rights, Vietnam, the Democratic convention in Chicago). I do not suggest that these large societal matters are directly related to the shifted scholarly accent. Noticing the context, however, does suggest that a simple reiteration of a model suited for the German church struggle was increasingly seen to be inadequate. The emergence of new scholarly paradigms is an inscrutable process. But there is no doubt that as Westermann moved beyond von Rad, and Cross decisively challenged Wright's categories, a shift was underway.

Renewal of Interest in Wisdom

We may pay attention to one other important development in scholarship, namely, a renewal of wisdom studies.[15] It is fair to say that wisdom studies had, in critical scholarship, been almost completely dormant. In the 1960s and 1970s, however, a vigorous new effort in wisdom was undertaken, surely as an alternative to, if not an escape from, the dominant model.[16]

I will refer in particular to the work of two scholars that I judge to be important in giving impetus to and categories for a new wave of scholarship. First, the work of Hans Heinrich Schmid of Zurich is singularly important. Four accents of Schmid's dissertation, published in 1966, have continued to be prominent in subsequent study: (1) the relationship between *ma'at,* an Egyptian notion of social-cosmic order, and wisdom, understood as an allegiance to that order, which is ordained in the fabric of creation and keeps the world and society coherent; (2) the relationship between Yahweh and wisdom, with particular reference to the hypostasis of wisdom as an agent of Yahweh, in the context of monotheism; (3) the anthropological accent in wisdom, which exposes as inordinate the stress on Yahweh's purpose and action in the theology of recital; and (4) the construct of "deeds-consequences" (*Tat-Ergehen*), whereby deeds themselves produce results, without the intervention of any active agent.[17]

In a somewhat different way, Schmid returned to these matters in 1968, in a study that is not aimed particularly at wisdom.[18] In this study, Schmid consider the notion of *sdq* (righteousness) as a notion of order (*Weltordnung*). He pays attention again to the Egyptian notion of *ma'at* and to the matter of "deeds-consequences." What should be especially noticed, however, is that the notion of *sdq* is treated as a matter of order, of the right ordering of the world, which intends *shalom* and eventuates in well-being when honored and in harm when not honored.

In 1973, Schmid, drawing upon his two book-length studies, published an essay that is fundamental to our topic.[19] Here, Schmid argued that creation forms the horizon of biblical theology, for the ordering of creation is the will of Yahweh as structured into the fabric of creation. It is impossible to overstate the importance of this thesis for the scholarship that has followed.

The second scholar from this same period who greatly advanced wisdom studies, astonishingly enough, is von Rad himself. In 1970, von Rad published his final book, which appeared in English in 1972.[20] It is a measure of the greatness of von Rad that he himself provided a study that moves well beyond his earlier work and, in fact, functions as the third volume of his theology of the Old Testament (though, of course, it is not identified as such).

His *Wisdom in Israel* is a fresh maneuver in theological exposition. Wisdom theology, as presented by von Rad and by many other scholars, is belief-ful reflection upon creation, its order, its gifts, its requirements, and its limits. In the middle of his book on wisdom, von Rad offers an exquisite exposition of Proverbs 8, Job 28, and Ben Sirach 24, which is clearly a theology of creation, though it was Walther Zimmerli who had enunciated the dictum "Wisdom thinks resolutely within the framework of a theology of creation."[21] In von Rad's general analysis, wisdom theology has as its subject the ongoing, generative order of creation, which is nourishing, sustaining, and reliable. For our purposes, what strikes one is that none of the older, pejorative phrasing about "Canaanite fertility religion" is anymore used. In the context of his treatment of "The Self-Revelation of Creation," von Rad has no hesitation about something like natural theology.[22] Thus, von Rad does not resist a departure from his own earlier categories, from Barth's either/or, and, we may believe, from the categories so urgent in the German church struggle.

A New Paradigm Develops

The extraordinary shift in the models for Old Testament theology in the 1970s, of which I have cited the very different contributions of Westermann, Cross, Schmid, and von Rad, has been followed by a rich literature that takes creation as the horizon (that is, scope, sphere, agenda) of Old Testament theological interpretation. Here I will briefly catalogue some of the more suggestive pieces of this new work that is committed to a very different set of categories.

1. In 1967, Bernhard W. Anderson published his book *Creation Versus Chaos* (which was reprinted in 1987).[23] We note again the date and context

of publication. Anderson, in any early attempt to make a move beyond the regnant hypothesis, takes up the theological theme of creation, with reference to history, covenant, worship, consummation, and conflict. All through this discussion, one can sense that Anderson is both paying attention to and struggling to move beyond the dominant model.

2. In 1969, Walter Harrelson published a little-noticed but enormously insightful book, *From Fertility Cult to Worship*.[24] As the title of the book indicates, Harrelson intends to show that Israelite worship in the Old Testament was concerned with the order and generativity of life in the world, themes that are ultimately related to creation:

> In the ancient world the gods gave life and fertility. . . . The Israelites certainly gave large place in their thinking and in their worship to fertility. . . . The theologians of ancient Israel came to understand Yahweh to be the creator of all fertility, providing within the natural order for a continuing appearance of life. It was Yahweh who at the time of creation provided their own seed, and animals and men who could procreate. . . . Fertility was related to the history of Yahweh's salvation also.[25]

Harrelson draws attention to the world and to the remarkable generative powers of God embedded in the processes of creation.

3. Among the more important contributions to the shifted paradigm is the suggestive and original book of Samuel Terrien, *The Elusive Presence*, published in 1978.[26] In this book, Terrien quite self-consciously sets out to break the grip of covenantal theology, now one of the code words of the Biblical Theology Movement that followed von Rad's and Wright's either/or model. The book is best recognized for its emphasis upon the "elusive," for Terrien does not countenance any obvious, direct, or easily accessible presence of God in Israel. God is hidden in the world. But for all the elusiveness, this God is present. To be sure, Terrien's book is not directly concerned with creation, and it mentions creation only in passing. It belongs, however, at the center of our consideration, because Terrien intends to speak of a hovering, haunting, pervasive presence that comes to Israel in, with, and under the experiences and processes of the world.

4. Rolf P. Knierim published an especially important essay in 1984, "On the Task of Old Testament Theology."[27] Knierim begins with the vigorous acknowledgement of plurality in the theological tendencies of the Old Testament.[28] This accent on pluralism seems innocent enough. In context,

however, the accent on pluralism is a protest against the reductionism of Old Testament faith to the simplistic either/or claim of recital theology.

Knierim sets up the problem of Old Testament theology as the need to find a universal basis for the claims of covenant and justice.[29] That is, the God who wills covenant is a God who must be before and behind the whole world. (There are echoes of Schmid here, whom Knierim cites.) The response to the need for a universal horizon is creation; Yahweh is not simply the enactor of deeds in Israel but the one who orders, guarantees, and commands the whole of reality.

5. Jon D. Levenson, who brings together the interpretive categories of Frank Cross and the passions of his own Jewish tradition, published an important book in 1988, *Creation and the Persistence of Evil*.[30] Levenson's book sets out to show, by citing specific texts, that the God of Israel does not yet exercise mastery of creation. On the one hand, <u>the power of chaos is still at large</u>. On the other hand, the elemental polytheism of the Hebrew Bible means that the God of Israel exercises governance only by the consent of the other gods. Thus, the ordering of creation is indeed a fragile, precarious business. Israel is promised that Yahweh will exercise complete mastery of the world, but that mastery is not yet at hand. Levenson's book, characteristic of the tradition of scholarship fostered by Cross, sees Israel as embedded in and participating in the religious world of its environment. It is impossible, in the face of Levenson's analysis, to appeal to any simplistic contrast any longer. The God of Israel is at work on a large front against the powers of chaos, which turn out to be resilient and unyielding.

6. Levenson's study, with its accent on Yahweh's struggle for creation against chaos, provides an introduction to Terence E. Fretheim's daring 1991 article, "The Plagues as Ecological Signs of Historical Disaster."[31] Fretheim begins by referring to the work of H. H. Schmid and proceeds from Schmid's understanding of creation.[32] In the second paragraph of his essay, Fretheim makes an amazing statement, one unthinkable under the old model: "Pharaoh's oppressive measures against Israel [in the book of Exodus] are viewed as fundamentally anti-life and anti-creation."[33] Fretheim then undertakes a detailed analysis of the plague cycle in the book of Exodus, and suggests that the plagues are disruptions of creation caused by the antilife, anticreation policies and practices of slavery. As a response to Pharaoh's destructiveness, Yahweh acts in the exodus not simply to save Israel but to restore creation. "Generally for Exodus, God's liberation of Israel is the primary but not the ultimate focus of the divine

reality. The deliverance of Israel is ultimately for the sake of the entire creation."[34]

The conclusion of Fretheim's study is that the plagues are the disruption of creation, so the exodus and its celebration in Exodus 15:1-18 are the restoration of the order of creation. Fretheim is able to show that this horizon of creation is not some foreign, "mythic" element in the narrative but Israel's very own affirmation of creation.

7. James Barr's 1991 Gifford Lectures were published in 1993 as *Biblical Faith and Natural Theology*.[35] The Gifford Lectures, by statute, must discuss natural theology. Two points in Barr's lectures interest us. First, Barr makes a sustained case for "natural theology" in the Bible. He begins with Romans 1 and Acts 17, works backward through Baruch, and gives extended attention to Psalm 104. Barr simply refuses the restrictive categories that von Rad laid out in 1936.

Second, it is of enormous interest that Barr articulates his verdict not only on Barth's construct of contrast but also on the reason for which Barth laid out his construct in the first place. According to Barr, Barth simply gave a "wrong diagnosis" about "natural theology."[36] Barr opines that Barth was wrong to insist that embracing natural theology would lead to resistance; Barr argues that no correlation can be found between revealed religion and resistance or between natural religion and collusion.

It is now increasingly clear that the sharp contrast between Israel and Canaanite fertility religion may have served as a reference point for the Confessing Church, but it cannot be sustained "on the ground" for the Old Testament. And it is equally clear that this contrast required the contemporary church to give up too much, when it read the Bible as having no interest in creation. This twin recognition means that Old Testament theology stands at a place where (*a*) it must abandon or treat with extreme care some favorite slogans of the mid-twentieth century and (*b*) it is open to very different categories of interpretation, which invite a major reconfiguration of the field.[37]

Some Advantages of the New Model

We are only beginning to see the implications of treating creation as the horizon of biblical faith. Here, I will mention three unmistakable advantages of the new perspective.

1. The paradigm that takes creation as the horizon of biblical faith (and therefore looks to God as creator) makes possible new contacts between

theology and science.[38] This interface is extremely complex, giv
history of hostility between the disciplines, and few if any scrip
ars are equipped for discussion at this interface. The resistance
theology, as demonized by the phrase "Canaanite fertility religi___, ...cant
that scripture scholarship—and to some large extent, Western, Protestant
theology—ceased to be engaged in critical reflection about the mystery of
the world. It can now be reasserted, in terms of biblical theology, that the
world has an inescapable theological dimension to it. It seems obvious that
scripture interpretation may contribute to a fresh science-religion conversation, which need not be one of hostility, at two points.

First, a biblical-theological discernment of creation attests to a generative mystery at the core of reality, a generative mystery that is intrinsic to
the reality of the world but is not finally and fully at the behest of the
world. This generative mystery grants to human knowledge a great deal of
freedom for exploration, but in the end, it invites wonder, astonishment,
celebration, gratitude, praise, and doxology. Second, scripture study that
refocuses upon creation attests to the claim that ethical insistence, limits,
and restraints are inherent in the processes of creation themselves. The
production of scientific knowledge, therefore, is not simply a matter of
power, resources, and technical capacity but also of responsibility, so that
scientific investigations must answer to the uncompromising claims of the
stuff of creation itself. The material of the world is invested by God with
what the Bible terms wisdom, a sense of life-giving, life-valuing, life-pro-
tecting coherence that cannot be mocked or shoved aside.

2. The recovery of creation as the horizon of biblical theology encour-
ages us to contribute to the resolution of the ecological crisis. New investigations in creation faith and its complement, wisdom theology, suggest
that the environment is to be understood as a delicate, fragile system of
interrelated parts that is maintained and enhanced by the recognition of
limits and givens and by the judicious exercise of choices.[39]

3. Creation theology permits us to acknowledge and appreciate that
human life is embedded in ongoing daily processes of generation and
decay, of birth and death, of alienation and embrace, of work and rest, of
rise and fall (Eccl. 3:1-8). And of course, these daily turns of reality are what
claim most of our energy and attention and produce the structures and
relationships of meaning whereby we exist as identifiable, self-conscious
creatures. While the emergence of a theology of blessing, which attends
to the daily embeddedness of generative processes, cannot be subsumed
under or equated with feminist consciousness, it also cannot be separated

from it.[40] It seems clear, in retrospect, that recital theology is indeed a quite masculine model of theology. I have learned, especially from Gerda Lerner's work, about male interpretive hegemony, which has taken the form of the "educational deprivation of women and male monopoly on definition."[41] Lerner writes of the social experience of women under the aegis of patriarchy:

> Yet, living in a world in which they are devalued, their experience bears the stigma of insignificance. Thus they have learned to mistrust their own experience and devalue it. What wisdom can there be in menses? What source of knowledge in the milk-filled breast? What food for abstraction in the daily routine of feeding and cleaning? Patriarchal thought has relegated such gender-defined experiences to the realm of the "natural," the non-transcendent. Women's knowledge becomes mere "intuition," women's talk becomes "gossip." Women deal with the irredeemably particular: they experience reality daily, hourly, in their service function (taking care of food and dirt); in their constantly inter- ruptible time; their splintered attention. Can one generalize while the particular tugs at one's sleeve? He who makes symbols and explains the world and she who takes care of his bodily and psychic needs and of his children—the gulf between them is enormous.[42]

I have no wish to reduce the matter of a changed paradigm to a trans- formation of gender consciousness. The theology of recital is more than patriarchy, and creation theology is more than feminist consciousness. But the linkages are important. When biblical theology has no interest in cre- ation, very much of the creation process of daily life is reassigned to the outer darkness of Canaanite fertility religion. The gains of the new para- digm are enormous on all of these issues.

Some Caveats about the New Model

Finally, I want to make three critical comments about this shifted paradigm:
 1. I must register some unease with the shift, an unease that runs through my writings on the subject: Creation theology, it seems to me, has a pow- erful propensity for the maintenance of the present system. Whether that propensity is intrinsic to the nature of creation theology or not, it is evi- dent in practice. For that reason, I want to insist that in some situations of interpretation and practice, a recital of Yahweh's transformative activities

that takes on the dimension of social revolution inherent in the substance of the text seems to me urgent and nonnegotiable. In revolutionary situations, it is the socially revolutionary part of the witness of biblical faith that is more likely to be heard and acted upon as God's live word. And in such revolutionary context, it may well be that creation as horizon is an inexcusable softening of the abrasive dimension of biblical faith.

2. It is possible to cling to a theology of recital as a reactionary defense of the status quo. Thus there are users of a theology of recital, who in the interest of established privilege (usually male but not always), continue to organize interpretation around saving deeds, and continue to demonize Canaanite fertility religion. Just as Karl Barth and Gerhard von Rad found a usable connection between Canaanite fertility religion and the National Socialist movement in Germany, so these latter-day interpreters find a usable linkage between Canaanite fertility religion and revolutionary feminism. My own judgment is that such a usage of the liberation trajectory employs revolutionary rhetoric in the service of social reactionism, which in substance is completely incompatible with the theological rhetoric used. In this case, then, a theology of recital, which had a powerful revolutionary bite in Germany, is used for exactly the opposite, ignoble purpose.

3. I have argued that the model of Barth and von Rad was peculiarly appropriate to (and therefore faithful to) its context. That is, the model is context-attested. Our own situation at the end of the twentieth century permits us to see that the model was in part context-determined, and we are compelled to move beyond it as context changes. Two temptations, however, attend this recognition. The first temptation is to regard the model of Barth and von Rad as an unfortunate experiment and to think that we can now get over it and get back to normal. But there is no getting over it or getting back to normal. That model now belongs to our history, and all subsequent paradigms will be articulated in light of it.

The second temptation is to imagine that whereas the theology of recital was context-evoked and lasted only for that context, our creation-as-horizon model is a better, more durable, less context-evoked model. Against the temptation to that self-deception, I have no doubt that "creation as horizon" is as context-evoked and circumstance-conditioned model as was that of Barth and von Rad. Ours is a time of synchronic systems thinking. And with the emergence of the crisis of ecology and the new sensibilities of feminism, "creation as horizon" is almost completely commensurate with our interpretive context. But that is no warrant for absolutizing this model, especially after we have witnessed the unfortunate absolutizing of another model. Indeed, it is important that scholarship not shift from one hegemonic model to another hegemonic model but recognize an irreducible pluralism in both the text and in interpretive habit. An accent on creation strikes me as especially hospitable to that pluralism. Such an awareness invites and requires us to be vigilant and self-critical about this paradigm, perhaps more vigilant and self-critical than were the advocates of the model of theology as recital.

CHAPTER SEVEN

The ABCs of Old Testament Theology in the United States

The developments of the last fifty years have brought us to a quite new place in Old Testament theology. Here I will reflect on these developments in the United States. I believe at the same time, *mutatis mutandis*, however, that U.S. developments are typical and representative. Reflection upon the development of the discipline is important for two reasons: (a) We continue to carry around in our midst all of the older ways of formulating the questions and answers in the discipline even when they have become clearly passé. The past, in a reflective discipline, is never past, but continues to operate with some authority. (b) Such a critical review helps us see that a certain way of putting questions and answers, any certain way, is highly contextual. A reflection on our past may help us to see how highly and peculiarly contextual is our own way of working in the discipline.

I

It is a truism to say that by 1960, Old Testament theology had reached something of a settled state, variously dominated by Gerhard von Rad and by Walther Eichrodt who, as is well known, had proposed that the "constancy" of Old Testament theology is to be found in "covenant," the single governing theme evident everywhere in the text.[1] It is unfortunate for Eichrodt's argument that the notion of covenant, in the 1950s through the work of Klaus Baltzer and George Mendenhall, was reduced to and came to be identified by a very specific notion of covenant linked to a particular form-critical pattern. Eichrodt's vista on the time was much larger, being informed by a strong Calvinist understanding of the theme; but scholarship forgot that, and settled for a very thin critical notion of covenant. In retrospect it is easy to say that Eichrodt's notion was too simplistic and reductionist, but it is important to recognize that Eichrodt in the 1930s was responding to the dominant "history-of-religion" approach and was wanting to reaffirm the *normative* character of Old Testament faith. In any case, it is fair to say that Eichrodt has not exercised great influence in the United States.

The case was much different with the work of Gerhard von Rad who wrote his theology in the 1950s and whose work appeared in English in the 1960s.[2] Whereas Eichrodt's approach was tilted in a *dogmatic* direction, von Rad, by contrast, was much more concerned with the *historical* dynamism of the text, an accent congruent with interest in the United States. The core accent of von Rad was the notion of a credo recital that was very old in Israel and very stylized, and that could be traced through many adaptations until it arrived at the full, secularized articulation of YHWH's mighty deeds. Retrospective assessments of von Rad include the recognition that he fully appreciated, much more than did Eichrodt, the rich pluralism of the text, so that he does not produce a single theology. Moreover, while von Rad's several points are endlessly insightful and generative, it is easy to conclude that they do not readily cohere. Whether this lack of coherence is a result of von Rad's failure to find an adequate unifying rubric, or whether the material itself is intractably pluralistic, is a subject for ongoing wonderment and debate.[3]

My own impression is that as Eichrodt is to be understood and appreciated contextually as a response against a "history-of-religion" approach, so von Rad is to be understood as a response to the German church crisis of the 1930s (in important ways those who subsequently appropriated von Rad's categories failed to reckon sufficiently with this context and so absolutized von Rad's categories in an unhelpful way). Specifically von Rad published two definitive articles in the 1930s that set much of the course of Old Testament theology in the 1960s. Most important, his article in 1938 on the problem of the Hexateuch proposed the notion of a credo recital.[4] It seems clear that von Rad, in the shadow of the Barmen Declaration, sought to provide "confessing" standing ground for the church against National Socialism. He did so by postulating that ancient Israel had to find confessional standing ground against the deep and pervasive threat of Canaanite "fertility religion." Having established that "Canaanite religion" was a counterpart to National Socialism, already in 1936 von Rad concluded that "creation" was an extraneous theme in the Old Testament and not central to its recital of faith.[5] He apparently made this judgment on the basis of and in response to the "Blood and Soil" claim of National Socialism that was in its own way a "fertility religion," albeit Aryan. These two claims concerning *credo* in 1938 and *creation* in 1936 produced a theology of a radical "either/or" for ancient Israel, in the service of the radical "either/or" of the German church in crisis. Clearly the pattern that von Rad articulated was picked up and extended well beyond von Rad's own German context. Specifically, the same radical "either/or" became intensely important in U.S. biblical theology of the 1960s, largely through the important work of G. Ernest Wright who worked in parallel categories.[6]

It is to be observed that the work at midcentury dominated by Eichrodt and much more by von Rad was largely at the impetus of Karl Barth.[7] As Barth's Romans commentary in 1919 drew the line against cultural, accommodationist religion, so Eichrodt, sharing Barth's Reformed rootage, sought to articulate normative faith-claims that show the Old Testament as a coherent, more-or-less self-contained statement without reference to cultural ingredients. And no doubt Barth's strictures against "religion" in the name of faith fed directly into von Rad's polemics against "Canaanite religion" that became a critique of all "religion" in the name of faith. It is surely correct to say that the shadow of National Socialism and the bold challenge issued by Barth set the pattern for theological interpretation of the Old Testament for several generations.

II

By the end of the 1960s and into the 1970s, all of that defining work had begun to unravel. Broadsides were issued against the so-called Biblical Theology Movement by James Barr and Brevard Childs, Barr on the grounds of poor semantic method and Childs because "history" had become the controlling reference point of interpretation.[8] It is not difficult to see, in retrospect, the limitations of the dominant patterns of interpretation that were propelled by Barth and offered by Eichrodt, von Rad, and Wright. But rather than focusing on those well-rehearsed critiques, it may be more helpful to consider two other matters that contributed to the breakup of that dominant pattern.

First, it may be said that the dominant pattern unintentionally had become deeply repressive of a great deal that was now found in the text that insisted upon articulation but that could not be admitted unto the dominant formulations. There was in the 1970s a moment of bursting of fresh energy that pushed in new directions. Rather than speaking of the loss through unraveling, I prefer to consider the gains. I shall mention six new facets in the field that contributed to as sense of disorder and confusion that was to last for two decades:

1. In a not very precise way, we may speak of the emergence of *postmodern pressures* in the field, by which I mean the growing awareness that the dominant patterns of interpretation were seen to be an interpretive monopoly that served and maintained a certain kind of hegemony. To be sure, neither Childs nor Barr had (or has) any sympathy for the general politicizing of interpretation; it cannot be doubted, however, that long before people in the field had heard of Jacques Derrida or Michel Foucault there came to be a sense that interpretive discourse is indeed a mode of power. And therefore the older consensus, sustained by a relatively homogenous community of interpreters, came to be deeply under assault.

2. As Brevard Childs and Langdon Gilkey came to see that "history" as an interpretive category is deeply problematic, we may notice the rapid disintegration of the *consensus claims of "history."*[9] From a theological side this critique came from Brevard Childs, but differently from the work of Thomas Thompson and John Van Seters.[10] Since that time, the problematizing of "history" has gone on apace among the minimalists—otherwise termed the nihilists—who include, along with Thompson and Van Seters, Keith Whitelam, Niels Lemche, and Philip Davies.[11] The tendency of this critique has been to deny any historicity to the early purported events in the Old Testament, and so to date everything later, or in the case of Whitelam in particular, to argue that what is represented as history is deeply ideological in a way that served ancient purposes and now served a contemporary ideological agenda.

The assault on "history" meant particularly the demise of the Albrightian synthesis in the United States, popularized in John Bright's *A History of Israel*.[12] Specifically I refer to Burke Long, *Planting and Reaping Albright*, which forcefully argues that the Albrightian reconstruction of the history of Israel was, from the outset, a quite tendentious enterprise that was remote from its own claims of "historical objectivity."[13] Whether Long's critique is fully sustainable or not, clearly "history" was on the way out as the defining category for interpretation. In 1979, Childs published his *Introduction to the Old Testament as Scripture*.[14] The phrase "as scripture" means, for Childs, a departure from historical questions toward the ecclesial and, for Childs, toward the canonical.

3. In the same year that Childs published his introduction, Norman Gottwald published his massive *Tribes of Yahweh*.[15] It is difficult to overstate the importance or influence of this book, even though it is poorly edited and has been much criticized. The "historical" intention of Gottwald's book was the reconstruction of early Israel as a revolutionary movement in a peasant revolt. The Moses-Joshua texts, moreover, are seen to be "functions" of the social revolution of the peasants against an entrenched economic monopoly. Informed by a Marxian interpretive grid, Gottwald kept his materialism dialectical, insisting that YHWH was a function of the revolution, even as the revolution is a function of YHWH.[16] The major importance of this declaration, for which Gottwald makes no apology, is the first of these, that YHWH is a function of the revolution.

While Gottwald's historical reconstruction has been critiqued and his Marxian categories of interpretation have been difficult for old-line historical interpreters, the decisive and surely irreversible gain of Gottwald is methodological. He has made a way whereby *sociology*, and derivatively the social sciences more generally, can be useful for interpretation. That is, texts are not simply reportage, but they are engines of social force that are embedded in and reflective of social transactions. This insight, carefully worked out by Gottwald, represents a huge move in the discipline, for it means that the texts are not safely "back there," but have immense and contemporary ideological force. To be sure, much of the social-scientific study since Gottwald has wanted to stay clear of his radical Marxian focus and have appealed afresh to Weber and Durkheim. But even so, the move from "history" to texts as *vehicles for social acts* has opened up a great deal of fresh interpretation and made the older "innocence" of interpretation no longer possible.

4. In 1978, one year before Gottwald and Childs, Phyllis Trible published *God and the Rhetoric of Sexuality*.[17] This book was the first sustained entry of *feminist* interpretation into the discipline, and it continues to be one of the finest and most careful exhibits of exegetical sensitivity toward feminist issues. As Gottwald served two purposes in his book—a reconstruction of early revolutionary Israel and a methodological move—so Trible's book has served a dual function in the field. Most clearly, her book is reckoned as a benchmark for rigorously text-based feminist interpretation that since her work has exploded in many directions, some much more radical than is Trible. It is important to recognize that Trible's feminist sensitivity in this book is not as a shrill manifesto but as the slow, delicate notice that the texts are immensely subtle and that close reading requires that one pays

attention to hints and silences that older historical criticism usually did not notice. Her work has been a harbinger of a great deal of feminist work that deprivileges older historical "summaries" and pays attention to conflicts and tensions in the text. Among those who have followed her lead are Cheryl Exum, Angela Bauer, Kathleen O'Connor, Alice Bach, David Gunn, and Danna Fewell.[18]

Most to be noticed, however, is the fact that Trible's second important contribution is her rhetorical criticism that she learned from James Muilenburg and has since treated more programmatically in her book, *Rhetorical Criticism*.[19] Trible has proposed the bracketing out or disregard of the usual historical-critical questions, with the insistence that what counts is the inner working of the text, so that the important reference points are those offered in the text itself, without appeal to external historical or theological reference points. So far as I know, we have as yet no close discussion of the interrelatedness of *feminist* hermeneutics and *rhetorical* methods, but it is to be noticed that historical criticism was the work of a largely male scholarly enterprise and even now functions especially among those who fence out all kinds of interpretive questions such as those raised by feminism. I do not suggest that the two—feminism and rhetorical criticism—are intrinsically connected, but the question warrants further study.

5. Not only did the so-called Biblical Theology Movement focus on "history," but it did so to the deliberate neglect of "creation." During the German struggle in 1936, von Rad had linked creation to "fertility religion," and thereby to the "Blood and Soil" slogans of National Socialism; as a consequence, "Mighty Deeds in History" became an alternative to "creation theology" that was too easily linked to racial politics. Because of the influence of that article and that interpretive linkage, Old Testament theological interpretation has largely stayed clear of creation themes, judging that they were not central to Old Testament faith.[20] But of course such a position is unsustainable and can be accepted only while staying closely within the early context of von Rad. In the 1970s that contextual claim was broken, and immense energy has since been expended on the exploration and reassertion of creation themes (alongside, perhaps as a by-product, has been the recovery of wisdom as a crucial datum for Old Testament faith). This work has included publications by Claus Westermann, Frank Cross, Samuel Terrien, James Barr, Jon Levenson, Hans Heinrich Schmid, Terence Fretheim, and Rolf Knierim, and even von Rad's final book in 1970 on wisdom.[21] Large vistas of interpretation were opened with the sugges-

tion of Patrick Miller that it is the covenant with Noah and YHWH's promise to humankind (of which Israel is a subset) that is the primary horizon of Old Testament faith.[22] Insofar as scholars could speak of "God's Mighty Deeds in History," the reclamation project of YHWH concerns the redemption and restoration of the whole of creation.

6. Finally, it is fair to say that in these decades there was a great tendency to retreat from the theological impetus of Barth that had been exploited by Eichrodt, von Rad, and Wright, and to return to a "history-of-religion" approach that echoed much of Wellhausen. That is, the dominant theological categories no longer convinced, and scholars relapsed into earlier critical approaches. The most important study in this regard is that of Rainer Albertz, published in the 1990s, but already inchoate in his book of 1978.[23] Albertz, however, is not a return to the unilateral evolution of Wellhausen, for the subtitle of his book concerns pluralism. It is the variegated quality of Israelite religion that concerns Albertz, as it does Erhard Gerstenberger, a clear rejection of the hegemonic force of the Biblical Theology Movement.

Now these six factors can all be documented in the literature and I have cited some of the most important works. It is important to recognize, however, that scholarship never happens in a cultural vacuum—thus the issue of history—and so the abrupt turn of the 1970s also needs to be understood contextually. The 1970s in the United States and in Western Europe generally witnessed a huge turn of affairs, all amounting to a deep distrust of established hegemonic authority. In the United States these are the days of the Civil Rights movement, resistance to the Vietnam War, and the Watergate affair. And in Europe the most obvious point of reference is perhaps the student revolt in Paris in 1968, of course the same year as the Democratic convention in Chicago that featured police brutality and the breakdown of civic order.[24] All of this contributed to an atmosphere for rejection of authority, a reaction to repression, and consequent withdrawal of allegiance to established authority. I do not suggest a direct or one-to-one linkage with developments in Old Testament study, for the matter is clearly more complex than that; but I do suggest that the context powerfully contributed to pluralism that refused to submit to consensus opinion and invited thoughtful people to engage in methodological experimentation. The critique of ideology is implicit in the work of Gottwald and Trible, the pluralism of Albertz, and the rejection of "history" by Childs; all of this ferment converged to create a disorder and reconstitution of the field. It is no wonder that by the end of the 1980s, many in the field had drawn the conclusion that the shattering of the field and its methodological splintering had made any larger work in Old Testament theology an impossibility. From the perspective of the old synthesis of von Rad, the 1970s and '80s are powerfully critical and deconstructive.

III

Given such a recent past, no one could have foreseen that the 1990s would feature such focus in Old Testament theology with enormous energy that created clear alternatives, but all of which were convinced that the doing of Old Testament theology is both possible and worth doing. For purposes of convenience, I will reflect on three theologies from the 1990s, all by senior and now retired U.S. scholars, leaving out some other important efforts, notable that of Rolf Knierim and John Goldingay.[25] The way in which I will proceed lets me nicely dub it as the "ABCs of Old Testament theology."

First, A is for *Anderson*. Bernhard Anderson was a distinguished teacher at Princeton Seminary before his retirement, and he continues his research and publication in retirement. He was a student of James Muilenburg and is much informed by the great generation of pre-war German scholarship. During the course of his long career, U.S. scholarship was largely dominated by the historical-archaeological concerns and judgments of the Albrightians, but Anderson kept at his distinct embrace of the theological task, most notably in his studies of creation, *Creation versus Chaos* and *From Creation to New Creation*.[26]

Anderson's recent theology, *Contours of Old Testament Theology*, is characteristic of his special gifts as a teacher; it is clear, accessible, balanced, and irenic.[27] It probably is fair to say that his book does not break new ground. He is not engaged in any of the interpretive conflicts that now seem important to the field, but instead offers an exposition that is rooted in the categories of the older Biblical Theology Movement, though with a fresh eye on how these categories are to be understood at the end of the century. The first two parts of the book provide a masterful synthesis on major themes. Part one[28] provides what I think is the best statement we have in English on the God of Israel as "the Holy One." Anderson takes up the required issues of the names of God, YHWH and the other gods, and insists with finesse on the God who is "Wholly Other," who is disclosed in the lived reality of the world.

The second, quite extensive section of the book[29] concerns the covenants of YHWH with Abraham, Moses, and David. The scope of the Abrahamic covenant in his discussion is noteworthy, for it includes creation and the Noah covenant, plus an extended consideration of the theology of Presence in the Priestly material. This is to stretch the rubric of covenant considerably, but the discussion itself is illuminating.

The third part of the book is more defuse and is, I believe, haunted by the issue of theodicy. The first topic is wisdom that culminates in Job.[30] The second topic is the linkage of prophecy to apocalyptic with attention to the "Dominion of Evil" and the claim of resurrection.[31] And the third theme is apocalyptic that leads to the New Testament, so that Anderson without apology understands his enterprise to be Christian, requiring the affirmation of Jesus as the resolution of the issues of the Old Testament.[32] None of this is stunningly new and certainly none of it is objectionable, but its fresh articulation is itself important.

I believe it correct to say that the subtext of Anderson's book that keeps recurring is the problematic of history. Anderson is committed to "God Acts in History," and yet he knows at the same time that history has become immensely problematic since the formulations of the 1950s, so that he permits himself none of the innocence of the earlier formulations.[33] Thus he is alert to the fact that "history" is close to "story," and he must attend to the matters of drama, imagination, and metaphor, ways of speaking about history that are recent in the field. The book is an important one because it is marked by (a) a deeply thought wisdom about the faith of the text that is not twisted by fad, (b) a pastoral sensitivity that recognizes the complexity and ambiguity of lived faith, and (c) a contemporaneity that is located at the front edge of the difficult interpretive, theological issues we face.

IV

B is for *Barr.* James Barr taught in Edinburgh, Manchester, and Oxford, and has recently retired from Vanderbilt. He first attracted notice and contributed powerfully to the demise of the midcentury theological consensus with his *The Semantics of Biblical Language* in 1961. Since that time his research and publication have been preoccupied with two major concerns: (a) a methodological interest in proper semantic method, whereby he has been vigilant about theological claims made for the text on the basis of what he regards as poor method, and (b) a running critique of fundamentalism that he has repeatedly shown to be objectionable and irresponsible. At first it may seem that these two agenda are very different, until one recognizes that much of his energy on proper method has been to expose illegitimate theological claims, the most extreme form of which is fundamentalism. Thus both concerns for Barr have made him primarily a critic of other scholars, vigorously deconstructing arguments of which he disapproves.

Barr's most recent contribution to the discussion of theology is his 1999 book, *The Concept of Biblical Theology*.[34] It is in many ways a curious book, because it is not and does not purport to be an offer of theological inter-pretation, nor is there any positive proposal for what Barr's own offer of theology might look like. Rather, the book is a survey of the field in its recent history and a critical assessment of current work from Barr's quite modernist perspective. The book is not well ordered, and it is not easy to identify a *Gestalt* to the whole. Nonetheless several elements of the book are of great importance. I will mention four aspects of the book.

1. Barr proposes a typology of five of the most influential Old Testa-ment theologies of the century, Koehler, Eichrodt, Vriezen, von Rad, and Childs.[35] While he alludes to a variety of issues, the point to which Barr repeatedly returns is the extent to which the faith of Israel is presented in a *descriptive* way, or alternatively, the way in which the text is read from a *confessional* Christian perspective. Barr believes that only descriptive work is legitimate and any confessional impetus is a discrediting mark. Not surprisingly, he is able to show that characteristically these five schol-ars are Christian, as indeed has been the entire enterprise of Old Testa-ment theology, and so there is regularly a direct linkage made to the New Testament, and an imposition of the categories of Christian dogmatics. There can be little doubt that this is the case, a point already made by Jon Levenson.

2. The most important part of the book, in my judgment, is an extended discussion of the ways in which Old Testament theology is related to and different from other disciplinary approaches, namely doctrinal theology, non-theological study, history of religion, philosophy and natural theol-ogy, and the New Testament.[36] Of these, perhaps the most important and the one where there is most at stake concerns the history of religion. Barr particularly notes the strong Swedish tradition in this matter with special reference to Professor Ringgren.[37] Positively, Barr insists on a historical analysis that is more or less objective and descriptive, with attention to "similarities with other peoples." Negatively, he proposes that the his-

tory of Israelite religion has been skewed by the way it has been related to the New Testament, and particularly by the imposition of "dialectical theology," with reference to Karl Barth and Brevard Childs. In passing, Barr notes Calvin's work in *Institutes of the Christian Religion* and makes the point, surely counting too much on the choice of terminology (poor semantic method!), that Calvin understood that "religion" could not be "abolished" as Barth sought to do.[38]

Barr pays particular attention to the recent two volumes of Rainer Albertz.[39] He appreciates Albertz's willingness to be "historical" and yet observes that (*a*) while the texts are very late, Albertz regards them as reliable for the early period; and (*b*) there is no real religious development in Albertz's perspective. Barr's acute analysis of Albertz indicates how exceedingly problematic the distinctions among disciplines are because, says Barr, at points Albertz "comes closer to Biblical theology."[40] While Barr sets out to make clear distinctions between theology and history of religion, his own discussion may suggest that the distinctions cannot be kept as neat and clean as he proposes, for eventually the material pushes beyond objective historicism. In the end, Barr suggests that the defining difference of approaches is that history of religion must attend to all of the text, whereas theology is related "to certain texts and to the theology implied by them."[41] If Barr is correct, then he seems to think that theology operates by censoring texts that it cannot bear. If that is true (and I would not dispute it), it may suggest fresh work whereby theological interpretation must take into account all of the texts and not engage in denial by censorship.

3. Barr's study permits him to consider special topics that have long concerned him. I suggest three of these are of special interest. First, he offers a chapter on "evolution and anti-evolution."[42] There are, as nearly as I can see, three aspects to this theme that interest Barr: (a) He wants to insist, with Wellhausen and against Barthian theology, that Israelite religion does have a developmental process in the Old Testament, and to pretend otherwise is to miss the data. Moreover, Barr insists that Albright fully conceded the point about development, even though he has been understood otherwise. Thus Barr's initial word on evolution concerns an affirmation of nineteenth-century hypotheses on developmentalism. (b) Barr comments briefly on "evolution and creation," as taken up by Claus Westermann. (c) But clearly what Barr finally is interested in is the notion of "development of doctrine" that precludes any final, absolutist statement. My impression is that Barr's attention to the history of religion is

instrumental to his resistance to finding in any mode of Israel's religion anything that might have normative status.

Second, Barr reiterates the argument of his Gifford Lectures on natural theology.[43] He offers natural theology as a way of fending off any narrow "theology of the word" and sees the positive implications of natural theology for morality and particularly for ecology.

Third, Barr offers a long discussion concerning how Old Testament theology is to be related to Jewish theology.[44] He considers in general the ongoing vitality of Judaism and takes up in particular the work of a number of contemporary Jewish scholars. Barr judges that the alienation between Christian and Jewish interpreters has been a tragic loss for what might have been an important and mutually productive exchange. One of the incidental gains of this discussion is his fine summary of contemporary work. There are a number of Jewish scholars at work on interpretive questions who can no longer be ignored. Like Barr, I judge that the most important of those is Jon Levenson, though Barr's critique of Levenson is more than I would consider warranted.

4. It is evident that Barr proposes that Old Testament theology should be a historical discipline that stays completely away from the tasks of ecclesial interpretation. My impression is that he has a quite rigid and classical notion of dogmatic theology, so that it becomes important to him to maintain space for biblical study not threatened by such an imposed agenda. In fact Barr is most comfortable with the historical categories of nineteenth-century historical criticism and so in fact continues the program of Philip Gabler who proposed Old Testament interpretation to be a historical project.

In light of this passion on his part, then, I mention finally the polemic note of the book. The polemic runs throughout the book against "dialectical theology," by which Barr means the work of Barth, but his particular strictures are against the work of Childs, and belatedly, against my work.[45] Indeed, the accent on historical developmentalism is precisely resistance against any claim that the Bible offers normative or authoritative teaching, for to make such a claim is to cease to be a historian and so to become a dogmatic theologian. This aspect of Barr's work is, in my judgment, more than a little embarrassing, for it is a polemic offered in a seemingly out-of-control, emotional form.

Nonetheless, his presentation that is so troubling in tone is an important one, because it joins issue on perhaps the most urgent question in the discipline, namely, whether interpretation is finally a historical enterprise done in an objective academy or an ecclesial matter designed for the instruction of the church. The latter obviously assumes a normative quality for the text and its claims, and it is this normative quality that evoked Philip Gabler and that clearly propels Barr. What is odd is that for the most part, specific interpretive disputes are not joined at all; what is offered is simply a loud generic protest against authoritative claims that clearly are felt by Barr as an unbearable authoritarianism. The book leaves me with a sense of disappointment, because what purports to be a judicious assessment of the field ends in a shrill emoting. My own sympathies are of course elsewhere than with Barr, and so I suggest that in the end, he imports into this conversation about Old Testament theology an authoritarianism that is clearly and sharply felt by him but, I have no doubt, is based in and felt from elsewhere and transferred here. It is clear to me that authoritative teaching that tends to be authoritarianism inevitably produces scholars committed to "objectivity" in a defense against a personally felt threat. Indeed, I only add that in the end, Barr becomes as authoritarian toward those who are "wrong" as anyone in the ecclesial tradition could possibly be.

V

This brings us directly to C, *Childs*. Through the confusing decades of the 1970s and '80s, when the task of Old Testament theology seemed impossible, it was Brevard Childs more than anyone else who kept determinedly at that task. His particular enterprise has focused on his sense of "canon," which he understands not to be a late ecclesial imposition on the text, but a theological decision made by the tradition that governs the church in its reading of scripture. His major publications on this project, supported by a series of journal articles, include: *Biblical Theology in Crisis, Introduction to the Old Testament as Scripture,* and *Old Testament Theology in a Canonical Perspective.*[46]

Finally, in 1993, he published *Biblical Theology of the Old and New Testaments.*[47] Childs is of course thoroughly trained at Basel in historical-critical methods; it is equally clear, however, that at Basel he was powerfully influenced by Barth, as has been the central work of Old Testament theology through this century. Over a long teaching career at Yale that ended with his retirement in 1999, Childs has been closely and thoughtfully developing his notion of canonical reading. His presenting problem has been preoccupation with history and awareness that historical-critical methods subject the text to references outside the text that are essentially misleading and distractive for the claim of the text itself.

His counter to such a historical practice has been an insistence that in ecclesial reading (which is his singular interest), the reference point is not external history but the internal claims of the canon, taken as a whole as normative text. Thus his introduction, entitled *Introduction to the Old Testament as Scripture,* meant an important departure from classic introductions, for "as scripture" means as the church's canon. It is clear at the outset how deeply Childs stands apart from Barr (a) in accepting the *church as matrix* for interpretation and (b) in taking the text as *normative* for the doing of theology.

His large book of 1993 represents something of a culmination of his continuing rumination on canon. It has as its thesis:

> A major task of Biblical Theology is to reflect on the whole Christian Bible with its two very different voices, both of which the church confesses bear witness to Jesus Christ.[48]

This bold central claim defines a task that in crucial ways sets Childs apart from his antecedents in the discipline and that clearly reflects the decisive influence of Barth upon him. Childs proposes nothing less than a massive redefinition and repositioning of the discipline. It is evident that Childs has set himself completely against the conventional perspectives of Old Testament theology and certainly against the "objective," historicist categories championed by Barr. Concerning his "canonical" project I will mention five aspects:

1. Childs quickly reviews contemporary ways of doing biblical theology, none of which interests him much.[49] His more important antecedents and reference points concern the master teachers of the church before the modern period. In this inventory he takes up Irenaeus, Origen, Augustine, Thomas, Luther, and Calvin, and at the present time, he is more intensely at work on Patristic exegesis.[50] It is clear that Childs intends to nullify the entire modern period of interpretation and the historical-critical project as a failed attempt, insisting rather that one should read as the church read before the Cartesian program of autonomy. It appears to me that Childs opts for a "Scripture and Tradition" approach not unlike Trent, a maneuver perhaps of special interest, given the recent rapprochement of Rome and

the Lutherans. It is difficult to overstate the radicality of this proposal to scuttle the critical project of modernity, even while it is clear that to some extent Childs must inevitably appeal to its critical gains. Indeed, Childs's own education in the modern critical tradition suggests that even as he protests, he inevitably appeals to that modern critical tradition.

2. As Childs has clarified and refined his sense of canon, he has begun to appeal much more to the "rule of faith" as the matrix of exegesis. Thus he references Irenaeus, who uses the phrase to locate the "order and connection" of scripture that are essential to its truth.[51] It is important to recognize that Childs's appeal to the "rule of faith" is not the same as any church confession, though Childs himself is a Calvinist. The rule of faith is broader and deeper than any of the church's confessions, but it is for Childs the normative limit of what texts can legitimately mean for the church. My own sense is that the notion of the "rule of faith" is enormously elusive and not clearly defined, so that it can be used more or less by such a learned scholar as Childs to sanction what he takes it to mean. That is, it permits high ground for quite subjective judgments, as Irenaeus understood in its use, for the rule of faith is a "living voice" that cannot be regarded as a "static deposit."[52] At points, nonetheless, Childs's strictures seem to treat it as a settled deposit to which he appeals.

3. Childs's book proceeds in three extended discussions that constitute the argument and the problem of the book. The first of these is "The Discrete Witness of the Old Testament" in which Childs takes up, in something of an "historical sequence," conventional themes of Old Testament study, moving from Creation through Patriarchs, Moses, Judges, Kings, Exile, and on to Apocalyptic, Wisdom, and the Psalms.[53] Childs is of course a first-rate reader and one can learn much; his presentation contains few surprises, however, except the surprise of how much he follows the "historical" account. It strikes me that he treats texts very much "in sum," without any consideration of the internal dynamic of any text, as though one only reads for conclusions. That is, Childs is not inclined to any of the newer "narrative" methods that go "inside" texts, but reads for theological outcomes.

4. The second substantive section is "The Discrete Witness of the New Testament" in which he treats in turn the early kerygma, Paul, the Gospels, Acts, and the "Post Pauline Age."[54] This discussion is, *mutatis mutandis,* parallel to that of the Old Testament. It is to be noticed that both discussions are "discrete" witnesses.

5. The final section, constituting half the book, is "Theological Reflections on the Christian Bible," in which he takes up conventional themes such as creation, covenant, reconciliation, law and gospel, and finally ethics.[55] Each of these headings is developed somewhat differently, but there is a pattern for each of them; the Old Testament material and the New Testament material are discussed and then come general comments that move things fairly far in a dogmatic direction toward the fullness of church teaching.

In passing, I mention three critiques that are not terribly important for Childs. First, the product of this analysis is an outline of prepositional conclusions that are given with almost no attention to the actual working of texts. Now it may be that Childs had neither space nor time for such attentiveness, but it is clear that Childs is focused on *conclusions*. I suggest that it is the *process* of the text itself that is more important for the theological enterprise and the dynamics that are revelatory. The point is an arguable one but an alternative to Childs is at least thinkable. Second, I think it is fair to say that in the last section, the Old Testament is so submerged as to disappear, being overwhelmed by the claims of the New Testament. Third, for all of Childs's careful articulation of discrete witnesses, his presentation has not at all solved the problem of how discrete witnesses relate to the final, coherent witness, for he has simply placed them side by side. I do not think he has at all solved the problem of continuity and discontinuity, which is his major agenda, and so his work in that regard does not seem to me to be an advance.

I would, however, not labor these points. What is finally to be said of Childs is that he has boldly and with sustained power articulated a fresh approach that is avowedly *ecclesial,* in a deliberate break with the more *academic* pattern championed by Barr. It should be clear, if one can get past the polemics, that Barr and Childs have offered models of work that set out the choices to be made by subsequent scholars.

VI

Before finishing, I want to situate my own work in my book of 1997 by acknowledging the critique made of my work by Anderson, Barr, and Childs. I proposed that Old Testament theology is essentially a rhetorical analysis of the actual, concrete utterance of the text to see what Israel says about YHWH and how it is said, that is, it is a study of Israel's testimony to the reality and character of God.[56] It is clear that a singular focus on testimony (utterance) requires me, as a strategy I sustained as best I could, to forgo questions of historicity and to bracket out dogmatic claims.[57] This is a strategic and provisional decision on my part (as is clear in the book), because I did not want historical or dogmatic claims to have the kind of priority that would curb the richness, boldness, and complexity of Israel's testimony. As one might imagine, such an attempt at antifoundationalism has evoked critical response:

1. Anderson has judged that my attempt to bracket out historical questions is unworkable, because the claims made for YHWH are claims in history.[58] The point is a sensitive one, but at least it needs to be recognized that the nature of "history" is highly problematic and one does not overcome the problem simply by insisting on an undifferentiated notion of "history," as though the term has agreed upon signification and is not a mere mantra. Anderson is of course aware of its problematic, for he can speak of "the symbolic world of the Mosaic covenant" and refer to the preaching of Deuteronomy as "imaginative construal."[59] Moreover, he can allow divine judgment from Mt. Zion to be distanced from history:

> From the very first the language about the Divine Warrior tends to move away from actual history into a world of imagination. . . . It is clear that the present form of the story invites the reader into a symbolic world, where the Divine Warrior calls for radical faith.[60]

In speaking of this imagery he concedes that it must be understood "with a poet's appreciation of the metaphorical language."[61] In using language of "imagination, symbolic, metaphorical," Anderson is quite close to my own intention. Anderson knows well that the notion of history is problematic, both because of the nature of the rhetoric of Old Testament claims and because of the probes of the historical "minimalists" in the field. But he is nervous that if we go "too far" we will lose the connection to lived reality.

That risk does not seem to me an issue, precisely because, as Paul Hanson says in his critique of my work, "history counted in Israel's account of God."[62] Precisely! But what we have is the *recount* ("account") in utterance, and what *counts* as history is given us only in the *recounting*. It is the *recounting* that lets history *count*, and my attempt is to pay attention to the recounting (testimony), which is what we have in hand. In any case, on the pivotal *theological* claims of faith in the Old Testament (as distinct from other aspects of Old Testament study), I believe that "history" is not a very substantive aid to us, except as given us in Israel's textual utterance. I may not have given quite the correct nuance, but I do believe that finally our interpretation must attend to the *what* and the *how* of utterance.[63] While Anderson has paid careful attention to the nuance of my work, Hanson has not. He has brusquely dismissed my work in a way that justifies a certain notion of "history" without taking into account the inescapable slippage between "testimony" and "happening."

2. Barr has issued a much more wholesale attack on my work.[64] I suspect that the real impetus for Barr's assault on my book is that in a rejection of Enlightenment reason as final arbiter, I have taken an antifoundational posture. Barr is unembarrassedly a foundationalist, and such antifoundationalism as mine strikes him as flimsy on the one hand and as absolutist and authoritarian on the other, because it attempts to make authoritative claims outside the domain of consensus reason. We shall simply differ on this critical matter. His shrill dismissal of such an antifoundationalism, however, does not so easily dismiss that epistemological option nor does his abrasiveness cover over the glaring problems of the rationalism he advocates.

My concern, a concern that has no legitimacy for Barr, is with the undeniable generative power of the texts for the community of faith, texts that attest to a God who inscrutably and inexplicably makes all things new. Now it is clear that an Enlightenment foundationalism must from the outset resist such an evangelical claim so that "the news" of the text necessarily evaporates into "explanation." I do not know how the generative power of the text for the church, generative power for missional energy, is possible if the text must be trimmed to fit modern reasonableness. Nor do I know how such manifest generative power is to be understood if the text can only legitimately be understood in flat and descriptive ways. I suggest that even if Barr's stricture against my work is valid, there remains this question of the generative power of the text, which is a historical datum that is both important and unanswered.

3. In his review of my book, Childs takes particular exception to my distinction between "core testimony," which includes Israel's account of YHWH's sovereign fidelity, and "countertestimony" that refers to the hiddenness and negativity of this God, a testimony that tells against the normative account of YHWH's fidelity.[65] On this dual focus, I wrote:

> Lived faith in this tradition consists in the capacity to move back and
> forth between these two postures of faith, one concerned to submit to

Yahweh, culminating in *self-abandoning praise,* the other concerned to assert self in the face of God, culminating in *self-regarding complaint* that takes a position of anatomy.[66]

Childs's judgment is that such a distinction bifurcates the unity of the character of God in a way that is "Gnostic." Hanson takes refuge in a usual theological ploy of "Mysterious Otherness" as a category that holds everything together in the testimony.[67] That of course is a convenient statement, but I do not see how that, *per se,* helps at all with the disjunction that is so evident in the text. My point is exactly that our conventional solutions to the problematic of the text do not adequately take into account the testimony itself. Simply an impervious statement to the contrary does not solve the problem that is so intractable and, I believe, defining for the text.

The problem with overriding the distinctions so evident in the text, so it seems to me, is that in asserting coherent unity, the homogeneity tends to be all on the side of sovereign fidelity with the near-evaporation of what I have pointed to in "countertestimony."[68] It seems to me that in the Old Testament, precisely in the parts not congenial to Christian convention (and likely Childs would say in the rule of faith), Israel candidly testifies negatively about YHWH, negatively without resolution. And of course Israel speaks so about YHWH precisely because in its lived history YHWH is "revealed" in this way as sometimes absent, silent, passive, or hostile.

Of course it is a matter of concern to settled theology whether the character of God can be seen to be available to Israel in more than one mode, in ways that contradict. I have no doubt that the text presents YHWH in such a manner, precisely because YHWH in the text is a full personal character with all the freedom that belongs to uncurbed personhood. Israel, moreover, cannot say everything about YHWH at once, and so makes its various utterances that tell the truth about YHWH. I understand that in "canonical" approach one holds this more easily together than I have done. I resist any canonical approach that has the effect of censuring what is uncongenial or letting the positive win easily. Such a reductionism not only violates the text but diminishes textual resources for living freely and honestly as the people of God in a world deeply conflicted and short on resolution.

VII

I take the trouble to review my own work with reference to A, B, and C, not because I need here to make a defense of what I have done, but because

I believe the exchanges attest to the vitality of the discipline and to some of its unfinished work. While Anderson tends to be quite irenic, Barr and Childs more readily are dismissive of those who depart from their norm, respectively modernist or canonical. My own judgment is that the emotional force of such dismissiveness is not simply about the study as such, but it is about *felt needs* and *felt threats* that propel our work, even if kept hidden. It is clear that the felt threat of Barr (authoritarianism) is very different from the felt threat of Childs (fragmentation).[69] Fair enough. But surely not all work in the discipline needs to be propelled by the same agenda or responsive to the same felt threat. I believe that the discipline now has energy for important work. But I also have no doubt that the field must be open enough to permit different agendas. There is no doubt that Childs's canon strikes Barr as authoritarian, and that Barr's foundationalism strikes Childs as avoidance of the truth of the matter. It is possible, however, instead of dismissing all those who "err" and depart from critical or canonical orthodoxy, to learn from each other. The text is complex, hidden, and irascible enough that it will finally elude all our categories, *historical, foundational,* and *canonical.*

CHAPTER EIGHT

Contemporary Old Testament Theology

A Contextual Prospectus

> White folks call their experience "tradition";
> they call our tradition "experience."
> —Will Coleman

I wish to reflect upon recent developments in Old Testament theology in context at the end of the century, of course paying some attention to my own efforts at the project. Old Testament theology is, in principle, problematic because the text itself is not intentionally "theological" in any recognizable or conventional sense, and because those of us who work at it, characteristically Christian, are inevitably caught and pulled (either attracted or repelled), between the immense, undeniable diversity of the texts themselves, and the consolidating claims of theology that are habitual, or between the pulls of a history-of-religions approach and what has come to be called a "canonical" approach that reads by the "rule of faith." In my judgment, moreover, no more than a provisional settlement of these matters is ever possible, because these pulls and tensions are inherent in the task even as they are intrinsic to the material itself. Thus all our proposals might properly have a modesty about them because having finished, we must always begin again.

The 1970s: Unraveling the Previous Historical Synthesis

It is well known that Old Testament theology reached a more-or-less stable point in the mid-twentieth century with the great accomplishments of Walther Eichrodt in the 1930s and Gerhard von Rad in the 1950s, with

G. Ernest Wright being the most dominant and influential interpretive voice in the critical context of the United States.[1] The gains of these more-or-less synthetic achievements are immense; they provide a baseline for all subsequent work, though the problematic character of their accomplishments becomes increasingly evident at a distance.

In retrospect it is now clear that the synthesis, which seemed so settled, had by 1970 already begun to unravel. Inside the field, we can notice the emergence of a "theology of blessing" by Claus Westermann, a recovery of wisdom as a theological datum by von Rad himself and H. H. Schmid, and a drastic recharacterization of the subtle relationship between the Bible and the Ancient Near East, especially by Frank Moore Cross.[2] All of these interpretive moves together made the single line of "God's Mighty Deeds in History"—focused as it was on Israel's historical-theological distinctiveness—less and less compelling as a reference point for theological interpretation.

These interpretive moves were matched, by the 1970s, by a larger, changing interpretive context. Inside the interpretive community of Old Testament study, there was within the decade an explosion of a new pluralism of perspectives and methods, soon followed by quite distinct communities of interpretation reflective of new vested interests, new self-consciousness, and new methods. The newness included, of course, feminist perspectives and a host of liberationist approaches that refused any longer to submit to the old dominant patterns of interpretation.

One outcome, it cannot be doubted, was the loss of a long-established coherence in the field, the loss of a pattern of hegemonic interpretation that trickled down from oracular centers of scholarly authority. New approaches have focused upon *contextualism*[3] (especially social sciences and especially sociology) and *imaginative construal* (especially literary and rhetorical criticism), all of which exposed old claims of "objectivity" to be less than persuasive, that is, a general rejection of what had been taken as "the established givens" of the field. Within a decade it became unmistakably clear that what had passed for "objectivity" was mostly unchallenged, monolithic dominance that appealed to the "historical" as a basis of "proof."[4] The newer approaches are largely unimpressed by such "historical appeals," holding in various ways that "historical" is an interpretive construal driven by and filtered through an angle of vision.[5] Indeed, the newer perspectives will not accept that there is any angle of vision that is not in some way also an angle of interest.

This deep change within the discipline is matched by a deeply changed interpretive world all around, to which the scholarly field itself is not immune. In the United States, the enduring conflicts over civil rights, Vietnam, and Watergate—matched by the student revolts in Paris in 1968 and the Democratic convention in Chicago—created a new climate of both rage and hope, a resolve not to settle for old answers or even old definitions of problems and surely not old offers of what is possible.[6]

It is my judgment that all of this collage of events and emergences has generated new interpretive options and possibilities that are irreversible; it matters very little in my judgment whether this is a gain or loss. Whether it is gain or loss tends to be adjudged by whether the newness is a loss of old influence (in which case it is bad and lamentable), or if the newness is the coming of interpretive power and influence never held before (in which case it is good). Either way, it is where we are and where we are likely to be for the foreseeable future or, as I would say, where God has now put us, and where we are called to be faithful, responsible theological interpreters.

One Text for Both Jews and Christians

As we might anticipate, the shattering of hegemonic interpretive categories in the 1970s created a great deal of confusion and bewilderment in the field, well into the 1980s, through which time Old Testament studies were finding their way in quite fresh paths. One can only begin to see, in the 1990s, something of the new shape of the discipline. While we may speak more generally about Old Testament studies with the dislodging of the preeminence of the "historical paradigm," here I want to speak specifically about Old Testament theology, and it will be evident to you that I have no warrant as a disinterested observer.[7]

I should like to suggest that the most difficult and interesting issue in the new discussion is the relation between *Old Testament attestations for God,* that is, "God talk" (*theos-logos* in the most simple and direct sense) and the more or less strong claims of the dominant *theological tradition.* Note well that in focusing upon *Bible* and *tradition* (by which I mean more or less settled and strong interpretive habits and categories), I am setting the issue as though it were a specifically Christian enterprise and, moreover, that the *Christian* enterprise is deeply linked to *classical* theological perspective. The twin notions that Old Testament theology has indeed focused on *Christian faith* in *classical formulation* constitute a truth that is also, at the same time, a key problem (as we shall see).

I digress only long enough to acknowledge the double problematic. First it is, in my judgment, surely not possible to accept uncritically Old Testament theology as a Christian project to the exclusion of Jewish faith and Jewish interpretation, both because the book is deeply Jewish and because of the deep moral failure of this stance throughout the twentieth century.[8] This is a major test point for the work to be done in the field.

Second, insofar as Old Testament theology is Christian, it is still deeply problematic to assume uncritically that the text leads directly to or can be delivered innocently for the classical formulations of Chalcedon, that is, Trinitarian and incarnational claims. It may be that those linkages can be voiced afresh, but we must recognize that such linkages are not easy or obvious, and surely must be dealt with in an awareness of their contested quality.[9]

The Felt Crisis

Having acknowledged these problematics, I will now return to the relation of the Old Testament text as theological voice and the difficulty of Christian, classical formulation. I will identify what I think are now three major perspectives on this issue of text and interpretation. In each case, I shall suggest that it is the *felt crisis* of interpretation that shapes the perspective, a crisis in religious claims, but more deeply felt than thought. I suggest that it is in each case *felt* crisis, precisely because in each case the argument receives passion and polemical tone that are well beyond what we might expect in a reasoned dispute.

I am aware that in setting up the problem in this way, I am insisting that each perspective is deeply contextual, including those positions that seek "high ground" and assert a truth beyond context. I believe that our theological work always and everywhere is *situated* work, and we do an honest and useful thing if we ourselves know how context shapes our sense of the question.

Position One: Minimalizing History and Theology

The first position I shall cite in a broad sketch of Old Testament theology is sometimes called "minimalist" and is perhaps not even intended as an argument in Old Testament theology. I cite Robert Carroll, a distinguished scholar at the University of Glasgow, as a representative figure of this perspective.[10] Carroll stands with a group of scholars, some Scandinavian and many British, who regard the classical interpretation of Old Testament directly toward Christian theology as *an authoritarian imposition* upon the text that itself makes no such claims at all. Indeed, it is argued variously that the text makes no such theological claims, or if it does, those claims are ludicrous and defy any modern credulity. Thus the felt crisis is one of authoritarian domination and imposition that is to be resisted by the identification of ideology in the text that is imposed belief as a form of social control that is characteristically patriarchal.

The closer strategies of this perspective are two. First, *critique of ideology* is a major enterprise that tends toward a Marxian direction of "distortion for the sake of control."[11] On occasion "ideology" is treated as would Clifford Geertz, as a synonym for "theology," that is, any large claim of meaning, but most often in this perspective the notion of willful *distortion* is at hand.[12] The second strategy is to date all texts as late as possible on critical grounds, so that the argument becomes a historical one, showing that any historical reliability as trustworthy reportage on events is impossible.[13]

In what I regard as a rather simplistic assumption, it is apparently thought to be the case that the undermining of historical reliability is a way of denying theological validity, a connection about which serious questions must be raised. (It has been recently suggested, moreover, that the historical minimalization of Old Testament tradition also has a consequence—intended or not?—of undermining the theological claims to the land that are central to the self-perception of modern Israeli Zionism.)

It is the practice of this perspective to "read against the grain of the text," which characteristically means to resist the assertion of Israel's normative faith tradition made in the text. Given a felt crisis of authoritarian imposition and a yearning for relief and freedom from that imposition, it is not difficult to see why such an argument is made; though it needs to be observed that "against *this* grain" requires a reading with some "*other* grain," here most often an uncritical modern Enlightenment rationalism in which familiar faith claims are in principle denied.

It is evident that this perception will not take us very far in Old Testament theology, nor does it intend to do so. It is nonetheless an important voice in the conversation, skeptical as it is, for it keeps cautioning against every easy fideism that is often simply an inherited reflex. It warns, moreover, against building hypothesis upon hypothesis that often are no more than repeated slogans. This view reflects the stringent honesty championed by the best of "modernism" and its appeals to the historical.[14] In the end, the *felt crisis* must be heard and honored, that the classical tradition has indeed been imposed in dishonest ways to the great hurt of those victimized by such hegemony. The hurt is a voice that belongs to the future conversation.

Position Two: The Canonical Reading

The second position I shall identify, of singular importance, is the "canonical," most often identified with Brevard Childs, who is surely the most important figure in the recovery and redefinition of Old Testament theology in the 1990s. Childs has offered a series of books in the last twenty-five years that stand in continuity with each other, but that keep advancing the argument in crucial ways.[15] His work is complex and erudite, and it is impossible to do justice to its importance here. I will focus briefly, first, on what I take to be his major critical position, and, second, on his major constructive proposal.

In his first summons to rethink biblical theology, in 1970, Childs raised the alarm against historical criticism as an inadequate lens through which to do theological interpretation. Since that time, Childs, as much as anyone, has kept raising this difficult question. On the one hand he observed, as anyone can see, that historical criticism of a certain kind is *fragmenting,* so that the text tends to dissolve into bits and pieces without any sustained, coherent claim.[16]

In response to such fragmentation, Childs insists that there is a theological coherence to the "final form of the text" that must be sustained and focused upon, without excessive preoccupation with the prehistory of the text. A more subtle argument he makes is the insistence that the text cannot finally be assessed by an appeal to "history" behind the text, as though the text must concur with history, even if that could be rightly reconstructed. Rather, the proper venue for adjudication and interpretation is the *larger context of the canon within the text* and not by any appeal outside the text to historical events. It is this issue that has put Childs most consistently at odds with his own great German mentors, all of whom were schooled in historical reference.

In Childs's hands, the text stands to itself and for itself and by itself, neither measured by nor subject to any external norm. This is what he means when he uses the telling definer "as scripture."[17] Childs thereby wants to free the text from context, so that the text is not in any way context-determined.

The constructive move he has made more recently is that the Old Testament must be read according to the "rule of faith." By this he means, I take it, the doctrinal coherence of the early church already voiced by Irenaeus but formulated in the great trinitarian-incarnational articulations of the Councils of Nicea and Chalcedon.[18] That is, Childs now proposes that the text should be a servant and echo of the normative, canonical, orthodox teaching of the church.

It appears to me that Childs has taken a move that is not unlike the Council of Trent in that it is the tradition that dictates what the text may and must mean. In his very great book, *Biblical Theology of the Old and New Testaments,* Childs's dictum is that the two testaments are "two witnesses" to Jesus Christ.[19] Thus the Bible, of course including the Old Testament, is now fully encompassed in the formulations of doctrine, so that in broad outline one knows beforehand the "plain sense" of the text.

It appears to me that Childs's felt crisis, in the end, is the *loss of the stability, fixity, coherence, and reliability of a tradition that witnesses to a single, reliable truth.* That is, Childs's "evangelical agenda" is that the Bible should show forth a gospel assurance of the truth claims of the faith. There is no doubt that he has seen that the fragmentation of historical criticism, along with the hermeneutical fragmentation of emerging communities of interpretation, have contributed to the fragmented meaning of the text, so that the text has so single, reliable, clear, sure theological focus. In part his resistance is to *historical criticism,* but his earlier polemics indicate that he also sees *pluralistic hermeneutics* as a threat, in one informal place terming it "neo-Gnostic." And therefore he proposes to retreat, to return to a time before the entire modern period of criticism (and, we may extrapolate, the postmodern movement of fragmented interpretation) to a "premodern" perspective. He appeals to the great claims of the Reformation and to the powerful patristic claims of the "rule of faith" as the keys to interpretation.[20]

My own sense of Childs's work, great as it is, is that it has not solved the problem that his program requires. He has made powerful appeal to the early, premodern theological interpretation of the church to good effect.[21] There are, however, two difficulties with this presentation.

First, his own presentation is bifurcated, whereby he presents "the discrete witness of the Old Testament" and then proceeds to "the discrete witness of the New Testament," and finally to "Theological Reflection on the Christian Bible."[22] Clearly Childs is a powerful expositor. The problem he faces (and that we all face) is that we are given no clear clue about the interrelatedness of these parts to each other, so that they must sit there side by side. Childs finally defers to the "rule of faith," but does not tell us what happens to his powerful readings that fall alongside the rule of faith but are not comprehended in it. Of course there are responses to be made to this query, but none that I find adequate.

Second, while Childs allows that the entire modern period of critical interpretation was a negative turn, it is simply not possible, in my judgment, to write it off and to proceed as though the "critical period" has not decisively happened among us. Indeed, the critical period has offered immense and irreversible gains, to which Childs himself has contributed. But the real issue is that reading communities, including canonical reading communities, live in history and are not outside history with a flat, absolute reading of the text. As Childs himself had earlier insisted, each reading stands in the presence of previous readings and that includes modern, critical readings.[23] Whatever may come next in theological interpretation must take into account the entire course of interpretation that includes the modern period. This is the crucial difference between postmodernism, which is a working through and a working out of modernity, and those approaches that attempt to deny modernity.[24]

While Childs is the most vigorous champion of an approach that reads the Old Testament directly toward the New Testament, toward Jesus, and toward classical Christian formulation, I wish also to mention two important books by Francis Watson, University of London.[25] In his earlier book, *Text, Church, and World* (1994), Watson takes up the claims of context in terms of autonomous texts, postmodernity, and feminist critique. His assessment is fair-minded, even if much more conservative than I would make it. His conclusion is that the Bible must be read as speaking about *reality,* resisting what he sees as the soft tentativeness of postmodern reading, and making direct appeal to the theological truth of the text.

In his more recent book, *Text and Truth* (1997), Watson takes up the hermeneutical projects of the nineteenth century, as well as Eichrodt, von Rad, and Childs, all of whom are found wanting. He concludes with a powerful theological exposition that he intends to be christological (not *christomonistic*).[26] It seems evident that Watson—like Childs, whom he finds too weak on these points—intends to resist autonomous, rationalistic exegesis and insist that proper reading asserts that "Christian faith, in a more or less definite form, actually has a right to exist."[27] While I fear the potential of reductionism in Watson, it is clear that he is an urbane and subtle reader who knows about these dangers and addresses them with theological sophistication. I suppose that with Watson it depends upon how stringently a "christological reading" is applied, whether room is given to the playful, elusive texture of the text in its God-speech. Watson, in my judgment, is more insistent than is Childs, but he has a much more sophisticated hermeneutical awareness that may protect from the very reductionism he seems to champion.

The outcome of what in Childs's hands is "premodern" is a Bible completely in the service of classical Christian formulation. It does yield *stability, coherence, and reliability,* but I find this a very one-sided proposal. At the same time, however, the *fragmentation* of the Western world and the apparent collapse of reliable metanarrative do produce anxiety and a hunger for coherence. This sort of program seems fundamentally a yearning for the way it used to be. But it is a *felt crisis,* and therefore it is one that belongs properly to the discussion.

Position Three: Postmodern Interpretations

The third perspective I wish to discuss is difficult for me to characterize specifically, partly because I identify with it and partly because it is much more diffuse in its articulation and less easily summarized. If not taken too narrowly, it can be termed "postmodern," by which I mean that the texts deliver no settled package of certitudes and assurances, but yield only traces and fragments and hints of an elusive kind that can be brought together in more than one credible coherence, but with no single credible coherence that is everywhere compelling.[28]

This perspective features interpretation "from below," admittedly contextual, and preoccupied with real questions of power, truth, control, and justice, factors that in any case always do impinge upon our reading. Socially and politically, this perspective would include liberationists of many kinds. Methodologically it pays attention to narrative, rhetoric, metaphor, and imagination, insisting that the readings are not *given* in the text so much as they are evoked and received by readers attentive to the text in concrete circumstance. The hermeneutical warrant for this perspective is a dialogical one in which texts arrive at ever-new disclosures when they must meet, address, and respond to evocative and particular contexts.[29]

This means that there is no single reading but a multiplicity of readings that withstand every absolutizing and every imposition of dominant or hegemonic category. This does not mean, however, that such readings need be "autonomous" or outside the scope of serious theological (even Christian) discourse. It means that the scope of such an interpretive community allows great freedom both because of the freedom-insisting requirement of the Subject and because of the work of the Spirit who reads with us in a spirit of freedom.

The felt need that can be identified in this perspective is that the text must be respected in all its *radical unfamiliarity*. It is Another in our midst who addresses us from outside our usual presuppositions. One can make a theological case for otherness by claiming that this text is inhabited by Another, unlike either our familiar creedal formulations or our rational modes of control. But if the appeal to the direct theological Agent is too much, one can argue that rhetorically and literarily this strange text speaks outside of our expectations—elusively and with polyvalence—yielding a Subject who is endlessly irascible.

This approach, then, yields fragments, hints, and traces of a dialogical kind, but it does not add up to a single claim. This claim of unfamiliarity that bespeaks Holy Otherness is illuminated in important ways, in my judgment, by Karl Barth's *Ganz Anders,* Buber's "Thous," and especially now with Emmanuel Levinas' *alterity,* whereby reducing text (or God) to Sameness is a killer strategy that denies holiness and eliminates human possibility.[30]

In this connection, I especially want to call attention to a remarkable book by Wesley Kort of Duke University,[31] which articulates a postmodern perspective on reading the Bible. Though put in a very different frame of reference, Kort's book provides an interesting and, I think, important challenge to the way of Childs and Watson. It is Kort's insistence that a canonical text is not only designed to lend support to settled, institutional conviction, but that it also "constrains, inhibits, creates fear, and sets limits."[32] That is, he is interested in the dynamic processes by which scripture constructs and defeats stable worlds of meaning for canonical communities.

He especially appeals to John Calvin, who forged new ways of reading from a combination of monastic practice, new learning from Paris, and the hermeneutics of Nicholas of Lyra. I wish to call attention to two accents Kort makes from Calvin. First, scripture reading always entails two moments: "the centripetal" (which Paul Ricoeur might term "retrieval"), but also "the centrifugal" which "involves and required above all divestment and dislocation."[33]

> A negative relation arises between the reader's world and self and the saving knowledge of God available only in and by reading Scripture, because the saving knowledge of God is not added to otherwise acquired knowledge of God but, rather, other knowledge of God now needs to be reconstituted in light of knowledge granted in and through centripetal reading. And this displacement and reconstitution is a part of reading Scripture every time it occurs. The act of reading centripetally is inseparable from a willingness to let go of everything else, including the self, and to count all that otherwise might be thought of as good as a potential obstacle, substitute, or diversion.[34]

Second, this leads Kort to observe that Calvin knows all about the challenging deconstructive work of scripture and precisely concerning the authority claims of the church (perhaps even the "rule of faith"). Calvin writes, as cited by Kort:

> But a most pernicious error widely prevails that Scripture has only so much weight as is conceded to it by the consent of the church. As if the eternal and inviolable truth of God depended upon the decision of men! For they mock the Holy Spirit when they ask: Who can convince us that these writings came from God? Who can assure us that Scripture has come down whole and intact even to our very day? Who can persuade us to receive one book in reverence but to exclude another, unless the church prescribes a sure rule for all these matters? What reverence is due Scripture and what books ought to be reckoned within its canon depend, they say, upon the determination of the church. Thus these sacrilegious men, wishing to impose an unbridled tyranny under the cover of the church, do not care with what absurdities they ensnare themselves and others, provided they can force this one idea upon the simple-minded: that the church has authority in all things.[35]

Kort focuses upon the "as if" (*sicut*) of Calvin:

> Hence the Scriptures obtain full authority among believers only when men regard them as having sprung from heaven, *as if* there the living words of God were heard.[36]

It is this "as if" that moves against every certitude and every settlement, insisting always upon divestment and dislocation. That is, the text reads, as is needed, against the certitudes of the church.[37]

After a sampling of the postmodern perspectives of Maurice Blanchot and Julia Kristeva, Kort draws a conclusion:

> But reading the Bible as scripture involves first of all movement away from self and world and toward their divestment and abjection. In centripetal reading the coherences and identities of the reader and the reader's situation are dissolved, and biblical coherences and identities, rather than being appropriated, are followed as indicators of an exit and then bypassed on the way to it. The reader accompanies biblical characters who leave the security of their homes and venture into forbidding uncertainties; the reader "walks," as Calvin liked to say, with the patriarchs away from cultural identities and locations or, like Job, past the theological certainties of culture's representatives in order to stand divested even of the questions that subvert the adequacy of biblical theologies. Biblical locations, plots, characters, and theological themes, when taken as directives toward this kind of reading, are invaluable and authoritative because they clarify the act of divestment and abjection, of departure and exit, and because they ask to be left behind. Centripetal reading is a process that leads to the divestment not only of one's world and sense of self but of biblical worlds and identities as well. It is a matter of accompanying and then going on alone.[38]

While I do not fully understand everything Kort has written, the primary point based on Calvin is that the Bible does not serve as an absolute "rule of faith." Rather, the Bible is itself still open beyond all settled assurances in Unfamiliarity, a deep, radical "Otherwise" who summons to live and toward death en route.

Of course I do not intend, out of such an argument, to sanction or approve everything done in the name of what is called postmodern. But I think that Kort has seen in Calvin—against much of Calvinism—a genuinely emancipatory, demanding word in scripture that is indeed Holy Address, the outcomes of which are not fully known ahead of time.

There are huge problems with such a fragmented approach that lacks visible coherence. But the need for *the Unfamiliar* is a deeply *felt crisis,* because the familiar has come to be known in some circles as settled, closed, fixed, certain, and eventually oppressive. Attention to fragment in its irascible elusiveness is to some extent strategic as a protest and alternative. But it is also, I believe, a way of seeing in the text what the old rabbinic, midrashic traditions had seen in any case. This is, then, a settling for "soft rhetoric" rather than "hard metaphysics";[39] but it is a move required, in my judgment, by too much hard metaphysics that tends to be control writ large and loud.

Summary, Synthesis, and the Live Word

I understand that this "Theology Update" is brief and schematic. So, let me propose some sense of the whole:

- *Modernist perspectives* (as in Carroll) have an experience of the text as *oppressive ideology of social control,* and therefore dismiss with aggressive skepticism the social control present in the dominant interpretive tradition. It is a *felt need* for exposure of abuse.

- *Premodern perspectives* (as in Childs) know an experience of *fragmentation and incoherence,* and therefore set about to conform the text to a rule of faith that has constituted the dominant reading that meets a *felt need* for grounded assurance.

- *Postmodern perspectives* (as in Kort) have an experience of the text under the aegis of the church as reduced to *sameness* that lacks power, and therefore a felt need for a text that is *unfamiliar* in its sheer, dread holiness.

I suspect it is possible to work out a series of provisional alliances in this triangle:

- *Modern and premodern* together insist upon the high claims against postmodernism. They part company because modernism knows the oppression of hegemony, whereas premodernism knows the claims to be true. They together have little patience for the elusiveness of the postmodern.

- *Modern and postmodern* together are agreed that premodern hegemony has been imposed and social control must be resisted, so that both are impatient with reductionist certitude. They part company, however, as modernism declines the claims completely, whereas postmodernism entertains the claims but refuses to bootleg with them the high institutional assurances that come with them.

- *Premodern and postmodern* together agree that this text is profoundly revelatory of God's holiness, against the emptying skepticism of modernism. They part company, however, over the character of that revelation, hegemonic or fragmentary and elusive.

Now if these alliances will hold momentarily and can be provisionally identified, they may make fresh, common work possible. The fact that they are *provisional* alliances, easily to be noticed, suggests a softening of the abrasive dismissal of alternatives, because each alternative may have something to teach the next.

If each of these perspectives goes its own way, as the current shrill cacophony may now suggest, then we will have only deep, irreversible division in which each talks only among its own. But what I propose as an alternative is that a contextual (pastoral?) approach to *felt crisis* needs to be honored and taken seriously in each case as the heart of the matter. The felt crisis, in each case, receives intellectual articulation. Without, however, reducing interpretive questions to therapeutic or power questions, each advocate is propelled by a hunch or a hurt or a fear that is deep and felt before it is thought. My urging is that a new conversation might be mutually productive if each advocacy is honored in its felt crisis:

- The felt crisis of *oppressive hegemony* is real; there is enough evidence.
- The felt crisis of *fragmentation and loss of coherence* is real; there is enough evidence.
- The felt crisis of *familiarity* is real; there is enough evidence.

The yearning in turn for emancipation, coherence, and unfamiliarity are not mutually exclusive. They are, when given, Holy Gifts beyond the largess of any interpretive sect. Kort says, *"Take, Read."* He might add, "Listen." Listen to the reading of the others. Listening is not first approving or resisting or defeating. The live word offered is given in, with, under, and against the listening church. There is common work for us.

Biblical Theology
Appropriately Postmodern

Even so classic a scholar as Horst Dietrich Preus can begin his Old Testament theology with this personal disclaimer, surely unthinkable in an earlier generation.

> Each effort to set forth an overview carries with it some of the personal idiosyncrasies or peculiarities of the author. This means that the present investigation contains my own peculiarities and weaknesses and reflects both the character and the limits of my knowledge.[1]

A New Context for Theological Interpretation

Such a disclaimer is representative of a quite new situation in scripture interpretation, which reflects what may be conveniently termed a "postmodern" context."[2] By that I mean simply the loss of hegemonic privilege among Christian interpreters or, alternatively, among the "ruling class" of critical scholars. This new post-hegemonic situation both permits and requires biblical theology to be done differently.

On the one hand, it requires Christian interpreters to notice for themselves a new interpretive position that no longer claims the field. Jon Levenson has well documented the supersessionist triumphalism of Christian Old Testament theology in times past.[3] The primary models of Gerhard von Rad and Walther Eichrodt are not the most offensive examples of supersessionism, but they do roughly participate in the Euro-Christian assumptions of transcendence, and with it the capacity to set forth a singular, comprehensive model for Old Testament theology that serves both the theological and cultural interests of Christian domination. My impression is that Childs's canonical perspective seeks to continue that enterprise, but with only limited success.[4]

Any Christian biblical theology in this new de-positioned locus must, in my judgment, lower its voice in a quite open interpretive conversation, and may expect to be instructed by many other voices, not only Jewish, but other Christian interpreters in other social locations. I do not expect for myself or others to give up a Christian locus of interpretation, nor to cease to claim Hebrew scriptures as authoritative for Christian faith, but I do expect that our long-standing assumption of privileged or dominating interpretation to be abandoned.

Conversely, the dislocation of Christian privilege in interpretation may permit renewed participation in a shared conversation of Jewish voices in what passes for biblical theological interpretation. Jon Levenson has made clear "Why Jews Are Not Interested in Biblical Theology."[5] I take Levenson's summary to be a fair representation of a mode of biblical theology that has prevailed in times past. And none can fault the negative conclusion Levenson draws of that enterprise. A new interpretive situation, however, may permit Jews back into common interpretive enterprise, as is evidenced in the judgment of M. H. Goshen-Gottstein.[6] Clearly such a participation, represented now in powerful ways by Levenson himself, does not proceed according to the long-privileged categories of Christian dogmatics, but more nearly permits the categories of interpretation to arise from the text itself.[7]

The de-positioning of Christian interpretation and the renewed entry of Jewish interpreters into a shared interpretive conversation may be based in a now widely shared recognition that the text of Hebrew scriptures is profoundly plurivocal and does not admit of settled, enforceable larger categories.[8] This reality in the text of course has long been recognized in Jewish interpretation that proceeded—since the ancient rabbis—by way of commentary, as distinct from a Christian propensity to systemization. This plurivocal quality intrinsic to the text is now deeply reflected in pluralism in interpretation: a plurality of methods, a plurality of interpreting communities, and a plurality of provisional grids of interpretation, all of which are reflected in the work of the Society of Biblical Literature. The plurality is reflected in Preus's opening disclaimer, which would have been unthinkable in the high days of Christian hegemony.

Leo Perdue has nicely suggested that the departure from hegemonic interpretation (my formulation, not his) is evidenced in a departure from *history* as the controlling category of interpretation.[9] It is, moreover, clear that the mesmerization of history is a peculiarly *modern* commitment, in which Christians have been deeply implicated.[10] The departure from "history" reflects a departure from modernist domination and, as Perdue makes clear, opens the way for other perspectives, notably hermeneutical enterprises concerned with narrative, metaphor, imagination—all inviting open-ended playfulness. The cruciality of such "playfulness" is that it does not insist upon conformity and leaves room for conversation among those who share much but who differ greatly.

Interpretive Themes Endlessly Processive

Acknowledging the plurivocal quality of the text, and consequently of the interpretive enterprise, one must nonetheless recognize that "theology of Hebrew scripture" is in some way—hopefully a self-aware and self-critical way—engaged in the process of thematization. Thematization is an attempt to notice claims (truth claims, normative claims, substantive claims) that are larger than the individual text.[11] There is no doubt that any thematization runs the risk of reductionism, and no doubt that thematization is a greater propensity for Christian interpreters than it is for their Jewish counterparts.[12] Having recognized both of these factors, I would judge "theology of Hebrew scripture" to be an enterprise of thematization, and it is such thematization that evokes not only the problematic of this volume but also the interest, inventiveness, and interplay that enlivens the discipline.

At the same time, every thematization is bound to fail because the text finally refuses thematization. The text is saturated with disjunctions and contradictions that mark it as an endlessly deconstructive enterprise and therefore our thematizations are likely to be quite local and quite provisional. Indeed, my judgment is that past thematizations pose problems precisely because these past interpreters rarely notice the local and provisional character of their work and come to regard such work as universal and enduring. It is easy to see, for example, that Eichrodt's thematization around the theme of covenant was pertinent to a time and place preoccupied with National Socialism in Germany, but we have more recently had to unlearn much of covenant. Von Rad's thematization is of course more open to an ongoing dynamic of the traditioning process, but in his own final work, *Wisdom in Israel*, von Rad himself had to recognize the inadequacy of the thematization of historical traditions on which he had spent his primary energy.[13]

As with Eichrodt and von Rad, so much more so with some lesser attempts in my own effort at theological interpretation, I have concluded that it is impossible to find a substantive thematization that is sufficiently comprehensive.[14] Either the thematization is so specific that it omits too much, or it is so inclusive as to be meaningless.

The primary interpretive move I have made, as a result, is to decide that the interpretive thematization I will pursue is not *substantive* but *processive*. That is, the theological substance of Hebrew scripture is essentially a theological process of vexed, open-ended interaction and dialogue between the Holy One and all those other than the Holy One.[15] In this dialogic transaction it is not possible to specify in large categories much substantive about the Holy One, though one may enumerate the usual inventory of actions and attributes. Conversely not much can be said in large categories about the other party to the transaction (variously Israel, creation, human persons, the nations). The most one can do is to notice, in particular texts, the processes there underway between the parties. In large, the *hermeneutical claim* that interests me is that *dialogic* transactions offer a crucial alternative to Cartesian positivism.

More specifically, I have adopted the juridical language of testimony to suggest that the text is *witness* to that rich and varied transaction. The witness, a category that brackets out all questions of being (ontology) and all questions of happening (history), proceeds in a dialectic of *core testimony* and *countertestimony*. By "core testimony" I refer to the articulation of basic claims made for the Holy One that are characteristic over time and through the text that in general are affirmative. But as in any serious juridical struggle for "truth," that core testimony is immediately under scrutiny and assault in cross-examination ("countertestimony"), whereby fresh evidence and new probing questions are put that expose the core testimony as not quite so full, so sure, or so compelling as at first glance.

I suggest three rubrics that I would pursue in this dialectic process of testimony:

1. *Covenant and Exile.* The covenant, rooted in either the ancestral narratives or in the Sinai materials, attests to an enduring relationship between a trustworthy God and a responsive community.[16] There are of course variations in the articulation of covenant. The Abrahamic covenant appears to be "less conditional" than the Mosaic, the Noachic more comprehensive than either that of Abraham of Moses.[17] But in all cases and in each case, the relationship is demanding and reassuring.

The pivotal focus of the Hebrew scripture on exile, however, destabilizes the assurances of covenant. Even if we regard the exile as a partisan, fictive construct rather than a historical event, it is clear that exile—which may be seen as punishment or as enraged abandonment—poses deep questions for covenant. And while enormous theological assurances arise from within exile, it is evident that the texts are not so sure or so simple or so neat as if the exile had not "happened."

2. *Hymn and Lament.* It is clear that the hymnic traditions, reaching all the way back to the Songs of Moses and Miriam, set out the baseline of Israel's faith. Indeed, these sweeping doxologies, rooted in particular transformations, constitute Israel's core testimony about the goodness, fidelity, and power of Yahweh.[18] But every interpreter of scripture knows that the core testimony of hymns is endlessly accompanied by lament and complaint, which subvert the great doxological claims. Indeed, Israel's relentless tradition of complaint finds a way of destabilizing every grand positive claim.

On the one hand, it is evident that these witnesses refused to lie in order to protect the Holy One, or to deny their own experiences of negation. They insisted not only on their experiences of negation as the truth of their life, but also insisted that the Holy One must be drawn into and subjected to the circumstance of suffering and negation. Indeed, Jacques Derrida goes so far as to suggest that justice—in the world and from God—is undeconstructable and therefore more ultimate than God.[19] The vigor of the complaints suggests that God is held to a norm of justice by ancient Israel.

On the other hand, in biblical interpretation and in theological reflection, Christians have much for which to answer in their disregard and refusal of this aspect of biblical disclosure and this aspect of human reality. Indeed, Christians are much more inclined to lie and to deny for the sake of "protecting God." It is my judgment that recent attention to complaints and laments in Christian interpretive conversations is both required and permitted by the end of cultural hegemony.[20]

It is beyond doubt that such a posture of "countertestimony" undermines and destabilizes the seemingly safe claim of the hymns. And therefore I suggest that the dialectic of hymn-complaint, as a mode of core and countertestimony, is a characteristic process of biblical theology.

3. *Presence and Theodicy.* In yet a third way I identify the governing dialectic of this material. There is no doubt that the presence of the Holy One is decisive for Israel's faith. This is evident in the promise of accompaniment

of Abraham. It is the source of dispute with Moses in Exodus 33, and it is the assumption of Israel's temple traditions.[21] This is none other than "The Holy One in your midst." In a variety of ways these texts bespeak presence. A more systematic extrapolation makes a parallel point about creation, for God is, as Eberhard Jüngel asserts, "The Mystery of the World."[22]

There is no doubt that God's presence is problematized in Hebrew scripture. Samuel Terrien had recognized this in his modifier "elusive." Indeed Terrien's splendid discussion is permeated with the recognition that the God of Israel is *Deus Absconditus*. In his first page, Terrien asserts, "Indeed, for most generations of the biblical age, Israel prayed to a *Deus Absconditus*."[23] But of course even that acknowledgment does not go far enough. Israel is given finally to theodicy, to the question of God's reliability, God's presence, God's willingness to be connected to Israel. The issue surfaces in many places, but of course most dramatically and powerfully in the book of Job. It is clear, moreover, that the resolution of the Joban question in 42:6 is fogged at best, perhaps a characteristic move in this tradition of affirmation.[24]

It is my judgment that in these several ways—*covenant and exile, hymn and lament, presence and theodicy*—and in many other ways that could be named, we are able to see the characteristic and definitional processes about which this testimony is concerned. And because there is this endless destabilizing—required by the body's truth of lived experience—no large claim for the Holy One of Israel can be made except locally and provisionally. The classic tradition of Christian interpretation has been uneasy with such a disclosure and so has felt obligated to skew the evidence.

Interpretation That Refuses Closure

It seems clear to me—and definitional—that this way of testifying to the Holy One of Israel is endlessly dialectical. As soon as one voice in Israel says it is so, another voice, or the same voice in a second utterance, is sure to counter the claim. What I think is most important for future shared work in Jewish and Christian interpretation is the recognition that the Christian tradition of interpretation has a deep propensity to give closure, to end the dialectic, to halt the deconstruction, and to arrive as quickly as possible at affirmation. Thus, characteristically, *covenant* is an enduring claim through and in exile, complaint characteristically ends in *doxology*, and *presence* will always trump theodicy. Well, yes and no. Yes, one can make such a case. But no, one cannot *clearly* make the case. And even if one could, the lived reality of the interpreting community knows better. The community has always known better, even if the decisive learning for us all now is the Shoah.

Church interpreters of Hebrew scripture, in my judgment, must resist the Christian propensity to closure. I am not clear why the pressure to closure is so strong a Christian propensity. It is perhaps the drive to Constantinian hegemony, which cannot tolerate instability and openness. Or it is perhaps the reasonableness of the Hellenistic traditions of interpretation, which refuses ambiguity. But now Christian interpreters are increasingly emancipated from the needs of political and intellectual hegemony. We have known for a long time, moreover, that this tradition of testimony sits ill at ease with Hellenistic reasonableness.

Thus, postdomination interpretation of Hebrew scripture is now situated to proceed without undue or premature closure. The closures to which we are tempted are of two kinds. First, it is to give closure that is *affirmative:* Finally God is gracious. All is well and all will be well. This temptation is enhanced by "therapeutic culture." Second, it is to give closure that is *christological:* Jesus fulfills all.

If, however, it is definitional in this material to resist closure, then Christian theology of the Hebrew scriptures cannot afford innocent affirmation because neither text nor life is like that. If it is definitional in this material to resist closure, then Christian theology of the Hebrew scriptures cannot be afforded an innocent, triumphal run to Jesus. As an alternative to that, interpretation in my judgment must attend to the endless dialectic of affirmation and negation and must attend to the ways in which the text is open to a Jesus reading as it is open at the same time to other faithful, responsible readings. A Christian theology of Hebrew scriptures may present the materials for Christian reading, but only an offer and not a direct hookup.

It is clear to me that the deconstructive dialectic of the Hebrew scriptures is indeed characteristically and intransigently Jewish in its openness to ambiguity and contradiction, as is reflected in midrashic interpretation, in Freudian depth psychology, and in the haunting interface of modernity and Shoah.[25] More than that, it is clear to me that a dialectic deconstruction belongs to the quality of the truth that is revealed here to which Israel testifies. The Only One of Israel is not innocently "omnipotent, omnipresent, and omniscient," as too much Christian theology has insisted, but is a God present with and absent from, a God to be praised in full adoration and assaulted as an abuser.[26]

The loss of hegemony in Christian theology invites a deep Christian rethink in these matters.[27] I suspect that what is to happen in the Christian connection is the recovery of the cross as *a symbol and mode of deconstruction* that is the pivot of faith and that lives in ongoing, unresolved tension with Easter. It is clear that in Christian reflection Easter does not put Friday to rest. And therefore a serious reader of Christian faith makes the deconstructive dialectic of Hebrew scripture an inescapable habit.

By accenting such a deconstructive dialectic, I mean to give no comfort to dismissive skeptics who have given up on the theological seriousness of the Hebrew scriptures. One would end in such easy skepticism if the deconstruction were only one step toward negation. But of course it never is only one step in Hebrew scriptures. Because in turn the negation is also regularly deconstructed with new affirmation. And it is the full dialectic that Israel endlessly enacts in its testimony.

Contextual Readings amidst Large Common Crisis

I do not wish to minimize or deny the divisions and distinctions that separate Jews and Christians in our interpretive responsibility. Least of all do I want to minimalize the historic asymmetry of Christian domination and Jewish suffering. It is my judgment that, important as they are, most of these differences and divisions stem from cultural, historical, and political realities propelled by Christian hegemony and domination, which has produced not only anti-Semitism and supersessionist interpretation but also a serious misconstrual of our own tradition.

If it is the case, as I have suggested, that the Hebrew scriptures are plurivocal and refuse closure, then conventional Christian closure (or any responding Jewish closure as a means of defense) is unfortunate and beyond the allowance of the text. I do not then concede to Childs that Jews and Christians read different Bibles, nor do I grant the same point when made from a Jewish perspective by Levenson.[28]

My own angle on interpretation is that we read together a testimony to the Elusive One who is endlessly rendered and re-rendered, around whom has gathered a rich inheritance of testimony, consisting in image, metaphor, and narrative—acts of imaginative construal that admit of no single reading but that generate many possible futures.

Like every interpreter, I read locally and provisionally. I read with certain habits and interests, as a tenured, white Christian male. All of my companion readers also read locally and provisionally. No apology for local, provisional reading. Apology is to be made for the cultural seduction of forgetting that our reading is local and provisional and imagining it is total and settled. That seduction, very strong in hegemonic Christianity, leads me to read only in isolation or in the company of other readers like myself. Precisely because the text advocates, sponsors, and insists upon many readings, my local, provisional reading must perforce be done in the presence of other serious readings—not white, not male, not tenured, not Christian—that endlessly subvert my own preferred reading.

Such a process, which evidently goes on within the text itself, does not lead to a new theological synthesis or harmonization. It leads rather to a human community in which every reading may be heeded and valued, but done in endless jeopardy, knowing that another text, another testimony, another reading will question my best truth.

I do not believe for an instant that critique of Christian supersessionism is misguided. I do not believe, moreover, that canonical reading in the Christian community is the wave of the future precisely because it continues old hegemonic assumptions. But I also do not believe that Christian reading by definition is wrong reading. A Christian claim of an exclusively right reading (like any exclusive Jewish claim of right reading) fails to take into account the elusiveness that is at the heart of the disclosure. And therefore it is my judgment that Jews and Christians may indeed read together as we wait together. I anticipate no easy overcoming of long habits of abuse and exclusivism. But I am sure that our sense of waiting matters to how we read. Martin Buber has said so well of our waiting:

> What is the difference between Jews and Christians? We all await the Messiah. You believe He has already come and gone, while we do not. I therefore propose that we wait for Him together. And when He appears, we can ask Him: Were You here before? And I hope that at that moment I will be close enough to whisper in his ear, "For the love of heaven, don't answer."[29]

Finally, however, my concern is not simply that Jews and Christians may make common cause in reading. In the end, I believe the risk of our reading-while-we-wait is situated in a much larger crisis. Our larger cultural crisis suggests that the reference point for theological interpretation of Hebrew scripture concerns the biblical chance for humanness of a dialectical kind that stands over against the flat, one-dimensional option of technological society. The intramural differences among us Jews and Christians in our several reading traditions are as nothing when set in the context of the loss of humanity that issues in uncurbed brutality. No doubt the Hebrew scripture is about the Holy One of Israel, but there issues from it a chance for humanness given nowhere else, albeit mediated through post-Hebrew scripture literatures of Jews and of Christians. And that should summon us to our shared, disputed reading.

In my judgment George Steiner has it right when he takes the deconstructive moments of Friday and Sunday and links them to the larger human crisis:

> There is one particular day in Western history about which neither historical record nor myth nor Scripture make report. It is a Saturday. And it has become the longest of days. We know of that Good Friday which Christianity holds to have been that of the Cross. But the non-Christian, the atheist, knows of it as well. This is to say that he knows of the injustice, of the interminable suffering, of the waste, of the brute enigma of ending, which so largely make up not only the historical dimension of the human condition, but the everyday fabric of our personal lives. We know, ineluctably, of the pain, of the failure of love, of the solitude which are our history and private fate. We know also about Sunday. To the Christian, that day signifies an initiation, both assured and precarious, both evident and beyond comprehension, of resurrection, of a justice and a love that have conquered death. If we are non-Christians or non-believers, we know of that Sunday in precisely analogous terms. We conceive of it as the day of liberation from inhumanity and servitude. We look to resolutions, be they therapeutic or political, be they social or messianic. The lineaments of that Sunday carry the name of hope (there is no word less deconstructible).
>
> But ours is the long day's journey of the Saturday. Between suffering, aloneness, unutterable waste on the one hand and the dream of liberation, of return on the other. In the face of the torture of a child, of the death of love which is Friday, even the greatest art and poetry are almost helpless. In the Utopia of the Sunday, the aesthetic will, presumably, no longer have logic or necessity. The apprehensions and figurations in the play of metaphysical imagining, in the poem and the music, which tell of pain and of hope, of the flesh which is said to taste of ash and of the spirit which is said to have the savour of fire, are always Sabbatarian. They have risen out of an immensity of waiting, which is that of man. Without them, how could we be patient?[30]

III.

A Conversation with Other Theologians

CHAPTER TEN

Theology of the Old Testament

A Prompt Retrospect

No one can doubt that theological interpretation of the Bible—most especially in the context of a Christian reading—is in a quite new, quite different, and quite demanding interpretive situation. It does not matter to me if that new circumstance is termed "postmodern," though I have used that term to describe it. What counts is a *pluralistic* interpretive community that permits us to see the polyphonic character of the text, and the *deprivileged* circumstance whereby theological interpretation in a Christian context is no longer allied with or supported by dominant epistemological or political-ideological forces. So long as Christian interpretation was dominant and normative, it could count on "intellectual reasonableness" to sustain it. That supportive alliance no longer pertains. Learning to do biblical theology outside the Western hegemony is demanding work, in order that Christian interpretation may come to know something of what Jewish interpreters have long known how to negotiate. Or more briefly, hermeneutical problematics and possibilities have now displaced positivistic claims—historical or theological—as the matrix of theological reflection.

I

As a consequence of that changed contextual reality, theological reflection concerning the Old Testament/Hebrew Bible must perforce move beyond the great twentieth-century achievements of Walther Eichrodt and Gerhard von Rad. Indeed, reading those works now strikes one as remarkably dated, and as largely innocent of the interpretive problems and possibilities that one now must face.

Having said that, however, I must add that no serious interpretive enterprise ever begins *de novo*, and certainly biblical theological work stands in important and grateful continuity with those contributions. Thus it is my intention to have worked carefully at issues of *continuity and discontinuity* with that scholarship, though it is likely that my appropriation and borrowing are more pervasive than I am aware. Eichrodt's effort to organize around the single conceptual frame of covenant was, in his time, an immense gain. It is unfortunate, moreover, that the theological grid of covenant got carried away into historical-critical matters with Klaus Baltzer, George Mendenhall, and Dennis McCarthy, because Eichrodt's governing theological insight—namely, that the God of Israel is characteristically a God *in relation*—was better than any of that. That insight, rooted for him in the Christian interpretation of John Calvin, is what Eichrodt sought to exposit.

It is clear that von Rad's work has been much more decisive for me, and indeed my opening section on "core testimony" is willfully von Radian. Von Rad's thesis of *recital* as a fundamental dynamic behind the Old Testament permitted a sense of openness, an acknowledgment of variation and plurality, and an accent upon "the said." All of that I have appropriated, though I have gone further than von Rad with the rhetorical, and have sought to avoid the morass of positivistic history from which von Rad was unable to escape. Thus the continuities with this scholarly work are important to me, and I have the sense that the thesis of *an alternative world voiced in Israel's testimony* is indeed a Barthian impulse on my part, which echoes G. Ernest Wright's thesis of "against."

II

Having said that and having acknowledged debts and continuities with gratitude, I want to suggest now the ways in which I have tried to move beyond those dominant models of the twentieth century, hopefully to contribute in a way congruent with our own interpretive context that is outside hegemony, pluralistic, and deprivileged. I will suggest six elements of my exposition that I consider to be *contributions to our ongoing work*.

1. At the outset it has seemed clear to me that a theology of the Old Testament *cannot appeal to "history,"* as evidenced by von Rad's inability to hold together "critically assured minimum" and "theological maximum":[1]

> But our final comment on it should not be that it is obviously an "unhistorical" picture, because what is in question here is a picture fashioned

throughout by faith. Unlike any ordinary historical document, it does not have its center in itself; it is intended to tell the beholder about Jahweh, that is, how Jahweh led his people and got himself glory.[2]

I do not for one instant mean to suggest, following Rudolf Bultmann, that there is nothing of "happenedness"; rather, the "happening" is not subject to the measure of modern positivistic categories.[3] The "happenedness" of the theological claims made for Israel's God is in, with, and under Israel's attestation; critical positivistic—and now nihilistic—judgments do not touch those claims. Indeed, Israel's recital and attestation at many points consciously assert a memory and a claim that is counter to dominant history, and our interpretation must attend to that impulse to counter. Thus the problematic is not Israel's claim made for its God, but the flattened criticism that refuses in principle to host such claims.

The issue, then, is not at all a particular claim that should be dissolved into universal assertion, for I have insisted everywhere on the particular and have refused a groundless universalism. The issue rather is particularity that has confidence in its own utterance and that refuses to submit its claim to any universal norm.

2. The counterside of eschewing modernist historical categories is to appeal to *the practice of rhetoric.* I understand Old Testament theology to be reflection upon the uttered faith claims of Israel concerning the God who is given to us precisely in and through those claims. In this regard, the focus upon utterance is congruent with von Rad's approach, which was unfortunately complicated by his appeal to critical history. Beyond von Rad, moreover, I am much influenced by Paul Ricoeur's awareness that utterance is an act of imagination that produces worlds and/or counterworlds.[4] More closely than Ricoeur, I am inescapably instructed by my teacher, James Muilenburg, who understood best about faith and rhetoric, so that in some general way Old Testament theology is "rhetorical criticism."

Such a focus upon rhetoric, in a context outside hegemony—pluralistic and deprivileged—is an effort at nonfoundationalism, an attempt to trade neither upon the stable claims of the Western theological-ontological tradition nor upon the claims of Western positivistic history, either in its maximal or now in its exceedingly minimalist tendency. Israel's rhetoric mediates a God not held in thrall by either mode of Western certitude or control.

3. I have increasingly found thematic approaches to biblical theology wanting, not only because they are inescapably reductionist, but because

they are characteristically boring and fail to communicate the open-ended vitality of the text. It is for that reason that I decided, early on, to focus not on substantive themes but on *verbal processes* that allow for dynamism, contradiction, tension, ambiguity, and incongruity—all those habits that belong peculiarly to interactionism.[5] What I hope I have offered is an interactionist model of theological exposition congruent with this believing community that is endlessly engaged with God, a God who is available for the extremities of praise and complaint, which are Israel's characteristic modes of speech in this conflictual engagement. The importance of this move *from theme(s) to process* cannot be overstated for me, because the interactive process seems crucial both to the Subject of Old Testament theology and to the pluralistic, deprivileged context of our own work.

4. More specifically, it is the focus upon juridical language of *testimony* that I hope will be the major gain of my work. I understand that "testimony" as a theme can be as reductionist as any other theme, but I intend it not as a theme but as a process whereby Israel endlessly gives an account of reality featuring the God of Israel as decisive, whether in presence and action or in absence and hiddenness.

It may be that the notion is reductionist because one can, I am sure, claim that not everything is testimony. Except that I think a case can be made that Israel, in all its utterances and writings, stays roughly fixed upon that single and defining claim for Yahweh.[6] Testimony about a single and defining claim permits two maneuvers that are important. There is, on the one hand, immense variation (as one would expect) in the detailed accounts offered the court by witnesses who nevertheless agree on the main point. On the other hand, there is a significant core of agreement among these witnesses, when heard in the presence of other accounts of reality that construe without reference to Yahweh.

It strikes me as odd that the genres of disputatiousness, given often in litigious tone, have not more centrally occupied theological interpreters. I would focus, for many reasons, on Second Isaiah wherein the poetry disputes about other gods. But the "speech of judgment" is dominant in the preexilic prophets.[7] The Deuteronomic history, informed as it may be by Deuteronomy 32, proceeds as an extended narrative speech of judgment. The psalms of complaint, culminating in the book of Job, proceed in similar fashion. I believe, moreover, that it is legitimate to conclude from such a core of material that even where the genre is not visible, Israel characteristically makes a case for a Yahwistic construal of reality against other construals of reality. Where the case is not disputatious, it is even there a lesser or softer advocacy for this rather than that. Thus I want to offer this focus on testimony as a gain, as long as it is taken as metaphor and not pressed too hard to a conclusion.

5. The process of litigation that gives great maneuverability allows for a *paradigmatic juxtaposition of core testimony and countertestimony,* a juxtaposition that I count as a major gain of my study. While Israel's utterances make a sustained case for a Yahweh-focused world, and in the face of rivals speak with one voice on the matter (acknowledging many traces of religious phenomenology not fully incorporated into that dominant voice), yet there is vigorous dispute with that unified claim among these advocates. It is my insistence that the counterclaims must be taken seriously as a datum of theological utterance.[8] My impression is that heretofore a coherent way has not been found for such an interface. Even von Rad's "answer" really did not exhibit the remarkable dynamic of that text.[9]

I take the countertestimony to be powerful evidence that Israel is resolved to tell the truth, to tell the truth of its own life, and to tell that truth even if it crowds the large claims made for Yahweh. This is no small matter, for it means that Israel's faith has little patience for religious softness or prettiness or cover-up in the interest of protecting or enhancing God. I am drawn to Jacques Derrida's verdict that, finally, justice is undeconstructible.[10] Or in another mode, Israel's faith will not compromise the undeniable givenness of bodily reality, especially bodily pain or pain in the body politic.

Such a procedure of claim and counterclaim is, in my judgment, definitional for theology in this tradition. This procedure appears to be deeply and endlessly open and unresolved, so that finally "claim" will not silence "counterclaim," nor, conversely, can "counterclaim" ever nullify "claim." This disputatious dialectic seems of absolute importance for the character of Yahweh rendered in this text, and consequently for the character of this people that renders and responds to Yahweh.

The refusal to give closure is a defining point of the data. This is a very different read from Bultmann's sorry verdict that the Old Testament is a failure, because the openness is not failure but a rigorous willingness to speak in dispute.[11] Christians exhibit an endless propensity to give closure to the matter in Jesus of Nazareth. I am, however, instructed by Jürgen Moltmann's suggestion that Friday and Sunday constitute a "dialectic of reconciliation," that is, both parts enduring and in force, so that the claim of Easter does not silence the counterclaim of Friday. The dynamic belongs to the process of faith and therefore inescapably to the parties in the process, Yahweh and Israel.

6. Finally, I have tried to extrapolate beyond Eichrodt's covenant the definitional *relatedness* of Yahweh, which I have voiced under the rubric of "Unsolicited Testimony." That is, everything said about Yahweh is said about Yahweh in relation. Yahweh is characteristically embedded in sentences with active verbs that have direct objects for whom the agency of Yahweh matters decisively.

I have, moreover, tried to make the case in some detail that what is said of Yahweh is, *mutatis mutandis*, characteristically said of Israel as well. Derivatively what is said of Israel as Yahweh's defining partner is said of all partners, so that Yahweh vis-à-vis Israel becomes the model for Yahweh vis-à-vis creation, nations, and human persons. This parallelism that I have suggested is in no way a move away from the privilege and particularity of Israel's status with Yahweh, but is the matrix through which all else is to be understood vis-à-vis Yahweh.

This relatedness that we subsume under covenant is crucial, because it not only draws the human-historical side of reality into the orbit of Yahweh's rule and reality—a point decisive in Calvinist theology since the first pages of the *Institutes*—but the relatedness bespeaks the truth of Yahweh as much as it voices the truth of Israel or any of Yahweh's derivative partners. That is, Israel can entertain the claim that this relatedness is not always a one-way deal: It does not always move from Yahweh to Israel (and the other partners). Nor is it adequate to suggest, as scholarship has done, that the relation is "bilateral." On occasion, so it seems to me, there is role reversal, so that Israel (or other partners) can take the initiative over against Yahweh, in complaint and in praise.[12] This prospect of role reversal, whereby the lesser party becomes provisionally the dominant party, seems to me a question for further probing, even though the possibility is beyond the horizon of conventional Christian understanding. This possibility is a learning that Christian interpretation may recover from Jewish tradition. It is an evidence of how radical and daring Israel is prepared to be in its dissent from Yahweh, as well as how capable it is in resisting the conventions of perennial Western philosophy.

This sense of relatedness is true to the text in broad outline. In parallel fashion, this construal of holiness represents a powerful alternative to Cartesian reductionism. Thus the interactionist model of holiness offered by

Martin Buber and Franz Rosenzweig, and now voiced afresh by Emmanuel Levinas, seems to be thoroughly rooted in the Bible, though it entails a drastic relearning for the dominant theological tradition of Western Christianity.[13] It will be evident that all of these elements I regard as gains are interrelated and of a piece in an interactionist model that refuses to take God either as a fixed object or as an empty cipher. Everything about this theological tradition insists, in the utterances of Israel, that there is Someone on the other end of the transaction who is decisive—even if absent, hidden, or in eclipse.

III

The gains that I suggest are commensurate with what will surely emerge as *points of contention and continued dispute*. I do not imagine that I have been able to see things convincingly through to the end. So I am glad to acknowledge at least four points where the argument is vulnerable, though other such points will surface in our discussion. I regard these as vulnerable points because they propose fresh perspectives for which we lack adequate categories. I incline to think that the vulnerability is only because things are not carried through, not because they are wrongheaded. It remains to be seen, of course, whether that judgment turns out to be acceptable to my colleagues.

   1. *A nonfoundationalist perspective.* There is now available a huge literature moving in this direction.[14] But no one in the biblical field known to me has tried to make the case as directly as have I. Thus my formulation of the matter leaves me with some considerable uneasiness.

A nonfoundationalist approach is open to criticism from two perspectives. First, it will not satisfy conventional theologians who have case matters in categories of Hellenistic ontology with the assumption that God is a stable, fixed point, because to do so is to conform the oddity of Yahweh to settled generic categories, a maneuver that is both an epistemological accommodation and an excessive political compromise. Anyone who reflects theologically on this text knows that the God of Abraham, Isaac, and Jacob, to say nothing of the God of Moses and Job, is not easily confused with the God of the philosophers.[15] Second, and more difficult, is my urging that the rhetorical claims for Yahweh in ancient Israel are not fully linked to the happenedness of history as it has been understood in positivistic categories. The current rage of historical minimalism (nihilism?), on the basis of positivistic claims, would love to nullify theological claims for Yahweh on the basis of the negation of historical data. But that is to fall into von Rad's dilemma. I prefer to insist that *history follows rhetoric*, so that the memory uttered is the memory trusted. This is, in my judgment, how it works in a reciting, testifying, confessing community, except that acceptance of the testimony creates a circle of affirmation in which it can be subsequently claimed that the rhetoric derives from the history. The difficulties are acute. I suppose I am more aware of the problem of "history behind rhetoric" than I am skilled at articulating the countercase against that long-standing Western assumption. Rhetoric is indeed "the weapon of the weak."[16] To the extent that ancient Israel lives its life and practices its faith "outside," to that extent its rhetoric is and must be profoundly originary, the only recourse held by "the weak" to remain outside hegemonic assumptions.

2. *Historical criticism.* The previous point leads to the question of historical criticism, which Brevard Childs has identified as the crisis point for doing biblical theology. I am sure that I have not done well in articulating the delicate relationship between historical criticism and theological exposition. Part of the problem is that I am so deeply situated in historical criticism that it is likely that I appeal much more to such categories than I am aware. And part of the problem is that it is increasingly difficult to say with precision what it is that constitutes historical criticism, given the eruption of methodological alternatives. What now is taken as historical criticism is certainly very different from what it was in ancient days when I was in graduate school.

But the real issue is neither of these two preliminary matters; the real issue is the work and import of such criticism. We must think critically about the Bible, because we live in an inquiring intellectual world. Taken on that basis, criticism is simply being intellectually responsible. A case is readily made, however, that what has passed for historical criticism has in fact been a commitment to something like Enlightenment rationality, whereby criticism has had the negative task of eliminating whatever offended reason and the positive task of rendering the claims of the text compatible with autonomous reason. That way of understanding criticism is supported by the so-called historical minimalists who have made a virtue out of skepticism, thus pushing criticism toward skepticism that is endlessly dismissive of the claims of the text.

The issue is nicely represented in Old Testament theological scholarship by comparing the work of Childs with that of James Barr. Childs has indicated that historical criticism is largely a deficit operation for theological exposition. But Barr, fearing authoritarian obscurantism, will insist that any credible theological claim from the text must be cast in the environs of critical categories. I suspect that what is made of historical criticism depends on what one most fears in the project of interpretation: *a debilitating fragmentation* (Childs) or *an excessive fideism* (Barr). It may be then that we do best to say that criticism is to be assessed dialectically in terms of the interpretive context. I have sought to occupy a mediating position. My sympathies are with Childs, but I do not want to follow him—as I shall clarify in a moment—toward his notion of "canonical," which strikes me as unfortunately reductionist. The issue, in the end, is how the odd claims of this text make their way in an intellectual environment inclined toward domestication and resistant to the scandal of particularity, a particularity that refuses the flattening that becomes predictable and replicable.

3. *Jewish and Christian reading.* Biblical theology in a conventional Christian context is often deeply supersessionist.[17] The assumption too often is that the Old Testament moves directly and singularly toward the New Testament and its christological claims, so that any other interpretive trajectory is excluded in principle.[18] There is no doubt that this is a deeply vexed question beyond my capacity to address, and that such conventional supersessionist interpretations have contributed powerfully, even if indirectly, to the anti-Jewish barbarism of the recent past. But it seems clear that exclusionary reading toward Christology is morally intolerable as well as theologically problematic.

I suspect that I do not know enough to deal adequately with the issue. My take on it, while waiting for further instruction, is that as a Christian I will by conviction and by habit read toward the New Testament. But because the text is endlessly polyvalent and because its Subject is endlessly elusive and beyond domestication, it is impossible, in my judgment, to pretend a monopolistic reading. Thus my reading toward the New Testament is done in the midst of other legitimate and valued readings—primarily Jewish—to which I must attend and by which I may expect to be instructed. It is my expectation that in the long run Jewish reading may also be open to the (not exclusive) validity of Christian reading, though clearly the issues are not symmetrical because of the long history of Christian hegemony and abusiveness. While I do not imagine any easy convergence in these readings, neither will I accept the verdict shared by Childs and Jon Levenson that we read different Bibles.[19] Rather we must read together as far as we can read and, beyond that, read attentively in each other's presence. Such a strategy, to be sure, has much to unlearn and to undo, but we must begin somewhere. I am encouraged that N. T. Wright has made a powerful case that the New Testament gospel is the retelling of the story of Israel through the life of Jesus, a retelling that does not preempt.[20] In all such common reading the particularity and primacy of Jewish claims are to be affirmed, and whatever else follows must follow from that primal affirmation. As I have indicated in my comments on the "partners" for God, Israel is the defining partner, and whatever else is to be said of other partners is derived from and informed by that claim and relationship. My sense, therefore, is that Christian reading must be done very differently from what we have done heretofore. The barbarism of the twentieth century is not an irrelevance, but is rather a primary datum that requires learning to read (and believe) differently.

4. *Toward the church.* The Christian enterprise of biblical theology, and specifically Old Testament theology insofar as it is Christian, has important responsibilities and limitations. This point is the counterside of my last point concerning the interface between Jewish and Christian modes of theological exposition.

There is now an important insistence, especially by Childs (and, from the side of systematic theology, by Francis Watson), that Old Testament theology must be deeply and exclusively linked to the New Testament because in Childs's terms, the two testaments are "two witnesses to Jesus Christ."[21] This tendency (that is, to assume that Christian interpretation of the Old Testament is distinctively and closely focused upon the church's claim for Jesus) assures that no competing or complementary interpretation—even Jewish—warrants any consideration. The several schemes of relation of Old Testament and New Testament—law-gospel, promise-fulfillment, salvation history—may all be utilized, but the common assumption is that the Old Testament awaits the New for a compelling reading.[22] The accent is completely upon the *continuity* between the testaments.

A student of the Old Testament, however, cannot help but notice the *disjunction and disconnection* from one testament to the other, so that the theological claims of the Old Testament do not obviously or readily or smoothly or without problem move to the New Testament. Indeed, if we are to claim some kind of continuity—as any Christian reading surely must—it is a continuity that is *deeply hidden* and *endlessly problematic.* For that reason, and given the intensely and consistently iconoclastic propensity of the Old Testament text, it may be suggested that the Old Testament stands as a critical principle over against any easy claims of New Testament faith, so that the God of Israel is not easily reduced to or encompassed by Christian claims.[23] After all of the adjustments from the faith of Israel to the faith of the church there is yet a deep "otherwise," which is uncontained and undomesticated, that must be acknowledged.

If the issue is to struggle with the ill fit between the two testaments, the problem is even more acute when one moves from the claims closely linked to Jesus in the New Testament to the developed dogmatic tradition of the church. It is well known that over the course of his long engagement with the intractable problem of canon, "canon" has meant several different things to Childs. In his *Biblical Theology of the Old and New Testaments,* surely his most mature articulation, the term *canon* has come to refer to the "rule of faith" (whereby Childs seems to mean the christological-trinitarian formula) as the way in which biblical theology is to be done.[24] Such perspective seems to me, in the end, both reductionist and excessively ideational, because it must gloss over the characteristic disjunctions of Old Testament rhetoric that mediate the disjunctive God of Israel. This same inclination is present in the essays collected by Carl Braaten and Robert Jenson in response to Childs.[25]

It seems to me that such a reductionist reading remains in the service of the hegemonic, triumphalist claims of the church, without at the same time recognizing the endlessly subversive intention of the text that is endlessly restless with every interpretive closure, whether Jewish or Christian. My own inclination is more congruent with the recent proposals of Wesley Kort—who considers Calvin's theory of reading as informed by *sicut,* "as if"—to read against every given conviction, to an unfounded (nonfoundational?) alternative that is given only in the text.[26] From Calvin, Kort's sense of scripture in a postmodern context is that scripture is too elemental, too primal, and too originary to be administered and shaped by established interpretation and doctrine:

> This is not to say that institution and doctrine are unimportant. The question is one of relative status. Reading the Bible as scripture must lead to an exit from them. For theology this means, first of all, freeing reading from theological determinations, particularly the substitution of doctrines of scripture for reading the Bible. . . . But unity and stability in the church are not necessarily good things, and certainly imposed or abstract unity and stability are not. . . . But reading the Bible as scripture involves first of all movement away from self and world and toward their divestment and abjection.[27]

It is my sense that Christian reading, long hegemonic in the West, must now face *divestment and abjection* of a social-political-economic kind that is best—perhaps inevitably—matched by a theological divestment as well. Although Israel has long understood that the force of the Holy One requires the exposure of the idols, any long triumphalist interpretation characteristically does not regard its own triumphalism as idolatrous.

Kort is against the stream in much current theological conviction. I think he has it proximately right and am reassured that he finds this guiding motif at the center of Calvin's own perspective. It is Calvin's (and Kort's) "as scripture" to which we must attend, in a phrasing parallel to that of Childs that comes to mean something very different. It is this "as scripture" that is *originary* and *undetermined by institutional force* that may help us face the demands of interpretation, for both the wounded and the wounder.

It is evident that such a stance toward church claims, a stance critical but not dismissive, is a complement to my suggestion concerning Christian theology vis-à-vis Jewish faith. The claim of scripture, endlessly problematic in the history of Christian reading and made poignant for our time by Karl Barth, is that the Holy One of Israel will not be held in church claims any more than in the temple claims of Solomon, for "Even heaven and the highest heaven cannot contain you, much less this house that I have built!" (1 Kings 8:27).

IV

It will be evident that I have opted for a *process* of testimony, dispute, and advocacy; I trust it will be equally evident why I have done so. The process of adjudication is not formal and vacuous, but endlessly implies *content* about the Subject of that testimony, dispute, and advocacy. The emphasis on the process, however, seems crucial to me because (*a*) Israel presented its most daring utterance in disputatious process, (*b*) the God of Israel characteristically engages in precisely such dispute, and (*c*) such ongoing, respectful disputation is the only interpretive option, in my judgment, in a pluralistic, deprivileged interpretive environment. I do not believe for a minute that deprivileged environment should itself dictate the terms of our exposition; I am, however, convinced that the shape of our interpretive environment is oddly congruent with Israel's preferred way to voice its faith. I have suggested, in my book, that the endless negotiation of core testimony and countertestimony, in Christian mode, takes the form of the dialectic of Friday and Sunday.[28] I have, moreover, been deeply moved and informed by the judgment of George Steiner that "ours is a long day's journey of the Saturday."[29] A Christian dynamic of Friday–Sunday regards post-Easter Monday as still under the aegis of Easter joy. In Christian perspective, Monday is very different from Saturday. But serious Christian discernment also knows that the problems of Saturday must continue to be faced on Monday, better faced with Jews who also wait. My attempt at theological interpretation is to engage the reading of our common calling, Saturday issues even on Monday.

CHAPTER ELEVEN

Israel's Creation Faith

Response to J. Richard Middleton

In 1994, J. Richard Middleton and I engaged in a dialogue, published in the Harvard Theological Review, *on my handling of creation theology in the Old Testament. I am grateful for his careful, critical assessment of my writings on this topic; the gist of his argument should be discernible from my references to his article that appear in the following response.*[1]

I am grateful to Richard Middleton for having commented upon my work with such care, precision, and generosity. On every point that matters for Middleton's analysis, he has understood me correctly and reported fairly. On the whole I must accept the critique he makes of my work. My response to his critique is not to justify what I have done, but to comment upon my own memory of the context and impetus for my work, and then, as far as I am able, to extend the conversation a bit further.

Multiple Models

Middleton rightly notes that in my work on creation in the faith and texts of ancient Israel, my thinking reflects either a development or a shift of models that suggests contradictory approaches. Among these he notes three: First, a dialectic of prophetic/royal consciousness which has been the dominant model of my work and which received its most extreme expression in *Israel's Praise*; second, a triadic model of orientation/disorientation/new orientation, a more recent development in my thinking which I use particularly in reference to the Psalms; and third, a world-affirming position in *In Man We Trust* which is rather an early oddity in my work. That is a fair summary of how my thinking has emerged.[2]

Three comments are in order. First, it is clear to me that my best interpretive work is the proposal of models of reading that look for larger patterns of meaning; these models are informed by historical criticism but seek to suggest interpretive possibilities for contemporary reading. That is, such models stand in a mediating position between criticism and contemporary reading. Such an enterprise is risky because it does not stay fully with critical matters, but dares to suggest analogues that are in part subjective and contextual. Moreover, such models for me emerge in conversation with contemporary partners, so that these three models had as primary conversation partners, in turn, Jose Miranda and his Marxist analysis, Paul Ricoeur, and Harvey Cox's early work.

It is clear that variant models are possible when reading the same material. Thus for example, in different contexts, I have situated Psalm 150 very differently, depending upon the model I was explicating. Middleton is correct that I did not directly seize upon or exploit Ricoeur's "multiple readings,"[3] but I was committed to that process long before I understood it conceptually. (The notion of "multiple readings" refers to the density of a text that permits different readers to find "correctly" different things in a text. The Enlightenment notion that a text has a single clear, recoverable meaning is an illusion.) Thus it is no problem for me or surprise to me that models that make different uses of "creation" materials emerge in my several studies. To a great extent, how a text functions depends upon how other texts are related to it.

Second, my work is invariably ad hoc because I am primarily and consistently interested in hermeneutical questions, most often questions that emerge in the process of studying a particular set of texts in a particular interpretive context. I have neither the interest nor the patience to spend my time defending or promoting a single theme, model, or segment of textual material. Thus I prefer to respond to what I perceive to be the questions that lie at the interface between theological claims and emerging cultural issues. I have not worried much about consistency, because in the articulation of models, one intends that at least for the moment, the model should be entertained and utilized on its own terms, in order to see what account of reality is made possible and what reading it alone generates, without respect to any competing interest, reality, or reading.

Thus, for example, my most positive treatment of wisdom-creation in *In Man We Trust* was completed in the wake of Harvey Cox's *The Secular City*.[4] My study was as "innocent" as his turned out to be; that is, it was informed by certain freighted convictions and assumptions that were in fact quite romantic. It also came just as Hebrew Bible scholarship was focusing on wisdom studies, and so my effort was to exhibit some of the possible linkages between current theological themes and the texts of Israel. In contrast, *Israel's Praise* was prepared for the Sprunt Lectures at Union Seminary in Richmond, Virginia. There I took as my subject the theme of lament as the ground of theology and liturgy, because I wanted to raise issues about what I perceived to be a "theology of glory" in the church establishment. I take some small comfort from the awareness that Karl Barth's great *Church Dogmatics,* while it is taken as a definitive and enduring statement, in fact represents in its various volumes responses to different issues and crises facing Barth along the way.[5] Even such definitive statements as those of Barth must be read in context and cannot be taken out of context and made absolute.

Third, there is no doubt that in spite of my building different models with a variety of perspectives, there is a resilience and recurrence of the "royal/prophetic" dialectic within my work. Part of that propensity is based in what I judge to be the claims of the texts themselves, and part is what I felt to be the overriding contemporary question of self-sufficiency grounded in technical competence and its seductive power of legitimation.[6] Behind such impressions, however, is the enduring criticism rising out of my own early growth and nurture in a situation of relative poverty amid a context of relative affluence, which has generated enough rage and urgency to last a lifetime, and which makes me adhere to what I take to be the revolutionary claims of the Mosaic-prophetic tradition. Thus my work is contextual in a very personal way. I concede that contextual impetus, even as Middleton does his Caribbean experience of otherworldly pietism. At the same time, I wish that others participating in the debate would examine and expose the factors that propel and influence their work, for I imagine that none of us is innocent.

Background and Influences

I must also recognize that my focus on the exodus-liberation texts in sharp contrast to creation texts reflects the mind-set of the scholarship in which I have been nurtured. I have belonged to that generation of students powerfully shaped by Albrecht Alt's notion of the distinctiveness of Israel, by Gerhard von Rad's credo hypothesis, and by G. Ernest Wright's *Old*

Testament Against Its Environment.[7] Recently, I have become more aware of how weighty and influential this background has been, as I have been reassessing, after fifty years, Eric Voegelin's *Israel and Revelation* and its sharp contrast of the cosmological and the historical.[8] It is clear that Voegelin's magisterial study is completely shaped by the assumptions of Alt and von Rad. I have no doubt, moreover, that the program centered in von Rad—from which he belatedly moved away in *Wisdom in Israel*[9]—was largely driven by Barth's way of contrasting the gospel and "religion," by his attempt to find "evangelical" territory in the face of the dominant ideology in his context of "blood and soil."[10] Von Rad's interpretive categories in his "credo hypothesis," which contrasts Israel's faith and Canaanite religion, are voiced under the influence of Barth's dismissal of "religion," which lacked a critical theological principle.

It is almost impossible for me to imagine the danger of the context that produced Barth's radical program and what I regard as the subsequent complementary articulation of von Rad. These arguments and models were justifiably found to be compelling, faithful, and urgent by many of their contemporaries, and I believe that it is foolish now to second-guess the efforts of Barth, von Rad, and cohorts.[11] Thus I regard this period of scholarship and its governing assumptions not as a lapse, as some are wont to do, but as producing a body of work that we must continue to take seriously. Nonetheless, such an extreme "over-againstness" in understanding Israel's distinctiveness, which led to a heavy accent on history, was a context-driven enterprise from which we can learn, but to which we do not need to continue to subscribe.[12] Thus neither embrace nor dismissal seems to me a proper response, but rather serious listening and learning. As Middleton rightly sees, at the end, von Rad himself was moving beyond the assumption that Israel's faith could be completely contrasted with the religions of its environment.

I have probably not differentiated enough in my own work between creation, royal thinking, Zion theology, and wisdom, instead lumping them together as having "establishment" inclinations. Middleton in large part seems to agree with me that these traditions most often function conservatively. The key element in his critique, however, is exposed by his use of the word "inherently" in his title and by my use of the word "inevitably" in my rhetoric. That is, is creation theology *inherently, inevitably* conservative, that is, does it legitimate the status quo? Of course, against my heretofore controlling models, which prefer "Mosaic covenant" to "creation faith" and "prophetic" to "Zionist" or "royal" modes of faith, the clear answer is "no . . . no, not inherently . . . no, not inevitably." Thus creation theology is neither inherently nor inevitably conservative, but functions most often in a conservative fashion.

In a more recent study, I have reflected on the way in which Psalm 37 can be read as a profound assertion of the status quo, as a self-affirmation of the virtue of the landed class.[13] It also can be read, however, as an act of radical hope by the disenfranchised, who are confident that current unjust land distribution cannot endure, and that the land eventually will be reassigned to "the righteous." While this psalm is not explicitly creation theology, it is a wisdom psalm that reflects the same world of faith. It does indeed allow for varied readings, providing an example of Ricoeur's plurivocality. I cite my work on Psalm 37 as a recent effort on my part to move beyond the powerful position of von Rad's confessional stances, and nuance more closely the complex issues that are operative in interpretation.

I have no doubt that von Rad's early position has been decisive in informing my own positions, but the reason for its compelling appeal is because of my own deep-rooted propensity to regard justice as a leitmotif of biblical faith. Thus scholarly nurture and personal inclination have converged.

New Developments in Creation Theology

I have great appreciation for the newer developments in creation theology in the study of the Hebrew Scriptures/Old Testament.[14] The work of Bernhard Anderson, James Barr, James Crenshaw, Terence Fretheim, Rolf Knierim, Jon Levenson, and Hans Heinrich Schmid, among others, is surely most important.[15] I have no doubt that I must continue to rethink these matters. Of great help in doing so is Middleton's important distinction between "creation-chaos" and creation as a transcendent reference that destabilizes all ideological claims, royal and prophetic.[16] Middleton rightly appeals to the deep transformative shift in the character of Israel's theological intentions—a shift that is permitted and required by the exile. The exile provoked a profound restatement and reinterpretation of Israel's central affirmations. In my judgment, our continued reflection and rethinking of this shift should be directed into four responses.

First, "biblical theology" must not conform too easily or quickly to dogmatic-creedal formulations or sequences which long concerned the

Christian enterprise of "Old Testament Theology."[17] Brevard Childs, for example, is intent upon again casting biblical theological interpretation in ways that are reflective of dogmatic claims if not subservient to them.[18] In his most recent and fullest articulation of biblical theology Childs requires the faith of ancient Israel to take a shape that is decisively amenable to Christian systematic theology. I do not suggest that adherents to the new accent on creation intend to follow this pattern, but we must be vigilant about the prospect of such a convergence between scholarly models and dogmatic categories. It is all too easy to assert with Knierim that "creation is the horizon of theology,"[19] but we must at least notice that the exodus—and not creation—has dominated the liturgical imagination of Judaism.[20] Creation faith is no doubt important to the shape of Old Testament theology. It is, however, far from clear that it is the inevitable clue to adequate interpretation, because Judaism characteristically does not begin there. Thus such a flat assertion as that of Knierim invites the question, "Whose horizon?"

Second, Barth's response to "liberalism" and von Rad's credo hypothesis reveal that these authors think in ways that are driven by their contexts.[21] Barth was completely disillusioned by liberalism and by his liberal teachers, because it was clear that their liberalism provided no critical principle against interpretive seductions. Von Rad's "credo hypothesis" is surely to be understood in light of the Barmen Declaration and the crisis of the Confessing Church of Germany. This in itself does not constitute a critique but rather a recognition that may help us better understand their intentions. In the renewed accent upon creation, it behooves us to think about the ways in which this scholarly inclination is also conditioned by context. I do not believe that such a shift in accents as is currently taking place in scholarship is completely unencumbered or just correcting a (Barthian) digression, but that the new move also needs to be assessed in context; that is, the new accent on creation is no more "innocent" than was Barth, and surely just as "theory laden." Such a shift may be driven in part by resonance with "new science,"[22] or may reflect a concern for order in an increasingly disordered Western world.[23] In a climate of religious pluralism, this shift may reveal a concern to work with larger, more comprehensive constructs and diminish the emphasis on Israel's "scandal of particularity,"[24] or it could reveal a desire to tone down the liberation thrust of Israel's confessional narratives.[25] I do not suggest any bad faith in the newer interpretive tendency, but I imagine that it is not "innocent"—it is not objective and disinterested. If such work is not innocent, we must note the contextual factors if we are to understand fully what is at issue.

Alongside a general cultural context, a third response to such a shift is to recognize the influence of the personal histories and inclinations of scholars, although I am not interested in making any *ad hominem* judgment. No scholar approaches interpretive questions completely disinterestedly, despite all of our efforts to be objective.[26] For example, my good friend Terence Fretheim, who has done some of the first work on creation thinking, has rightly critiqued my work in *Israel's Praise* as being excessively narrow in its "canon" of the lament psalm.[27] Fretheim, in turn, now focuses intensely upon creation, showing that even the exodus narrative is better understood with reference to creation concerns. I have wondered if his work is in part a response to his context of Lutheranism, which has underplayed creation. One can always wonder what motivates scholarly work. I have no doubt that the intellectual and social environment of any scholar is important, even as it is for me. Thus Middleton sees creation theology from his own setting, appreciating the claim of creation as an "explosive category" in a "postcolonial" setting.[28] Middleton evidently has a very different personal impetus from that of many North American scholars who have not lived in his context.

I also recommend a fourth response: What concerns me most is that Israel's vision of reality must be interpreted and then practiced "on the ground," that is, in particular situations of socioeconomic and political crisis. I believe, therefore, that Israel's vision of society or, more largely, of the world must be seen in relation to concrete issues of justice, issues that involve, for example, power, goods, and access. Insofar as Israel's faith is revolutionary, it is not a set of ideas but it is indeed a praxis. I do not resist the move from emphasis upon Mosaic-prophetic-historical texts to creation texts, but I wonder what the move from praxis (as evoked by the Passover imagination) to the horizon of creation means, and if the move from liberation to creation is at the same time a move from *praxis* to *ideas*. By "Passover imagination" I refer to the regular Passover festival recital and reenactment of the exodus narrative and the life-world of freedom and justice that is generated by this recital. It concerns me that some of the proponents of a move to creation theology do not seem to have read Marx and seem to be more or less innocent about social criticism. Thus the issue of importance, in my judgment, is not this or that theme, but the hermeneutical posture about which we must continue to struggle.

Conclusion

I conclude with reference to the comments of three authors. First, in his positive analysis of Zion theology, Ben Ollenburger makes almost lyrical claims for Zion theology, which is a mode of creation theology:

> It is fundamentally a theology of creation. . . . It means at the very least that since creation is by definition a universal category, the possibilities open to all humankind are not determined by history or by nature, but by creation.
>
> We know that at various points in human history we have been told that it is impossible to have a world without slavery, or the inferiority of some peoples to others is part of the essential fabric of history, or it is grounded in the immutable order of nature. We have been told that the idea that men and women could govern themselves in a democracy is impossible, for the monarchy is part of the essential fabric of history, or it is grounded in the immutable order of nature. We have been told that it is impossible for women to hold positions of significance or assume equal responsibility with men, for the domination of women by men is part of the essential fabric of history, or it is grounded in the immutable order of nature. In the present day we are being told that a world without poverty is impossible, for poverty is part of the essential fabric of history—the poor we have always with us, or it is part of the immutable order of nature. And we are being told that a world without war is impossible, for war is an essential part of the fabric of history, or it is part of the immutable order of nature. However, at the very heart of the "Jerusalem tradition" is the affirmation that our vision of what is *possible* is to be determined not by history or by nature, but by *creation*.[29]

I appreciate Ollenburger's comments, but he does not point out that all these fixities are sometimes credited not only to history and to nature, but also to creation itself. Thus his powerful rhetoric is not completely convincing, since his contrast of "history/nature" and "creation" is facile.[30]

Second, my teacher, George Landes, has offered an acute reflection upon the interrelatedness of creation and liberation.

> Some of the biblical traditions indeed probably did find their earliest expression from among the oppressed, but we must also keep in mind that much of the Bible, particularly the OT, was shaped, expanded, redacted, and edited by those associated with the royal court and the religious establishment, whom we would hardly identify with the

oppressed. And the message of the Bible is certainly for the liberation
of the oppressed, but also for the liberation of the oppressors, in fact for
everyone, regardless of their status or condition.[31]

While I agree with Landes' statement, it leaves all of the interpretive questions still before us, for if the message of the Bible is "for everyone," then
the class distinctions that Landes himself presupposes evaporate. Clearly
his judgments come at the beginning of the interpretive discussion, and
not at the end.

Third, in his penultimate footnotes, Middleton, modifying a quotation
of Emil Brunner's, suggests that "it is the task of our theological generation to find the way back to a true creation theology."[32] In taking up this
task, we must note that an emphasis on liberation is not self-evident in the
creation texts that focus upon order; in each case, the commentator who
is concerned with issues of justice must shift the language of "oppressed-
oppressor" from the liberation tradition to creation theology. Taken alone,
the creation traditions are somewhat removed from liberation issues. This
may suggest that von Rad was not so far off base in his judgment that creation is reread in light of Israel's narratives of rescue and transformation.[33]

Finally, what is at stake, in my judgment, is an interpretive posture that
concerns not only the function of the text, but the social location of the
interpreter. The quest for order in an anxious culture such as ours cannot
be permitted to crowd out a core insight of Israel, that exploitative order
in the name of creation or of law is *disorder.* As Schmid has seen so well,
a theological understanding of *Weltordnung*—a "world system"—concerns
Gerechtigkeit—"righteousness."[34] It takes all of Israel's traditions to keep
before us the *Gerechtigkeit* that constitutes *Weltordnung.* I end with thanks
to Middleton and with resolve to think and think again.

CHAPTER TWELVE

Against the Stream

Brevard Childs's Biblical Theology

Since 1970, when he published *Biblical Theology in Crisis,* Brevard Childs has authored a series of important books, swimming upstream against the interpretive consensus of critical scripture studies. He has been preoccupied with the canonical shape of the text, though in his several books, he has approached canonical matters from a variety of directions. Apparently, he has been exploring how best to articulate and respond to the interpretive crisis that has consistently preoccupied him. His latest book, *Biblical Theology of the Old and New Testaments: Theological Reflection on the Christian Bible,*[1] is the culmination of his long, reflective work. It is an achievement worthy of his passion, erudition, interpretive sensitivity, and courage. With almost no conversation partners in the twentieth century whom he regards as consistently reliable or worthy of consideration (with the decisive exception of Barth), Childs has staked out a position and vocation for biblical theology that is sure to reshape our common work and that will require intense engagement by any who dare take up the task.

I

Childs's focal point is to insist that "canonical" in Christian understanding means to see that both testaments of the Bible are "witnesses" to a single "reality," that is, "two distinct witnesses to a common subject matter who is Jesus Christ." With this definitional commitment, Childs is able to overcome quickly a host of interpretive problems, and so to clear the field for a single task. The problem he takes up is to see how these two witnesses share the task, while insisting that the two testaments are not to be coalesced but are to be kept clearly distinct from each other in character and function. Biblical theology, in this view, has no other work than to interpret around this single christological focus. A corollary of this commitment, everywhere evident but, I think, never explicitly stated, is that biblical theology is to move very far toward systematic-dogmatic theology (in Childs's case in the Reformed tradition), to shape the reading of texts for ready use in systematic categories.

As will be expected from Childs's previous books, his organization of material is overly complex, which makes for a good bit of repetition. Moreover, one is not always clear on the different functions intended for the several parts of the discussion. The "pay dirt" of the book is the last half, which takes up major theological themes in order to show how the two witnesses are derived from and directed toward the one reality of Jesus Christ. In each of these chapters, Childs regularly has sections on Old Testament witness, New Testament witness, "Biblical Theological Reflection," and "Dogmatic Theological Reflection." Occasionally, there is a special discussion of the Jewish dimension of the issue. Whereas the Old Testament discussion tends to be brief and with a unified statement, Childs spends much more time on the variegated evidence of the New Testament. In these chapters, Childs brings to bear his masterful theological sensitivity and his ready capacity for critical dismissal of views other than his own, which are often excessively either "biblicist" or "liberal." These chapters provide carefully honed material for more systematic reflection, though Childs often goes a good way on such reflection himself. Indeed, he regards such a move toward systematic reflection as a proper and essential element of doing biblical theology.

Preparation for this meaty and impressive final section of the book is made in several earlier sections. First, there is a review of recent approaches to biblical theology, all of which are found to be inadequate and wanting in important ways. This critical assessment of recent work is offset by a brief section considering six classical theological interpreters in the church, from Irenaeus to Calvin. Childs's strategy here, I take it, is to show how thin, unsure, and mistaken most recent work is when contrasted with the classical work which is sure and focused in its tone, catholic in its scope, and unbothered by all sorts of problems (for example, history of religion, sociological analysis) that excessively vex recent interpretation and vitiate the theological nerve required for the work that needs to be done. The case is well made that our own work might better be modeled after these great teachers of the church.

Having set up this powerful and (perhaps inevitably) one-sided contrast between classical and modern, Childs then voices in some detail his own canonical view of the task of biblical theology. One aspect of his view is the insistence that, in doing theological interpretation, we deal not only with texts and with witnesses but finally with "the reality, the substance," that is, with the truth of God. In making this claim repeatedly, Childs surely means to overcome the relativizing of recent study that detracts from and is excessively nervous about an "innocent" acceptance of this truth. While I share such a view of the text and its witness to "reality," the echoing of the tone of early Barth on this point does not make the claim "more true" simply by its repeated and insistent assertion. It would be enough, in my judgment, to take the subject of the text as the text gives it, without a rather shrill affirmation to support it, for such shrillness adds nothing to the textual claim. It is sufficient that God is referenced in the text, without a loud insistence for the ontological claim beyond the specific assertion of the text. On this fundamental claim for the "reality" of God, Childs wants to override the very point in question in interpretive work. Even though I think such an accent unnecessary and unhelpful, such an insistence is necessary to his program.

After these matters of definition, Childs offers long sections on the "discrete witness" of the Old Testament and of the New. Here good use is made of Childs's vast critical learning. The outcome of these sections is rather routine and not exceptional, for what is exceptional is the author's brilliant and determined way of juxtaposing, interfacing, combining, and setting in tension what is commonly shared by interpreters about these texts. (Almost as an aside and without any orienting introduction, Childs offers two extended exegeses, which I assume are given as models for how canonical interpretation is to be done.)

Childs's proposal is magisterial in scope, depth, and power, and will provide "nerve" for all of us who seek to do church interpretation. (He of course has no interest in any other kind of interpretation.) When the dust settles, I suspect (as Childs no doubt anticipates) that it is his main claims, which mark the strength and distinctiveness of his work, that will also be the places of sharpest attack. His critics will likely judge his accent points to be points of question and vulnerability, because he dismisses by dictum problems that must indeed be faced. I imagine Childs will consider that he is criticized on these points (including in this review) because he has made clear that modern interpretation has missed the boat. I suspect that this will lead, yet one more time, to a critical impasse. In the meantime, however, Childs's book will be there as a powerful summons, invitation, and model for what the claims of the gospel are at root, and how we are to speak boldly about them.

II

In the midst of my enormous gratitude for the book, I suggest from my own reading three further talking points:

1. *Childs operates from very high ground.* That is, the tone is impatiently "apodictic" (an accusation he makes against H. J. Kraus). Childs proceeds as though "canonical" were a self-evident reading that anyone can see, because it is there in the text and stands in corrective opposition to all those views Childs regards as mistaken. Indeed, Childs allows for "reader response," but requires that "canonical restraints" be used and that "reader response be critically tested in light of different witnesses of the whole Bible." Fair enough. Except that it is, of course, Childs who will determine what is "canonical," so that the "reader response" of other readers is to be corrected by his "canonical." He seems unwilling or unable to acknowledge that his own "canonical" is also another form of "reader response," for he proceeds as if the "canonical" is simply there and involves no reader, not even Childs. Thus, for example, his "canonical" conclusion expressed in his repeated and acrimonious dismissal of "so-called liberation theology" is, in my judgment, simply his own contextual response. The outcome is a reading that has all sorts of sociopolitical implications, though Childs will not or cannot recognize these, for it would jeopardize his high ground.

2. *Childs proceeds with a heavy dose of hermeneutical innocence.* I once heard Childs lecture on Barth's postcritical exegetical method and remarked to him that it sounded quite precritical as he explicated it. My impression of his presentation of Barth is roughly the same for Childs's own work here. It is not accidental, I take it, that Childs prefers Calvin above all and prefers to go behind the biblicalism of the eighteenth century, behind the developmentalism of the nineteenth century, and behind the inconvenience of socially conflicted readings of the twentieth century to a reading that is not intellectually impinged upon or disrupted by these cultural realities. I would wish for the same, as it would make our work easier and more readily compelling. I do not believe, however, that we can proceed as if suspicion is not among us in ways that require the argument to be made differently. And here, Childs does not help us much, for he will entertain

no suspicions of his own interpretive certitude. I do not for a moment believe that the claims of the Bible are to be conceded to those eroding critical, epistemological categories of more recent time. But I also do not believe we can pretend they are not among us, and, therefore, a response in this kind of innocence is not without its own problems. My own sense is that our interpretive claims must be made more honestly in the fray of epistemological challenge rather than above it, as though the fray was not close at hand. In my judgment, any so-called canonical reading must be made as a competitor to other readings, as an advocacy among many advocacies.

Specifically, Childs regularly recognizes "diversity" in the witnesses but then works promptly and readily toward a unity of witness that is voiced in christological categories. While Childs acknowledges diversity in the witnesses, he insists that the text is stable, that it has a persistent, clear meaning. I submit that this is a reader-response decision on Childs's part to which he is entitled, but it is not self-evident. The notion of the instability of the text, which would impede his ready cognitive closure, is not simply a postmodernist invention but has for a very long time been recognized by careful readers and interpreters. When one arrives at the stability of the text as quickly as does Childs, much of the power, energy, and, I dare say, truth of the text is lost in a kind of reductionism. The notion of instability is not an enemy of faith but, in fact, an honoring of the detail and nuance of the text that dogmatic closure does not easily entertain or allow. Childs's hermeneutical innocence is not only against our own interpretive context, but more important, against the very character of the text itself, which refuses to be so innocent.

3. *Biblical theology has long had a tense relation with dogmatic-systematic categories.* The importance of Childs's project is that he draws biblical theology very close to dogmatic categories and seems to put biblical theology in the service of dogmatic claims. That intention, however, is not without problem, for it is half of a dialectic without the other half. That is, biblical theology lives not close to the history of religion but to the delicate, detailed rhetorical voice of the text and, therefore, at some distance from dogmatic categories, which notoriously do not honor such detailed voice. Childs's mode of biblical theology is flatly cognitive, as though the Bible were simply a set of ideas. Thus, he traces the witnesses in assertions that are large and, to my mind, "flattening and homogenizing" (again a criticism made of Kraus). On the one hand, such an approach fails to take

seriously the detail of the text, which is not so flat or homogeneous. On the other hand, it is difficult to see how biblical theology can protest against or correct dogmatic claims (a role Reformed faith fully affirms) if it must proceed in such a fashion. In the end, the faith of the church in Jesus Christ is well served by such a procedure, but the liveliness of the biblical God and the unsettling work of the witnesses seem to me to be oddly muted.

III

Now I understand, of course, that Childs is not unaware of these issues. He has thought them through long and carefully, and has determined that the claims he wants to make are more important than any deterrence offered by these strictures. Indeed, given his own programmatic concerns, the issues I have raised fall outside what he terms "canonical," so that the criticisms themselves are only evidence of and symptomatic of what he regards as the problem of most contemporary interpretation. But that, of course, is the point in question, and the point to be further probed. "Canonical" is scarcely useful or faithful if it means to preclude all readings of the Bible save a dogmatic one on a text that clearly precludes such ideational clarity. But, of course, Childs's program means to combat exactly the weakening of sturdy, sure-voiced witnesses to a reality that these questions seem to invite.

Given these not inconsiderable wonderments, I have no doubt that, once again, Childs is the teacher of us all. He will move theologians, teachers, and preachers to greater nerve and passion, a nerve and passion not grounded in the methodological cleverness or shrewdness but in nothing less than the truth, the "solid rock on which I stand." And even where one disagrees, we are mightily instructed, informed, and admonished. The late twentieth century is not an easy place for faithfulness. In a daring way, Childs has shown us what faithfulness might now mean. His reading is indeed "against the stream." He may, in the end, even reverse the flow of soft-minded, embarrassed theological accommodation, a hope I fully share with him.

CHAPTER THIRTEEN

Walter Brueggemann's
Theology of the Old Testament: Testimony, Dispute, Advocacy
A Review by Brevard S. Childs and a Response

When Walter Brueggemann wrote his *Theology of the Old Testament*,[1] he was very much aware that the field appears to be stalled in an impasse. No recent volume comparable in influence to Walther Eichrodt's in the 1930s or Gerhard von Rad's in the 1950s has appeared. In response to this lacuna he mounts a case for the urgent need of a fresh approach, which he then characterizes as postmodern. It would seek to do justice, to the radical unsettlement evoked by the new postmodern epistemological situation with its insistence on pluralism of faith affirmations, pluralism of methodologies, and pluralism of diverse communities, all of which have shattered the earlier hegemonic assumptions of biblical studies. Accordingly, interpretation is defined by Brueggemann as an ongoing process of negotiating among the full range of conflictional testimonies which avoids any absolute claims—whether historical or ontological—beyond the court of appeal found in the biblical text itself.

To achieve this end, the author structures his material around the metaphor of Israel's testimony of witness to Yahweh. He first describes Israel's core testimony, then Israel's countertestimony, next the unsolicited testimony, and finally the embodied testimony. The core testimony encompasses the normative shape of Israel's utterance, which he examines with close attention to its grammatical forms. The countertestimony derives from a study of competing voices calling into question the adequacy of the established forms of confessional expression. Under the rubric of unsolicited testimony are included a discussion of the human person, the nations, and creation as Yahweh's partners. Finally, under the heading of embodied testimony are treated the presence of Yahweh, Torah, king, prophet, and sage as mediators. The volume closes with a reflection on the prospects for theological interpretation with a further defense of his postmodern proposal.

The reader is immediately impressed with Brueggemann's rhetorical skills in offering a fresh and challenging new construal of the Old Testament material by focusing on the trial imagery of two rival voices. The imagery of disputation finds its strongest biblical warrant in 2 Isaiah, but also from its widespread usage in Job and in the Psalter. One is also appreciative of Brueggemann's ability to incorporate such a large amount of very diverse material within his net. It has been a standard criticism of the earlier approaches that some of the proposals have been forced to omit or severely limit some important topics. The author has worked hard to mute this criticism with his imagination and learning.

Some of his chapters appear more successful than others. In his presentation of the core tradition his focus on verbs, adjectives, and nouns within the sentence tends to lose the dynamic of Israel's narrative, the discovery of which has been a hallmark of much recent Old Testament scholarship. Then again, to include wisdom theology under the category of countertestimony is largely artificial since, as we now recognize, wisdom functioned throughout the entire spectrum of Israel's witness—narrative, law, hymnody—and as a positive formulation of the core testimony of its faith. Finally, just as Eichrodt had difficulty in his final volume in extending the category of covenant to include anthropology, one senses some elements of structural strain in parts of sections III and IV. Still these features do not seriously distract from the brilliance of the attempt.

Far more substantive are the issues raised by Brueggemann's hermeneutical challenge. His major contribution lies in having forcefully raised the theological stakes regarding many basic questions relating to the nature and authority of the Bible for the Christian church.

1. What Does One Understand by the Testimony of the Old Testament?

Initially Brueggemann stands on the side of those scholars who view the Hebrew Bible simply as a record of the religion of Israel to be studied phenomenologically, and thus he recognizes in the biblical text the confessional element of Israel's voice offering a witness to its experience with its God. But now the crucial hermeneutical issue turns on how one evaluates Israel's own testimony.

The present form of the biblical literature emerged during a long process of collecting, shaping and transmitting a wide variety of different traditions arranged in sections of Torah, Prophets, and Writings toward the end of serving communities of Israel as an authoritative guide of faith and practice. In this process various editors exercised a critical function in registering from the received traditions that which they deemed truthful and authoritative. This shaping thus involved a *Sachkritik* which was not simply reflective of private, idiosyncratic agenda, but which arose from actual communal practice and belief. Accordingly, Moses not Korah, Jeremiah not Hananiah, were judged to be faithful tridents of divine revelation. In a word, Israel shaped its literature confessionally to bear testimony to what it received as containing an established range of truthful witness. At the same time, the biblical editors subordinated other voices, either by placing them within a negative setting, or omitting them altogether as deleterious to Israel's faith.

In contrast, when Brueggemann seeks to describe a category of countertestimony to the so-called core tradition, he feels free to reconstruct voices on which Israel's authors had already rendered a judgment. Thus, it is the "fool" who says "there is no God" (Ps. 14:1). Or, when Jeremiah complains to God, "You are to me like a deceitful brook, like waters that fail," the editor interprets this outburst as "worthless and without merit" (Jer. 15:19). Finally, the biblical editors retained the radical skepticism of the book of Ecclesiastes largely in an unredacted form. But they added in an epilogue a rule for properly interpreting the book, namely, it is to be heard within the framework of Torah (Eccl. 12:13f.). When Brueggemann assigns an independent role to such traditions as countertestimony, he is running in the very face of Israel's canonical witness.

Yet it is also obvious that Israel's genuine complaints before God constitute a major positive witness within a large portion of the Bible. They are present in the Psalter, Prophets, and Wisdom literature as a truthful testimony to Israel's experience before God in order not to contradict, but rather to establish, its core tradition of faith. A major task of Old Testament interpretation lies in understanding the rich variety of ways in which the complaint truthfully depicts Israel's life with God. When Brueggemann sets up the relationship as a countertestimony to be constantly juxtaposed in a contrived "dialectic," he cuts off the real access to the theological significance of the complaint as a constitutive element of Israel's true faith.

2. The Identity of God in the Hebrew Bible

By juxtaposing Israel's core testimony with his so-called countertestimony, Brueggemann sees the task of interpretation to be a never-ending activity of negotiating between conflicting voices. There is never a final testimony, but every interpretation is described as provisional and shaped by shifting "socio-ecclesial-political-economic contexts" within this active process of disputation.[2] The result is that the God of Israel is both gracious and merciless, truthful and deceptive, powerful and impotent, which is constitutive of the very nature of this deity.

In spite of Brueggemann's constant reference to the "Jewishness of the Old Testament," the irony emerging from his description of God is one that no serious, religious Jew can tolerate. Israel's faith in God rests on Torah, covenant, and eternal promise, which are non-negotiable because of the truth of God's Word. The stability of God in relation to his people sets Israel's faith apart from all the arbitrariness and confusion of paganism. Of course, there remain continuous threats, demonic terrors, and persistent evil, but these do not alter God's unswerving commitment forever to the Patriarchs. Israel continues to suffer because of its confession that God has not, and will not, change toward his people in spite of experiencing life on the very edge of extinction.

3. The Hermeneutical Choice

Brueggemann rejects any appeal to an ecclesial reading of scripture, whether by church or synagogue, as reductionist and hampering of the genuine creativity of unimpaired human imagination. It may be that one is philosophically justified in characterizing Brueggemann's approach as postmodern. However, from a theological perspective the closest analogy is found in the early church's struggle with Gnosticism, especially in the second century of the Christian era. The Gnostics rejected the great church's appeal to the God of Israel as truthful and authoritative for faith. Rather they established their own speculative systems of interpreting the Bible with a mixture of mythology, rationalism, and intuition. Their deities emerged in constant flux within a primordial struggle between the forces of light and darkness, truth and falsehood.[3]

One does not have to look far to discover the striking analogies between Brueggemann's postmodernism and ancient Gnosticism. Both operate within an overarching philosophical system in which "imaginative construal" closely parallels Gnostic "speculation" as a means for correcting the received biblical tradition. Both approaches work with a sharply defined dualism between a God of creation who is known and predictable, and one who is hidden, unknown, and capricious. Brueggemann even projects this "dialectic tension" into the divine reality itself. Both contrast competing claims of divine justice and cosmic evil without any resolution.

When Irenaeus countered the Gnostic threat (*Adversus haereses*), he appealed to a *regula fidei* (rule of faith)[4] grounded in the truth of Israel's faith, which he confessed to find incarnate in the person of Jesus Christ. Such a confessional interpretation of scripture Brueggemann now characterizes as "oppressive, hegemonic, and reductionist." The early Christian church saw it as freeing, salvific, and the sure grounds for an unswerving truth in God in the battle against recurring paganism.

To conclude, I would agree with Brueggemann that the challenge of postmodern interpretation of the Bible is real, and that the issue may well dominate the theological debate for many decades to come. It is also true that how Christians respond will also decide the identity of the church for future generations.

A Response to Professor Childs by Walter Brueggemann

In the 1970s, when Old Testament theology had more or less fizzled out and lost its vitality, Professor Childs decisively intervened in his series of influential books to turn the discussion in a very different direction. By his passion, imagination, courage, and great learning, he has single-handedly generated an entirely new perspective in Old Testament theology. He is the teacher of us all; my own debts to him are very great (and I think quite evident in my work), even if he thinks I have acquitted those debts poorly. It is a source of satisfaction to me that he would engage my book so closely—even if, as I believe, mistakenly.

The major charge against my book in his critique is that its "closest analogy is found in the early church's struggle with Gnosticism." I take the word "analogy" to be a term that allows a wee bit of wiggle-room, but nonetheless believe that the suggestion of the analogy is a deep distortion of what I have done.

Professor Childs has elsewhere indicated that he takes the phrase "imaginative construal" negatively, and here he links it to "Gnostic speculation." Of course that is not at all what is meant by the phrase, for I regard his so-called canonical perspective as an impressive "imaginative construal," not made more authoritative because he terms it "canonical." To term my work anything like "speculative" is very much overstated, given my close and endless attention to texts.

Professor Childs asserts that "the biblical editors subordinated other voices" through "an established range of truthful witness." But of course that conclusion is exactly the project of our common study. He has decided, apparently well ahead of specific texts, about the nature of that subordination or even elimination. In the case he cites of Ecclesiastes 12:13f., the case for subordination has been argued by Gerald Sheppard; one may, however, wonder whether such "canonical" subordination could not have been more successful or worked at harder, if that is so obviously what is intended. Childs writes as though he already knows what "an established range" is, when in fact in church practice texts are being endlessly subordinated and recovered for use in particular circumstances.

Professor Childs suggests there is a "dualism" in my presentation. Of course nothing could be more of a distortion of what I have written. What I have done is to give "other voices" a serious hearing, for there is no doubt that in scripture there are voices of witness in profound tension with each other. The issue turns on which witnesses are truthful, but it has been the lived reality of the church that different witnesses in scripture have been heard as truthful on different occasions; in different circumstances serious people of faith have found in various witnesses in scripture something truthful in their attestations. It does happen in the lived reality of the church that sometimes in good faith, an "established range of truthful witness" has been seen to be a cover-up and a sham. I understand that this recognition allows for more contextual power than Professor Childs would accept, but such variation does operate in the lived testimony of the church. This does not suggest any dualism, but a tension in lived witness and interpretation that each time requires fresh adjudication. The church inescapably does this all the time.

Professor Childs suggests that I have assigned "an independent role" to what he believes a subordinate witness. Of course nothing could be further from the truth. I have consistently said that the different testimonies are endlessly in tension with and corrected by other testimony. None is free-standing, none is isolated, none is cut off, not even the ones he regards in "an established range." (Incidentally Professor Childs's passing comment on my reference to Psalm 14 is a complete misinterpretation, perhaps based on a too-quick reading. He fails to notice the point being made.)

Professor Childs judges that I have rejected "any appeal to an ecclesial reading." While I have strategically and provisionally sought to hear and read the text on its own terms as much as possible—as has he in his attempt to read the Old Testament witness first of all apart from the witness of the New Testament—I have framed my discussion of countertestimony as a "theology of the cross," surely a perspective that could only be ecclesial. He may have noticed that my attempt to get at the issue was written on Good Friday in an effort to discern—impossible as it finally is—what the church means by the three hours of darkness and chaos. Reading ecclesially, moreover, has caused me to be more attentive to the reading among serious believing communities who notice that the silence and absence of God is indeed a lived reality that must be fully taken into account. I have not wanted to let any "large" ecclesial claims censor the lived reality of the believing church.

Of course my perspective is not "gnostic"; such a judgment is a caricature of my work. I do not believe that this is a deliberate caricature by Professor Childs, but one that derives from his determined interpretive agenda. Indeed my work is no more gnostic than is that of Childs docetic in his attempt to arrive at a closed set of theological certitudes that are not seriously impinged upon by the brokenness or absence that wells up in the text and in the lived life of the church. This is not an exchange between a gnostic and a docetist, but rather an exchange before a strange text that defies all our categories, canonical, postmodern, or whatever.

I suppose it is fair to say that the differences in our perspectives, which are as important to him as they are to me, arise from different mind-sets and different senses of what is needed. My own way of approach to interpretive issues is through the drama of liturgy and through the pastoral reality of the church. In both liturgy and pastoral reality, one is endlessly aware of the disjunction and tension that must be faced and embraced and not overcome rationally. It is therefore not surprising that I am drawn to a particular range of texts in a certain way. Professor Childs, so it seems to me, is drawn in a dogmatic direction and for that reason wants to find an articulation that is comprehensive and, so to say, "foolproof." My hunch is that as he sees "dualism" in my work, he is alert to the fragmentation of theological thought in what may be termed "postmodern" perspective; at the same time I am much more attentive to the ways in which subordination and silencing of texts has been and is a recipe for denial about the real brokenness that constitutes important theological data. The difference or accent is in fact much less than appears when cast in pejorative labels. My own sense is that there is not any single, one, right way to frame interpretation. I myself am unpersuaded by a "canonical" approach that knows an outcome to all of these matters that can be final, absolute, and not open to further examination and adjudication. In my estimation, such a reading is much too costly for the faith of the church.

I agree with Professor Childs that it would be a useful undertaking to consider further the theological function of complaints in the life of faith. If, however, he means by that to subordinate, silence, eliminate, or explain them away by "canonical" maneuver, then I am resistant to such a project. It seems to me that such a "canonical" perspective functions, *mutatis mutandis,* too much like historical criticism in its propensity to reduce or eliminate texts that are unwelcome in a certain interpretive horizon. It is true, even if unwelcome, that the lived reality and lived articulation of faith in the church is more open and raw than any such construal—critical or canonical—characteristically allows.

There is no doubt that Professor Childs's "canonical" approach occupies the center of the field and will continue to do so. The slight variation between his approach and mine I believe to be a more benign variation than his rhetoric suggests. What is at issue is the endlessly tricky relation between "The Great Tradition" and the "little texts." It may be that the little texts witness on occasion to God's "alien work," so deeply alien that it disrupts every "canonical" conclusion. Childs champions the "Great Tradition," and for good reason. One of the responsibilities of careful interpretation, however—even as it is one of the responsibilities of pastoral, liturgical attentiveness—is to pay attention to the life, the text, the sensibility that is too soon excluded and censored by The Great Tradition. We are increasingly aware that "The Great Tradition," in its many forms, has been powerfully exclusionary of some truth-bearers. That awareness should be a caution to the "canonical" enterprise. I agree with Professor Childs's final statement about the future "identity of the church." It is my concern that in future generations, the church will be able to attend to the "little texts," even as it commits to the Great Tradition. If it does not so attend, then the cross will have evaporated into a "theology of glory."

There is an awareness that in the earliest form of the "rule of faith" to which Professor Childs appeals, the phrase did not yet specify a full dogmatic formulation of the faith. Even before such a full dogmatic formulation, the "rule of faith" was the rule of love lived toward neighbor as a response to the love of God. In adherence to such a rule of faith, it may be that we should be asking about something other than a closed articulation of dogmatic formulation. In any case we will not run out of work to do. Again my thanks to Professor Childs for identifying and shaping, as he does so well, the issues about which we share a common responsibility, a common calling, and in large part a common reading.

Abbreviations

BHTh	Beiträge zur historischen Theologie
BibInt	*Biblical Interpretation: A Journal of Contemporary Approaches*
BZAW	Beihefte zur Zeitschrift für die alttestamentliche Wissenschaft
CTJ	*Calvin Theological Journal*
CBQ	*Catholic Biblical Quarterly*
ConBOT	Coniectanea biblica: Old Testament series
EKL	*Evangelisches Kirchenlexikon*
HBT	*Horizons in Biblical Theology*
HTR	*Harvard Theological Review*
IDB	*The Interpreter's Dictionary of the Bible*. Edited by G. A. Buttrick. 4 vols. Nashville, 1962.
IDBSup	*The Interpreter's Dictionary of the Bible: Supplementary Volume*. Edited by K. Crim. Nashville, 1976.
Int	*Interpretation*
IBC	Interpretation: A Bible Commentary for Teaching and Preaching
JAAR	*Journal of the American Academy of Religion*
JBL	*Journal of Biblical Literature*
JR	*Journal of Religion*
JSOTSup	Journal for the Study of the Old Testament Supplement Series
OTL	Old Testament Library
PTMS	Princeton Theological Monograph Series
SBT	Studies in Biblical Theology
SJT	*Scottish Journal of Theology*
StTh	*Studia Theologica*
ThTo	*Theology Today*
USQR	*Union Seminary Quarterly Review*
VTSup	Vetus Testamentum Supplements

Notes

Preface

1. Karl Barth, "The Strange New World within the Bible," in *The Word of God and the Word of Man*, trans. Douglas Horton (New York: Harper & Brothers, 1957 [1928]), 28–50.

2. See Brevard S. Childs, *Biblical Theology of the Old and New Testaments: Theological Reflection on the Christian Bible* (Minneapolis: Fortress Press, 1993); Ronald Clements, "Patterns in the Prophetic Canon," in *Old Testament Prophecy: From Oracles to Canon* (Louisville: Westminster John Knox, 1996), 191–202; James A. Sanders, *Torah and Canon* (Philadelphia: Fortress Press, 1972).

3. The literature in the current discussion of ideology is cited by James Barr, *History and Ideology in the Old Testament: Biblical Studies at the End of the Millennium* (Oxford: Oxford University Press, 2000), though Barr's own modernist perspective has little appreciation for the enterprise and does not seem to sense what is at stake in the discussion. On Barr's own position, see the crucial discussion of Keith W. Whitelam, "Interested Parties; History and Ideology at the End of the Century," *Reading from Right to Left: Essays on the Hebrew Bible in Honour of David J. A. Clines*, ed. J. Cheryl Exum and H. G. M. Williamson, JSOTSup 373 (Sheffield: Sheffield Academic, 2003), 402–22.

4. See, for example, Regina M. Schwartz, *The Curse of Cain: The Violent Legacy of Monotheism* (Chicago: University of Chicago Press, 1997); and David Jobling, *1 Samuel*, Berit Olam (Collegeville, Minn.: Liturgical, 1998).

5. See George Lindbeck, *The Nature of Doctrine: Religion and Theology in a Postliberal Age* (Philadelphia: Westminster, 1984).

6. Amos N. Wilder, "Story and Story-World," *Int* 37 (1983): 361.

7. See Phyllis Trible, *Rhetorical Criticism: Context, Method, and the Book of Jonah*, Guides to Biblical Scholarship, Old Testament Series, ed. Gene

M. Tucker (Minneapolis: Fortress Press, 1994), and especially her discussion of the pivotal contribution of James Muilenburg.

1. Biblical Authority in the Postcritical Period

1. David H. Kelsey, *The Uses of Scripture in Recent Theology* (Philadelphia: Fortress Press, 1975).

2. Alan Richardson, "Scripture, Authority of," in *IDB* 4:248–51; James Barr "Scripture, Authority of," in *IDBSup,* 794–97.

3. Karl Barth, *Anselm: Fides quarens intellectum,* trans. I. W. Robertson (Pittsburgh: Pickwick, 1975 [1960]); Robert E. Cushman, *Faith Seeking Understanding: Essays Theological and Critical* (Durham, N.C.: Duke University Press, 1981).

4. Harold Lindsell, *The Battle for the Bible* (Grand Rapids: Zondervan, 1976).

5. For instance, Jack B. Rogers and Donald K. McKim, *The Authority and Interpretation of the Bible: An Historical Approach* (New York: Harper & Row, 1979).

6. Langdon Gilkey, *Society and the Sacred: Toward a Theology of a Society in Decline* (New York: Crossroad, 1981); Michael Harrington, *The Politics at God's Funeral: The Spiritual Crisis of Western Civilization* (New York: Holt, Rinehart and Winston, 1983).

7. Robert L. Heilbroner, *An Inquiry into the Human Prospect: Updated and Reconsidered for the 1980s* (New York: Norton, 1980).

8. Robert N. Bellah, "Biblical Religion and Social Science in the Modern World," *NICM Journal for Jews and Christians in Higher Education* 6, no. 3 (1982): 8–22.

9. Ibid., 21–22.

10. Robert N. Bellah et al., *Habits of the Heart: Individualism and Commitment in American Life* (Berkeley: University of California Press, 1985).

11. Richard L. Rubenstein, *The Age of Triage: Fear and Hope in an Overcrowded World* (Boston: Beacon, 1983).

12. Ibid., 230–40.

13. Bruce Chilton, *A Galilean Rabbi and His Bible: Jesus' Use of the Interpreted Scripture of His Time* (Wilmington, Del.: Michael Glazier, 1984).

14. Carl A. Raschke, "On Reading Romans 1–6 or Overcoming the Hermeneutics of Suspicion," *Ex Auditu* 1 (1985): 147–55.

15. David Tracy, *The Analogical Imagination: Christian Theology and the Culture of Pluralism* (New York: Crossroad, 1981).

16. Ibid., 102.

17. Ibid., 115–16.

18. Ibid., 116.

19. Paul Ricoeur, "Biblical Hermeneutics," *Semeia* 4 (1975): 29–148; Bellah, "Biblical Religion and Social Science"; Rubenstein, *The Age of Triage.*

20. Langdon Gilkey, "Scripture, History and the Quest for Meaning," in C. T. McIntire and Ronald A. Wells, eds., *History and Historical Understanding* (Grand Rapids: Eerdmans, 1984), 3–16, esp. 12–13.

21. Gerhard Ebeling, "The Bible as a Document of the University," in Hans Dieter Betz, ed., *The Bible as a Document of the University* (Chico, Calif.: Scholars Press, 1980), 5–23.

22. Robert W. Lynn, *The Big Little School: 200 Years of the Sunday School* (Birmingham, Ala.: Religious Education, 1980); John H. Westerhoff III, *McGuffey and His Readers* (Nashville: Abingdon, 1978).

23. Brevard S. Childs, "Some Reflections on the Search for a Biblical Theology," *HBT* 4 (1982): 1–12.

24. Morton Smith, "The Present State of Old Testament Studies," *JBL* 88 (1969): 19–35.

25. Walter Wink, *The Bible in Human Transformation* (Philadelphia: Fortress Press, 1973); Brevard S. Childs, *Introduction to the Old Testament as Scripture* (Philadelphia: Fortress Press, 1979).

26. Max Horkheimer and Theodor W. Adorno, *Dialectic of Enlightenment* (New York: Continuum, 1972 [1944]).

27. Parker J. Palmer, *To Know As We Are Known: Education as a Spiritual Journey* (San Francisco: Harper & Row, 1983).

28. Northrop Frye, *The Great Code: The Bible and Literature* (New York: Harcourt Brace Jovanovich, 1982).

29. Robert N. Bellah, *The Broken Covenant: American Civil Religion in Time of Trial* (New York: Seabury, 1975); see also Martin Marty, "America's Iconic Book," in Gene M. Tucker and Douglas A. Knight, eds., *Humanizing America's Iconic Book,* Biblical Scholarship in North America 6 (Chico, Calif.: Scholars Press, 1982), 1–23.

30. Michael Walzer, *Exodus and Revolution* (New York: Basic, 1985).

31. James H. Smylie, "On Jesus, Pharaohs, and the Chosen People," *Int* 24 (1970): 74–91.

32. Bellah, "Biblical Religion and Social Science"; Rubenstein, *The Age of Triage.*

33. Tracy, *The Analogical Imagination.*

34. Ronald J. Sider, *Rich Christians in an Age of Hunger* (Downers Grove, Ill.: InterVarsity, 1977).

35. Robert J. Schreiter, *Constructing Local Theologies* (Maryknoll, N.Y.: Orbis, 1985).

36. Walzer, *Exodus and Revolution*.

37. Emmanuel Levinas, *Totality and Infinity: An Essay on Exteriority*, trans. Alphonso Lingis (Pittsburgh: Duquesne University Press, 1969).

38. Martin Buber, "The Man of Today and the Jewish Bible," in *On the Bible: Eighteen Studies*, ed. Nahum N. Glatzer (New York: Schocken, 1968), 5.

39. Karl Barth, *The Word of God and the Word of Man*, trans. Douglas Horton (New York: Harper & Brothers, 1957 [1928]), 33–34.

40. Ibid., 39–40.

41. Ibid., 43.

42. Raymond E. Brown, *The Sensus Plenior of Sacred Scripture* (Baltimore: Saint Mary's University Press, 1955).

43. Ernst Fuchs, "The New Testament and the Hermeneutical Problem," in James M. Robinson and John B. Cobb Jr., eds., *The New Hermeneutic* (New York: Harper & Row, 1964), 111–45; Gerhard Ebeling, "Word of God and Hermeneutic," in *The New Hermeneutic*, 78–110.

44. Amos Wilder, "Story and Story World," *Int* 37 (1983): 353–64.

2. Biblical Authority: A Personal Reflection

1. The phrase is an allusion to the famous essay of Karl Barth, "The Strange, New World within the Bible," in *The Word of God and the Word of Man*, trans. Douglas Horton (New York: Harper & Brothers, 1957 [1928]), 28–50.

2. While many folk in many traditions lay claim to this aphorism, I have it on the authority of my colleague Lowell Zuck that its origin is deep in German pietism.

3. My first reading out of the generativity of von Rad was in a little-noticed book by B. Davie Napier, *From Faith to Faith: Essays on Old Testament Literature* (New York: Harper & Brothers, 1955). It was this book that decided for me a life of study in the Old Testament.

4. I deliberately make allusion to Martin Luther, "A Treatise on Christian Liberty," in *Three Treatises* (Philadelphia: Muhlenberg, 1943), 251–90.

5. The hiddenness, of course, pertains no less to the disclosure of God in Jesus of Nazareth, a truth not given to "flesh and blood" (Matt. 16:17).

6. Nor did Luther intend such self-interpretation, for all of the popular misunderstanding of his emancipation of the text from the hold of the church's magisterium.

7. See, e.g., Jon D. Levenson, *Creation and the Persistence of Evil: The Jewish Drama of Divine Omnipotence* (San Francisco: HarperCollins, 1988), 131–568.

8. See Gerhard von Rad, "Endeavors to Restore the Past," in *Old Testament Theology*, vol. 1: *The Theology of Israel's Historical Traditions*, trans. D. M. G. Stalker (San Francisco: Harper & Brothers, 1962), 69–77, 219–31; and Martin Noth, "The 'Re-Presentation' of the Old Testament in Proclamation," in Claus Westermann, ed., *Essays on Old Testament Hermeneutics* (Richmond: John Knox, 1963), 76–88. On Moses as the engine of interpretation, see Walter Brueggemann, *Theology of the Old Testament: Testimony, Dispute, Advocacy* (Minneapolis: Fortress Press, 1997), 578–90.

9. Herbert Donner, "Jesaja lvi 1–7: ein Abrogationsfall innerhalb des Kanons—Implikationen und Konzequenzen," VTSup 36 (1985): 81–95.

10. See Michael Fishbane, *Biblical Interpretation in Ancient Israel* (Oxford: Clarendon, 1985), 284.

11. The literature on the subject is immense and growing. See, among the better representative examples, Sean McDonagh, *To Care for the Earth: A Call to a New Theology* (Quezon City, Philippines: Claretian, 1986); and Carol J. Dempsey and Russell A. Butkus, eds., *All Creation Is Groaning: An Interdisciplinary Vision for Life in a Sacred Universe* (Collegeville, Minn.: Liturgical, 1999).

12. George Steiner, *Real Presences* (Chicago: University of Chicago Press, 1989), 225. The polyvalence of Jewish interpretation has been forcefully exposited by James L. Kugel, *The Bible as It Was* (Cambridge, Mass.: Belknap, 1997).

13. See my summary of the force of imagination in interpretation, *Texts under Negotiation: The Bible and Postmodern Imagination* (Minneapolis: Fortress Press, 1993).

14. On this theme, see Walter Brueggemann, "The Faithfulness of Otherwise," in *Testimony to Otherwise: The Witness of Elijah and Elisha* (St. Louis: Chalice, 2001). My phrase intends to allude to the phrasing of Emmanuel Levinas.

15. On the parables as a mode of generativity for the future, see Paul Ricoeur, "Biblical Hermeneutics," *Semeia* 4 (1975): 114–45, and "The Bible and Imagination," in *Figuring the Sacred: Religion, Narrative, and Imagination,* trans. David Pellauer, ed. Mark I. Wallace (Minneapolis: Fortress Press, 1995), 144–66.

16. On the category of "wonder," see Martin Buber, *Moses* (Atlantic Highland, N.J.: Humanities Press International, 1946), especially 75–76;

and my discussion of Buber's insight, *Abiding Astonishment: Psalms, Modernity, and the Making of History*, Literary Currents in Biblical Interpretation (Louisville: Westminster John Knox, 1991), 30–33 and passim.

17. Karl Barth, *Church Dogmatics*, III/1, *The Doctrine of Creation* (Edinburgh: T. & T. Clark, 1958), 81, 91. See the discussion of the cruciality of imagination after Wittgenstein, and especially on Barth, by Fergus Kerr, *Theology after Wittgenstein* (London: SPCK, 1997).

18. For an example of "ideology critique," see David Penchansky, *The Betrayal of God: Ideological Conflict in Job*, Literary Currents in Biblical Interpretation (Louisville: Westminster John Knox, 1990).

19. Distinctions can be made in the use of "ideology" in a Marxian sense (as here) and after the manner of Clifford Geertz. A helpful guide on the concept is Paul Ricoeur, *Lectures on Ideology and Utopia*, ed. George H. Taylor (New York: Columbia University Press, 1986).

20. The passionate intentionality of the authors of texts has been forced upon the awareness of biblical scholarship by Norman K. Gottwald, *The Tribes of Yahweh: A Sociology of the Religion of Liberated Israel, 1250–1050 B.C.E.* (Maryknoll, N.Y.: Orbis, 1979). After Gottwald, a host of scholars have joined issue on the matter.

21. On what follows, see Walter Brueggemann, *Texts under Negotiation*, 61–64.

22. On "felt threats" as propulsions for interpretation, see Walter Brueggemann, "Contemporary Old Testament Theology: A Contextual Prospectus," *Dialog* 38 (Spring 1999): 108–16; reprinted in this volume as chapter 8.

23. See Carolyn Pressler, *The View of Women Found in the Deuteronomic Family Laws*, BZAW 216 (Berlin: de Gruyter, 1993).

24. See Henri Mottu, "Jeremiah vs. Hananiah: Ideology and Truth in Old Testament Prophecy," in *The Bible and Liberation: Political and Social Hermeneutics*, ed. Norman K. Gottwald (Maryknoll, N.Y.: Orbis, 1983).

3. Biblical Authority and the Church's Task of Interpretation

1. David Tracy, *The Analogical Imagination: Christian Theology and the Culture of Pluralism* (New York: Crossroad, 1981), 101–4, 115–24.

2. This phrase, of course, comes from the Medellin Conference of 1967. See Gustavo Gutiérrez, *The Power of the Poor in History: Selected Writings*, trans. Robert R. Barr (Maryknoll, N.Y.: Orbis, 1983). It embodies a fundamental interpretive decision from which much else follows. In a paper offered to the American Academy of Religion, Lee Cormie explored a

posture of interpretation and politics that practices "the preferential option for the rich."

3. This matter has been shrewdly critiqued in Elisabeth Schüssler Fiorenza, *Bread Not Stone: The Challenge of Feminist Biblical Interpretation* (Boston: Beacon, 1984). A blatant example of the power of ideological theology is found in Robert P. Ericksen, *Theologians under Hitler: Gerhard Kittel, Paul Althaus, and Emanuel Hirsch* (New Haven: Yale University Press, 1985).

4. Frank Kermode has written of the formation of canon and the monopoly of interpretation as twin aspects of the effort to control the meaning of literature. He has observed this phenomenon not only in relation to the Bible but with reference to the dominant literary tradition of the West. See his *Forms of Attention* (Chicago: University of Chicago Press, 1985), 78–93; and *The Art of Telling: Essays on Fiction* (Cambridge, Mass.: Harvard University Press, 1983), 168–84.

5. On the epistemological crisis now concerning Enlightenment modes of knowledge and control, see Langdon Gilkey, *Society and the Sacred: Toward a Theology of Culture in Decline* (New York: Crossroad, 1981); Michael Harrington, *The Politics at God's Funeral: The Spiritual Crisis of Western Civilization* (New York: Holt, Rinehart and Winston, 1983); and Colin Gunton, *Enlightenment and Alienation: An Essay towards a Trinitarian Theology* (Grand Rapids: Eerdmans, 1985).

6. Robert Bellah et al., *Habits of the Heart: Individualism and Commitment in American Life* (Berkeley: University of California Press, 1985), have fully explored the nature of the therapeutic society and the dangerous costs that are related to it.

7. On theology and interpretation as a form of social legitimation, see Walter Brueggemann, "A Shape for Old Testament Theology, 1: Structure Legitimation," *CBQ* 47 (1985): 28–46; reprinted in Brueggemann, *Old Testament Theology: Essays on Structure, Theme, and Text*, ed. Patrick D. Miller (Minneapolis: Fortress Press, 1992), 1–21.

8. See Walter Brueggemann, "Trajectories in Old Testament Literature and the Sociology of Ancient Israel," *JBL* 98 (1979): 161–85; reprinted in Brueggemann, *A Social Reading of the Old Testament: Prophetic Approaches to Israel's Communal Life*, ed. Patrick D. Miller (Minneapolis: Fortress Press, 1994), 13–42.

9. The delicate relation between authority and interpretation is evident, for example, in the discussion of Clark H. Pinnock, *The Scripture Principle* (San Francisco: Harper & Row, 1984), chap. 9.

4. Twentieth-Century Old Testament Studies: A Quick Survey

1. Originally published in German in 1878. The English translation is Julius Wellhausen, *Prolegomena to the History of Israel*, trans. J. S. Black and A. Menzies (Edinburgh: Adam & Charles Black, 1885).

2. Karl Barth, *The Epistle to the Romans*, trans. from the 6th ed. by Edwin C. Hoskyns (New York: Oxford University Press, 1933).

3. The early 1930s was a time of great "model building" in German scholarship, especially by Albrecht Alt and Martin Noth; their monographs in this period posited a "tribal confederation" that became the home of Gerhard von Rad's "credo" and helped to make the case for the early location of the generative theological traditions of the Old Testament.

4. Walther Eichrodt, *Theology of the Old Testament*, 2 vols., trans. J. A. Baker, OTL (Philadelphia: Westminster, 1961, 1967).

5. On the Calvinist use of the notion of covenant, see Charles S. McCoy and J. Wayne Baker, *Fountainhead of Federalism: Heinrich Bullinger and the Covenantal Tradition* (Louisville: Westminster John Knox, 1991).

6. George E. Mendenhall, *Law and Covenant in Israel and the Ancient Near East* (Pittsburgh: Biblical Colloquium, 1954); Klaus Baltzer, *The Covenant Formulary in Old Testament, Jewish, and Early Christian Writings*, trans. D. E. Green (Philadelphia: Fortress Press, 1971).

7. The formative essay is Gerhard von Rad, "The Form-Critical Problem of the Hexateuch," in *The Problem of the Hexateuch and Other Essays* (New York: McGraw-Hill, 1966), 1–78. Derivatively came his *Old Testament Theology*, 2 vols., trans. D. M. G. Stalker (San Francisco: Harper & Brothers, 1962, 1965).

8. Gerhard von Rad, *Wisdom in Israel* (Nashville: Abingdon, 1972).

9. Von Rad, *Old Testament Theology*, 1:108. He comments further on the vexing question: "But our final comment on it should not be that it is obviously an 'unhistorical' picture, because what is in question here is a picture fashioned throughout by faith. Unlike any ordinary historical document, it does not have its center in itself; it is intended to tell the beholder about Jahweh, that is, how Jahweh led his people and got himself glory. In Jahweh's eyes Israel is always a unity; his control of history was no improvisation made up of disconnected events: in the saving history he always deals with all Israel" (1:302).

10. Albright's programmatic book is *From the Stone Age to Christianity: Monotheism and the Historical Process* (Baltimore: Johns Hopkins University, 1957). For an appreciation of his life of stunning contributions, see

Leona Running and David Noel Freedman, *William Foxwell Albright: A Twentieth-Century Genius* (New York: Two Continents, 1975).

11. John Bright, *A History of Israel* (Philadelphia: Westminster, 1959). This popular textbook has gone through a series of editions.

12. Burke O. Long, *Planting and Reaping Albright: Politics, Ideology, and Interpreting the Bible* (University Park: Pennsylvania State University Press, 1997).

13. See his popular summary: George Ernest Wright, *Biblical Archaeology* (Philadelphia: Westminster, 1957).

14. G. Ernest Wright, *The Old Testament against Its Environment*, SBT 2 (London: SCM, 1950); *God Who Acts: Biblical Theology as Recital*, SBT 8 (London: SCM, 1952).

15. The encyclical was *Divino Afflante Spiritu*. See Thomas Aquinas Collins and Raymond E. Brown, "Church Pronouncements," in Raymond E. Brown et al., eds., *The Jerome Biblical Commentary* (Englewood Cliffs, N.J.: Prentice-Hall, 1968), 628.

16. James Barr, *The Semantics of Biblical Language* (Oxford: Oxford University Press, 1961).

17. Brevard S. Childs, *Biblical Theology in Crisis* (Philadelphia: Westminster, 1970).

18. John Van Seters, *Abraham in History and Tradition* (New Haven: Yale University Press, 1975); Thomas L. Thompson, *The Historicity of the Patriarchal Narratives: The Quest for the Historical Abraham*, BZAW 133 (Berlin: de Gruyter, 1974).

19. Langdon Gilkey, "Cosmology, Ontology, and the Travail of Biblical Language," *JR* 41 (1961): 194–205.

20. Norman K. Gottwald, *The Tribes of Yahweh: A Sociology of the Religion of Liberated Israel, 1250–1050 B.C.E.* (Maryknoll, N.Y.: Orbis, 1979). See his more programmatic statement, "Social Class as an Analytic and Hermeneutical Category in Biblical Studies," *JBL* 112 (1993): 3–22.

21. James Muilenburg, "Form Criticism and Beyond," *JBL* 88 (1969): 1–18. His programmatic statement has been best exposited by his most important student, Phyllis Trible, *Rhetorical Criticism: Context, Method, and the Book of Jonah*, Guides to Biblical Scholarship, Old Testament Series, ed. Gene M. Tucker (Minneapolis: Fortress Press, 1994).

22. Brevard S. Childs, *Biblical Theology of the Old and New Testaments: Theological Reflection on the Christian Bible* (Minneapolis: Fortress Press, 1993).

23. Rolf P. Knierim, *The Task of Old Testament Theology: Method and Cases* (Grand Rapids: Eerdmans, 1995); Bernhard W. Anderson, *Contours of Old Testament Theology* (Minneapolis: Fortress Press, 1999); James Barr, *The Concept of Biblical Theology: An Old Testament Perspective* (Minneapolis: Fortress Press, 1999); Rolf Rendtorff, *A Theology of the Old Testament*, New Canonical Hebrew Bible (London: SCM, 2004). See also my proposal, *Theology of the Old Testament: Testimony, Dispute, Advocacy* (Minneapolis: Fortress Press, 1997).

24. See Philip R. Davies, *In Search of Ancient Israel* (Sheffield: Sheffield Academic, 1995); Niels P. Lemche, *Ancient Israel: A New History of Israelite Society* (Sheffield: Sheffield Academic, 1988); and Keith W. Whitelam, *The Invention of Ancient Israel: The Silencing of Palestinian History* (London: Routledge, 1996).

25. See Robert P. Carroll, *The Bible as a Problem for Christianity* (Philadelphia: Trinity Press International, 1991), and *Wolf in the Sheepfold: The Bible as Problematic for Theology* (London: SCM, 1997); David Penchansky, *The Betrayal of God: Ideological Conflict in Job*, Literary Currents in Biblical Interpretation (Louisville: Westminster John Knox, 1990).

26. See Jon D. Levenson, *The Hebrew Bible, The Old Testament, and Historical Criticism: Jews and Christians in Biblical Studies* (Louisville: Westminster John Knox, 1993).

27. Michael Fishbane, *Biblical Interpretation in Ancient Israel* (Oxford: Clarendon, 1985); Jon D. Levenson, *Creation and the Persistence of Evil: The Jewish Drama of Divine Omnipotence* (San Francisco: HarperCollins, 1988), and his *The Hebrew Bible*.

28. Childs, *Biblical Theology of the Old and New Testaments*; Levenson, *The Hebrew Bible*.

29. Fredrick C. Holmgren, *The Old Testament and the Significance of Jesus* (Grand Rapids: Eerdmans, 1999); Norbert Lohfink, *The Covenant Never Revoked: Biblical Reflections on Christian-Jewish Dialogue*, trans. J. J. Scullion (New York: Paulist, 1991); and R. Kendall Soulen, *The God of Israel and Christian Theology* (Minneapolis: Fortress Press, 1996).

5. Biblical Faith as Narrative, Recital, Confession: An Introduction to von Rad's *Old Testament Theology*

1. On the life and work of Gerhard von Rad, see James. L. Crenshaw, "Von Rad, Gerhard (1901–1971)," in Donald K. McKim, ed., *Historical Handbook of Major Biblical Interpreters* (Downers Grove, Ill.: InterVarsity,

1998), 526–31; Crenshaw, *Gerhard von Rad* (Peabody, Mass.: Hendrickson, 1991); Rudolf Smend, "Rad, Gerhard von (1901–1971)," in John H. Hayes, ed., *Dictionary of Biblical Interpretation, vol. K–Z* (Nashville: Abingdon, 1999), 364–65.

2. Julius Wellhausen, *Prolegomena to the History of Israel*, trans. J. S. Black and A. Menzies (Edinburgh: Adam & Charles Black, 1885).

3. An abridgement of his address in English is offered by John H. Sandys-Wunsch and Laurence Eldredge, "J. P. Gabler and the Distinction between Biblical and Dogmatic Theology: Translation, Commentary, and Discussion of His Originality," *SJT* 33 (1980): 133–58. See also Rolf P. Knierim, "On Gabler," in *The Task of Old Testament Theology: Method and Cases* (Grand Rapids: Eerdmans, 1995), 495–556.

4. Karl Barth, *The Epistle to the Romans*, trans. from the 6th ed. by Edwin C. Hoskyns (New York: Oxford University Press, 1968).

5. See Jan Rohls, "Weimar, the German Church Struggle, and the Barmen Theological Declaration," in *Reformed Confessions: Theology from Zurich to Barmen* (Louisville: Westminster John Knox, 1998), 293–302.

6. Walther Eichrodt, *Theology of the Old Testament*, 2 vols., trans. J. A. Baker, OTL (Philadelphia: Westminster, 1961, 1967).

7. Gerhard von Rad, "The Theological Problem of the Old Testament Doctrine of Creation," in *The Problem of the Hexateuch and Other Essays* (New York: McGraw-Hill, 1966), 131–42.

8. G. Ernest Wright, *The Old Testament against Its Environment*, SBT 2 (London: SCM Press, 1950); *God Who Acts: Biblical Theology as Recital*, SBT 8 (London: SCM Press, 1952).

9. It is difficult to know whether the exclusion of "natural theology" in the face of National Socialism was a requirement of evangelical faith. That of course was the assumption and passionate conviction of those who risked the most in the dispute. For a later dissenting judgment, see James Barr, *Biblical Faith and Natural Theology: The Gifford Lectures for 1991* (Oxford: Clarendon, 1993), 112–13: "Thus the understanding of pro-Nazi theology as basically a kind of natural theology was probably a vast misdiagnosis."

10. Gerhard von Rad, "The Form-Critical Problem of the Hexateuch," in *The Problem of the Hexateuch*, 1–78.

11. Karl Barth, *Credo: A Presentation of the Chief Problems of Dogmatics with Reference to the Apostles' Creed* (London: Hodder & Stoughton, 1936). On testimony before the authorities, see the comments of Choan-Seng Song, "The Politics of the Resurrection," in Justo L. González, ed., *Pro-*

claiming the Acceptable Year (Valley Forge, Pa.: Judson, 1982), 25–39, concerning Luke 21:12-15. See also Kevin J. Vanhoozer, "The Trials of Truth," in J. Andrew Kirk and Kevin J. Vanhoozer, eds., *To Stake a Claim: Mission and the Western Crisis of Knowledge* (Maryknoll, N.Y.: Orbis, 1999), 144–56.

12. H. Richard Niebuhr, *The Meaning of Revelation* (New York: Macmillan, 1962 [1941]) is often credited with having established a self-conscious basis for narrative theology. See Stanley Hauerwas and L. Gregory Jones, eds., *Why Narrative? Readings in Narrative Theology* (Grand Rapids: Eerdmans, 1989). James Barr, "Story and History in Biblical Theology," *JR* 56 (1976): 1–17, suggested that "history-like story" is a way to understand the problem of history in scripture. It is unfortunate that later on, critics of von Rad, perhaps including Barr himself, have not heeded this important distinction that von Rad understood so well.

13. See James B. Wiggins, *Religion as Story* (Lanham, Md.: University Press of America, 1975), for an important sampling of the earlier discussion on the connection between faith and narrative.

14. The Hexateuch rather than Pentateuch as the narrative corpus was necessary to von Rad's presentation, though the notion of Hexateuch is intrinsically problematic. On the Pentateuch as Hexateuch without fulfillment, see James A. Sanders, *Torah and Canon* (Philadelphia: Fortress Press, 1972), 20–30.

15. On the oral character of the recital, see Susan Niditch, *Oral World and Written Word: Ancient Israelite Literature*, Library of Ancient Israel (Louisville: Westminster John Knox, 1996).

16. I have cited some of Barth's appeal to testimony, as well as commentaries on Barth's notion of testimony in Walter Brueggemann, *Theology of the Old Testament: Testimony, Dispute, Advocacy* (Minneapolis: Fortress Press, 1997), 119 n. 6.

17. On the questions of foundationalism, see Paul K. Moser, "Foundationalism and Some Alternatives," in *Knowledge and Evidence*, Cambridge Studies in Theology (Cambridge: Cambridge University Press, 1989), 166ff.; John E. Thiel, *Nonfoundationalism*, Guides to Theological Inquiry (Minneapolis: Fortress Press, 1994); and F. LeRon Shults, *The Postfoundationalist Task of Theology: Wolfhart Pannenberg and the New Theological Rationality* (Grand Rapids: Eerdmans, 1999).

18. Gerhard von Rad, *Old Testament Theology*, vol. 2, *The Theology of Israel's Prophetic Traditions*, trans. D. M. G. Stalker (San Francisco: Harper & Brothers, 1965), 4.

19. Brevard S. Childs, *Introduction to the Old Testament as Scripture* (Philadelphia: Fortress Press, 1979), 325–34.

20. See Henning Graf Reventlow, *Problems of Old Testament Theology in the Twentieth Century*, trans. J. Bowden (Philadelphia: Fortress Press, 1985), 125–33.

21. Von Rad, *Old Testament Theology*, 1:3–102.

22. Ibid., 1:69–77 [Deuteronomy]; 1:77–80 [Priestly].

23. Ibid., 1:105–305.

24. Ibid., 1:187–279.

25. Accent on the first two commandments was programmatic for the work of Walther Zimmerli, *Old Testament Theology in Outline*, trans. D. E. Green (Atlanta: John Knox, 1978).

26. Von Rad, *Old Testament Theology*, 1:306–54.

27. Ibid., 1:334–47.

28. Ibid., 1:355–459.

29. Thus, for example, James Barr, *The Concept of Biblical Theology: An Old Testament Perspective* (Minneapolis: Fortress Press, 1999), 46.

30. Von Rad, *Old Testament Theology*, 1:369–70. Von Rad's phrasing is perhaps an unintentional but wondrous echo of the phrasing of George Herbert, that the human person is assigned by God as "Secretary of thy praise." See Diana Benet, *Secretary of Praise: The Poetic Vocation of George Herbert* (Columbia: University of Missouri Press, 1984); and Daniel W. Hardy and David F. Ford, *Praising and Knowing God* (Philadelphia: Westminster, 1985), 81–82.

31. Von Rad, *Old Testament Theology*, 1:392.

32. Ibid., 1:377.

33. Ibid., 1:435.

34. Gerhard von Rad, *Wisdom in Israel* (Nashville: Abingdon, 1972). Of this book Rudolf Smend, in "Rad, Gerhard von [1901–1971]," *Dictionary of Biblical Interpretation, Vol. K–Z* (Nashville: Abingdon, 1999), 365, writes:

> During the last years of his life he consciously applied himself to the correction of the one-sidedness of his earlier work by the study of Wisdom, which he had earlier considered a fringe phenomenon. His 1970 book surprised many scholars. Still, the fundamental problem that stood behind the rich and vital presentation of this thought-world was the one that had motivated R. in his work on the historical biblical witnesses and that had imprinted his entire theological existence: the relationship of faith to reality.

35. Von Rad, *Old Testament Theology*, 2:viii.

36. Von Rad on the promises may be considered the crucial mediating figure who took up the analysis of the ancestral promises by Albrecht Alt, "The God of the Fathers," in *Essays on Old Testament History and Religion*, trans. R. A. Wilson (Oxford: Blackwell, 1966), 1–77, and turned it to theological contemporaneity (Alt's essay was first published in 1929). From von Rad's instruction and exposition, the theme of promise was taken up by Jürgen Moltmann, *Theology of Hope: On the Ground and the Implications of a Christian Eschatology*, trans. James W. Leitch (Minneapolis: Fortress Press, 1993 [1967]). This is one of the rare and spectacular cases in which biblical exposition feeds directly and influentially into theological interpretation.

37. It is stunningly obvious that von Rad had no sense of the ways in which the future of the old tradition came to be embodied in the faith of Judaism. This exclusionary vision is a key issue in the critique of von Rad's work, on which see below.

38. Von Rad, *Old Testament Theology*, 2:3–125.

39. Ibid., 2:4, 117, 118.

40. Ibid., 2:129–315.

41. Ibid., 2:263–77.

42. Ibid., 2:301–8.

43. Ibid., 2:306.

44. Ibid., 2:319–429.

45. Ibid., 2:viii.

46. Ibid., 2:361, 422.

47. Ibid., 2:413. The dialectic of old and new is illuminated in an important way by R. W. L. Moberly, *The Old Testament of the Old Testament: Patriarchal Narratives and Mosaic Yahwism*, Overtures to Biblical Theology (Minneapolis: Fortress Press, 1992). Moberly's approach is not without important points of contact to that of von Rad.

48. While I term the matter "deeply problematic" because von Rad paid no attention to Jewish trajectories of ongoing faith, it is the case that Brevard Childs and Jon Levenson are quite content to settle for the fact that Jews and Christians read different texts and are not obligated to pay attention to the alternative trajectory of ongoing faith. The issue is complex, but I nonetheless view von Rad's approach as, in the end, deeply problematic.

49. Von Rad, *Old Testament Theology*, 2:330.

50. Ibid., 2:329, 332–33. Note well that von Rad carefully says "proper for Christians." This seems to me the correct way to nuance the matter, for it

allows that in a particular tradition of faith, certain warrants are allowed and recognized. This is very different from claims that do not acknowledge the specificity of the interpretive tradition but seem to make sweeping, universal, and therefore exclusionary statements. Von Rad on occasion offers both kinds of claims.

51. Ibid., 2:333.

52. Ibid., 2:327.

53. Rudolf Bultmann, "The Significance of the Old Testament for the Christian Faith," in Bernhard W. Anderson, ed., *The Old Testament and Christian Faith: A Theological Discussion* (New York: Harper & Row, 1963), 8–35.

54. Von Rad, *Old Testament Theology*, 2:382.

55. It is commonplace to observe that for von Rad and his remarkable generation of biblical interpreters, the Shoah did not figure as a theological datum that had to be taken into account. Perhaps the stunning reality of the event was so overwhelming that it has taken extended time even to recognize the Shoah as a defining datum that changes all interpretive work. The point is made unmistakably clear in Tod Linafelt, ed., *Strange Fire: Reading the Bible after the Holocaust*, Biblical Seminar 71 (Sheffield: Sheffield Academic, 2000).

56. See Hans Walter Wolff, "The Hermeneutics of the Old Testament," in Claus Westermann, ed., *Essays on Old Testament Hermeneutics* (Richmond, Va.: John Knox, 1963), 160–99.

57. At the turn of the new century, an accent on "Christian culture" has again become an ominous reality in German politics. Certainly von Rad needs to be appreciated in the context in which he wrote, because he was characteristically immensely attuned to his context.

58. See a summary of the assault on the "Biblical Theology Movement" in Brueggemann, *Theology of the Old Testament*, 42–49.

59. Brevard S. Childs, *Biblical Theology of the Old and New Testaments: Theological Reflection on the Christian Bible* (Minneapolis: Fortress Press, 1993), 103.

60. James Barr, *The Concept of Biblical Theology*, 35; see also 47. It is curious that Barr qualifies the distinction he makes with the parenthetical comment, "if we may be permitted that phrase!" In addition to speaking with a curious royal "we," the phrase seems to compromise Barr's critique by an acknowledgment that "history as it really happened" is in fact not history as it really happened: after all, this is very close to von Rad's own careful point.

61. Barr, *The Concept of Biblical Theology*, 45.

62. Von Rad, *Old Testament Theology*, 1:107–8, 302.

63. It may seem odd to include Childs among modernists, and perhaps the point is not quite correct. When he speaks of "real history," however, he makes distinctions that sound modern in their intent.

64. Karl Barth, *Church Dogmatics* III/1, *The Doctrine of Creation* (Edinburgh: T. & T. Clark, 1958), 81–82; see also 91. See also *Church Dogmatics* IV/1, *The Doctrine of Reconciliation* (Edinburgh: T. & T. Clark, 1956), 336, 508.

65. On the general problematic, see Richard R. Niebuhr, *Resurrection and Historical Reason: A Study of Theological Method* (New York: Scribner's, 1957).

66. James Barr, "Story and History in Biblical Theology," *JR* 56 (1976): 1–17, later came to see the legitimacy of "story" for reading these texts. It is odd that even later Barr holds von Rad to a critique that his own distinctions might have redressed differently.

67. Jon D. Levenson, "Why Jews Are Not Interested in Biblical Theology," in *The Hebrew Bible, the Old Testament, and Historical Criticism: Jews and Christians in Biblical Studies* (Louisville: Westminster John Knox, 1993), 41.

68. Barr, *The Concept of Biblical Theology*, 46.

6. The Loss and Recovery of Creation in Old Testament Theology

1. Thomas S. Kuhn, *The Structure of Scientific Revolutions* (Chicago: University of Chicago Press, 1963) has made available to us this crucial dynamic of interpretive activity.

2. Gerhard von Rad, "The Theological Problem of the Old Testament Doctrine of Creation," in *The Problem of the Hexateuch and Other Essays* (New York: McGraw-Hill, 1966), 131–42. The essay was first published in *Werden und Wesen des Alten Testaments* (Berlin: Töpelmann, 1936).

3. Gerhard von Rad, "The Form-Critical Problem of the Hexateuch," in *The Problem of the Hexateuch*, 1–78.

4. This connection is confirmed by Norbert Lohfink, "God the Creator and the Stability of Heaven and Earth: The Old Testament on the Connection Between Creation and Salvation," in *Theology of the Pentateuch: Themes of the Priestly Narrative and Deuteronomy* (Minneapolis: Fortress Press, 1994), 118: "Since its origin in the year 1935, when Gerhard von Rad proposed this theme for the first time at a meeting in Göttingen, it has

been far too closely connected with the narrowing of the question necessitated by the conflict of the Confessing Church with the tendencies of the churches to accommodate themselves to the ideology of the Third Reich, an accommodation that sought legitimation in a theology of creation, even though this is scarcely evident in the subsequent literature."

5. G. Ernest Wright, *The Challenge of Israel's Faith* (Chicago: University of Chicago Press, 1944); *The Old Testament against Its Environment,* SBT 2 (London: SCM, 1950); *God Who Acts: Biblical Theology as Recital,* SBT 8 (London: SCM, 1952).

6. Wright, *The Old Testament against Its Environment,* 9.

7. Ibid., 17–19, quotation from p. 17.

8. Claus Westermann, "Creation and History in the Old Testament," in Vilmos Vajta, ed., *The Gospel and Human Destiny* (Minneapolis: Augsburg, 1971), 11–38. Westermann's other important discussions of this theme include *Creation* (Philadelphia: Fortress Press, 1971); *Elements of Old Testament Theology* (Atlanta: John Knox, 1982); and *What Does the Old Testament Say about God?* (London: SPCK, 1979).

9. Westermann, "Creation and History," 17, 32.

10. Ibid., 24, 34.

11. Ibid., 32. See Claus Westermann, *Blessing in the Bible and in the Life of the Church,* trans. K. R. Crim, Overtures to Biblical Theology (Philadelphia: Fortress Press, 1978).

12. Frank Moore Cross, *Canaanite Myth and Hebrew Epic: Essays in the History of the Religion of Israel* (Cambridge, Mass.: Harvard University Press, 1973). Brevard S. Childs has recognized the important contribution of Cross in moving beyond the models of the so-called Biblical Theology Movement (*Biblical Theology in Crisis* [Philadelphia: Westminster, 1970], 75–77). Cross's program is imaginatively reflected in the work of a number of his students. See, for example, Patrick D. Miller, *The Divine Warrior in Early Israel* (Cambridge, Mass.: Harvard University Press, 1975); Patrick D. Miller and J. J. M. Roberts, *The Hand of the Lord: A Reassessment of the "Ark Narrative" of 1 Samuel* (Baltimore: Johns Hopkins University Press, 1977); Thomas W. Mann, *Divine Presence and Guidance in Israelite Traditions: The Typology of Exaltation* (Baltimore: Johns Hopkins University Press, 1977); and Jon D. Levenson, *Creation and the Persistence of Evil: The Jewish Drama of Divine Omnipotence* (San Francisco: HarperCollins, 1988).

13. Cross, "The Song of the Sea and Canaanite Myth," in *Canaanite Myth and Hebrew Epic,* 112–44.

14. Ibid., 143–44.

15. For the fullest, most recent summary of scholarship on the wisdom traditions, see John G. Gammie and Leo G. Perdue, *The Sage in Israel and the Ancient Near East* (Winona Lake, Ind.: Eisenbrauns, 1990).

16. For representative treatments of the problems and the possibilities of taking wisdom into account in Old Testament theology, see Samuel Terrien, "The Play of Wisdom: Turning Point in Biblical Theology," *HBT* 3 (1981): 125–53; Alan Jenks, "Theological Presuppositions of Israelite Wisdom Literature," *HBT* 7 (1985): 43–75; and John J. Collins, "Proverbial Wisdom and the Yahwist Vision," *Semeia* 17 (1980): 1–17. My book *In Man We Trust: The Neglected Side of Biblical Faith* (Atlanta: John Knox, 1972) was an early attempt to take seriously the emerging accents of scholarship.

17. Hans Heinrich Schmid, *Wesen und Geschichte der Weisheit: Eine Untersuchung zur altorientalischen und israelitischen Weisheitsliteratur* (Berlin: Töpelmann, 1966).

18. Hans Heinrich Schmid, *Gerechtigkeit als Weltordnung: Hintergrund und Geschichte des alttestamentlichen Gerechtigkeitsbegriffes*, BHTh 40 (Tübingen: Mohr/Siebeck, 1968).

19. Hans Heinrich Schmid, "Schöpfung, Gerechtigkeit, und Heil," published in English as "Creation, Righteousness, and Salvation: 'Creation Theology' as the Broad Horizon of Biblical Theology," in Bernhard W. Anderson, ed., *Creation in the Old Testament*, Issues in Religion and Theology 6 (Philadelphia: Fortress Press, 1984), 102–17.

20. Gerhard von Rad, *Wisdom in Israel* (Nashville: Abingdon, 1972).

21. Ibid., 144–57; Walther Zimmerli, "The Place and Limit of the Wisdom Framework of the Old Testament Theology," *SJT* 17 (1964): 148.

22. Von Rad, *Wisdom in Israel*, 144.

23. Bernhard W. Anderson, *Creation versus Chaos: The Reinterpretation of Mythical Symbolism in the Bible* (Philadelphia: Fortress Press, 1987 [1967]). We are now fortunate to have a reprinting of Anderson's many groundbreaking essays on creation, under the title *From Creation to New Creation: Old Testament Perspectives*, Overtures to Biblical Theology (Minneapolis: Fortress Press, 1994). See also the book he edited, *Creation in the Old Testament*.

24. Walter J. Harrelson, *From Fertility Cult to Worship* (Garden City, N.Y.: Doubleday, 1969).

25. Ibid., 12, 68.

26. Samuel Terrien, *The Elusive Presence: Toward a New Biblical Theology* (San Francisco: Harper & Row, 1978).

27. Rolf P. Knierim, "On the Task of Old Testament Theology," *HBT* 6 (1984): 25–57.

28. Ibid., 29–31.

29. Ibid., 42–43.

30. Jon D. Levenson, *Creation and the Persistence of Evil: The Jewish Drama of Divine Omnipotence* (San Francisco: HarperCollins, 1988).

31. Terence E. Fretheim, "The Plagues as Ecological Signs of Historical Disaster," *JBL* 110 (1991): 385–96.

32. Ibid., 385.

33. Ibid.

34. Ibid., 392. Fretheim's article was an adumbration of his commentary *Exodus*, IBC (Atlanta: John Knox, 1991), which in a programmatic way boldly reinterprets the exodus narrative in terms of creation theology. This commentary compellingly demonstrates how the shift away from "mighty deeds" touches even those texts that had been pivotal for the older approach. The commentary is a model for this newer perspective and a baseline for much that is still to come.

35. James Barr, *Biblical Faith and Natural Theology: The Gifford Lectures for 1991* (Oxford: Clarendon, 1993).

36. Ibid., 113.

37. Barr's is the definitive statement on creation in recent interpretation. I parenthetically add one other reference, however, because it pertains to me particularly and intensely, even if awkwardly; it reflects my own struggle with this major shift in paradigms, to which a student of the Old Testament must now respond. I refer to J. Richard Middleton's careful, critical assessment of my handling, throughout the course of my writings, of creation theology in the Old Testament ("Is Creation Theology Inherently Conservative? A Dialogue with Walter Brueggemann," *HTR* 87 [1994]: 257–77). My published response to Middleton indicates that I accept his critique as largely on target ("Response to J. Richard Middleton," *HTR* 87 [1994]: 279–89; reprinted in this volume as chapter 11, "Israel's Creation Faith"). There are no doubt many reasons for my vacillation on the issue, only some of which are known to me. The one of which I am most aware and wish to accent here is the power of paradigm. Von Rad's 1936 essay has been decisive for me, as for many others. I take my struggle with this matter as a reflection of the struggle within the discipline since the appearance of von Rad's article. The immediate point is the power of von Rad's essay. The larger point is the power and authority of paradigm. Every interpreter

lives in and with a paradigm of interpretation, either a dominant one or a protesting one. Paradigms are inevitable, and every one of them hardens even as it reveals.

38. See Knierim, "On the Task of Old Testament Theology," 39. On the interface between biblical-theological thought and the natural sciences, see Jürgen Moltmann, *God in Creation: A New Theology of Creation and the Spirit of God*, trans. Margaret Kohl (Minneapolis: Fortress Press, 1993 [1985]); Langdon Gilkey, *Nature, Reality, and the Sacred: The Nexus of Science and Religion*, Theology and the Sciences (Minneapolis: Fortress Press, 1993); and Sallie McFague, *Metaphorical Theology: Models of God in Religious Language* (Philadelphia: Fortress Press, 1983). Clearly none of these theological thinkers is burdened with the specificity of the text as are biblical scholars. But then, none of them has such resources of a concrete kind readily available either.

39. Of course, reference to the Bible and ecology cannot fail to evoke thoughts of the now famous thesis of Lynn White Jr. that the biblical notion of dominion is the taproot of the abusive exploitation of the earth ("The Historical Roots of Our Ecological Crisis," *Science* 155 [March 10, 1967]: 1203–7). The urgent issues surfaced by White have been carefully reviewed by Cameron Wybrow in *The Bible, Baconianism, and Mastery over Nature: The Old Testament and Its Modern Misreading*, American University Studies, Series 7 (New York: Peter Lang, 1991). Wybrow makes clear that it was the misreading of scripture in the service of modern technology that led to the abuse of the earth about which White writes.

40. "Creation theology undercuts patriarchy," says Phyllis Trible in her essay "Treasures Old and New: Biblical Theology and the Challenge of Feminism," in Francis Walton, ed., *The Open Text: New Directions for Biblical Studies?* (London: SCM, 1993), 47.

41. Gerda Lerner, *The Creation of Patriarchy* (Oxford: Oxford University Press, 1986), 219.

42. Ibid., 224.

7. The ABCs of Old Testament Theology in the United States

1. Walther Eichrodt, *Theology of the Old Testament*, 2 vols., trans. J. A. Baker, OTL (Philadelphia: Westminster, 1961, 1967).

2. Gerhard von Rad, *Old Testament Theology*, 2 vols., trans. D. M. G. Stalker (San Francisco: Harper & Brothers, 1962, 1965).

3. The quest for a "center" (*Mitte*) has proved endlessly elusive to scholars who have tried to overcome the pluralism of which von Rad made so much.

4. Gerhard von Rad, "The Form Critical Problem of the Hexateuch," in *The Problem of the Hexateuch and Other Essays* (New York: McGraw-Hill, 1966), 1–78.

5. Gerhard von Rad, "The Theological Problem of the Old Testament Doctrine of Creation," in *The Problem of the Hexateuch*, 131–43.

6. G. Ernest Wright, *The Challenge of Israel's Faith* (Chicago: University of Chicago, 1944); *The Old Testament against Its Environment*, SBT 2 (London: SCM, 1950); *God Who Acts: Biblical Theology as Recital*, SBT 8 (London: SCM, 1952).

7. See Walter Brueggemann, *Theology of the Old Testament: Testimony, Dispute, Advocacy* (Minneapolis: Fortress Press, 1997), 16–20.

8. James Barr, *The Semantics of Biblical Language* (Oxford: Oxford University Press, 1961); Brevard S. Childs, *Biblical Theology in Crisis* (Philadelphia: Westminster, 1970).

9. Langdon Gilkey, "Cosmology, Ontology, and the Travail of Biblical Language," *JR* 41 (1961): 194–205.

10. Thomas L. Thompson, *Early History of the Israelite People from the Written and Archaeological Sources* (Leiden: Brill, 1992); *The Historicity of the Patriarchal Narratives: The Quest for the Historical Abraham*, BZAW 133 (Berlin: de Gruyter, 1974); John Van Seters, *Abraham in History and Tradition* (New Haven: Yale University Press, 1975); *The Life of Moses: The Yahwist as Historian in Exodus-Numbers* (Louisville: Westminster John Knox, 1994); *Prologue to History: The Yahwist as Historian in Genesis* (Louisville: Westminster John Knox , 1992).

11. Keith W. Whitelam, *The Invention of Ancient Israel: The Silencing of Palestinian History* (London: Routledge, 1996); Keith W. Whitelam and Robert B. Coote, *The Emergence of Early Israel in Historical Perspective*, The Social World of Biblical Antiquity 5 (Sheffield: Almond/Sheffield Academic, 1987); Niels Peter Lemche, *Ancient Israel: A New History of Israelite Society* (Sheffield: Sheffield Academic, 1988); *Prelude to Israel's Past: Background and Beginnings of Israelite History and Identity* (Peabody, Mass.: Hendrickson, 1998); *The Israelites in History and Tradition*, Library of Ancient Israel (Louisville: Westminster John Knox, 1998); Philip R. Davies, *In Search of "Ancient Israel,"* JSOTSup 148 (Sheffield: JSOT Press, 1992). This skeptical posture toward historicity in the Old Testament is

nicely presented in "Virtual History and the Bible," ed. J. Cheryl Exum, *BibInt* 8, 1/2 (Leiden: Brill, 2000).

12. John Bright, *A History of Israel*, 2nd ed. (Philadelphia: Westminster, 1972).

13. Burke O. Long, *Planting and Reaping Albright: Politics, Ideology, and Interpreting the Bible* (University Park: Pennsylvania State University Press, 1997).

14. Brevard S. Childs, *Introduction to the Old Testament as Scripture* (Philadelphia: Fortress Press, 1979).

15. Norman K. Gottwald, *The Tribes of Yahweh: A Sociology of the Religion of Liberated Israel, 1250–1050 B.C.E.* (Maryknoll, N.Y.: Orbis, 1979).

16. Ibid., 603–21.

17. Phyllis Trible, *God and the Rhetoric of Sexuality*, Overtures to Biblical Theology (Philadelphia: Fortress Press, 1978).

18. J. Cheryl Exum, *Fragmented Women: Feminist (Sub)Versions of Biblical Narratives*, JSOTSup 163 (Valley Forge, Pa.: Trinity Press International, 1993); *Plotted, Shot, Painted: Cultural Representations of Biblical Women*, JSOTSup 215 (Sheffield: Sheffield Academic, 1996); Alice Bach, *Women, Seduction, and Betrayal in Biblical Narrative* (Cambridge: Cambridge University Press, 1997); Danna Nolan Fewell and David Gunn, *Gender, Power, and Promise: The Subject of the Bible's First Story* (Nashville: Abingdon, 1993); *Compromising Redemption: Relating Character in the Book of Ruth*, Literary Currents in Biblical Interpretation (Louisville: Westminster John Knox, 1990); Angela Bauer, *Gender in the Book of Jeremiah: A Feminist-Literary Reading*, Studies in Biblical Literature 5 (New York: Peter Lang, 1999); Kathleen M. O'Connor, "The Tears of God and Divine Character in Jeremiah 2–9," in Tod Linafelt and Timothy K. Beal, eds., *God in the Fray: A Tribute to Walter Brueggemann* (Minneapolis: Fortress Press, 1998), 172–85; Kathleen M. O'Connor and A. R. Pete Diamond, "Unfaithful Passions: Coding Women Coding Men in Jeremiah 2–3 (4:2)," in *BibInt* 4 (1996): 288–310.

19. Phyllis Trible, *Rhetorical Criticism: Method and the Book of Jonah*, Guides to Biblical Scholarship, Old Testament Series, ed. Gene M. Tucker (Minneapolis: Fortress Press, 1995).

20. An important exception is the work of Bernhard W. Anderson, *From Creation to New Creation: Old Testament Perspectives*, Overtures to Biblical Theology (Minneapolis: Fortress Press, 1995); *Creation versus Chaos: The Reinterpretation of Mythical Symbolism in the Bible* (Philadelphia: Fortress Press, 1987 [1967]).

21. I have cited and summarized this material in "The Loss and Recovery of 'Creation' in Old Testament Theology," *ThTo* 53 (1996): 177–90; reprinted in this volume as chapter 6.

22. Patrick D. Miller, "Creation and Covenant," in Stephen J. Kraftchick et al., eds., *Biblical Theology: Problems and Perspectives: In Honor of J. Christiaan Beker* (Nashville: Abingdon, 1995), 155–68.

23. Rainer Albertz, *A History of Israelite Religion in the Old Testament Period*, 2 vols., trans. J. Bowden, OTL (Louisville: Westminster John Knox, 1994); *Persönliche Frömmigkeit und offizielle Religion: Religionsinterner Pluralismus in Israel und Babylon*, Calwer theologische Monographien A, 9 (Stuttgart: Calwer, 1978).

24. See Bernard E. Brown, *Protest in Paris: Anatomy of a Revolt* (Morristown, N.J.: General Learning, 1974).

25. See Rolf P. Knierim, *The Task of Old Testament Theology: Method and Cases* (Grand Rapids: Eerdmans, 1995); John Goldingay, *Theological Diversity and the Authority of the Old Testament* (Grand Rapids: Eerdmans, 1987); *Models for Scripture* (Grand Rapids: Eerdmans, 1994).

26. See n. 20.

27. Bernhard W. Anderson, *Contours of Old Testament Theology* (Minneapolis: Fortress Press, 1999).

28. Ibid., 37–78.

29. Ibid., 79–236.

30. Ibid., 251–74.

31. Ibid., 275–85.

32. Ibid., 287–324.

33. The context and the intention of Anderson's study is illuminated by the fact that the book is dedicated to the memory of G. Ernest Wright, his long-time friend and colleague.

34. James Barr, *The Concept of Biblical Theology: An Old Testament Perspective* (Minneapolis: Fortress Press, 1999).

35. Ibid., 27–51.

36. Ibid., 62–76 (doctrinal theology), 77–84 (non-theological study), 100–139 (history of religion), 146–71 (philosophy and natural theology), 172–88 (the New Testament).

37. Ibid., 113.

38. Ibid., 109.

39. Ibid., 118–29. For Albertz, see n. 23.

40. Ibid., 121.

41. Ibid., 133.

42. Ibid., 85–99.

43. Ibid., 468–96.

44. Ibid., 286–311.

45. Ibid., 401–38 (Childs), 541–62 (Brueggemann).

46. Brevard S. Childs, *Biblical Theology in Crisis*; *Introduction to the Old Testament as Scripture*; *Old Testament Theology in a Canonical Context* (Philadelphia: Fortress Press, 1985).

47. Brevard S. Childs, *Biblical Theology of the Old and New Testaments: Theological Reflection on the Christian Bible* (Minneapolis: Fortress Press, 1993).

48. Ibid., 78.

49. Ibid., 11–29.

50. Ibid., 30–51.

51. Ibid., 31–32.

52. Ibid., 32. For a discussion of the "rule of faith" with which Professor Childs would likely agree, see Peter Stuhlmacher, "The Christian Canon, Its Center, and Its Interpretation," in *How to Do Biblical Theology*, PTMS 38 (Allison Park, Pa.: Pickwick, 1995). T. H. Polk, *The Biblical Kierkegaard: Reading by the Rule of Faith* (Macon, Ga.: Mercer University Press, 1997), however, leaves things much more open and undetermined; see especially pp. 8f. on Augustine and chapter 2.

53. Childs, *Biblical Theology of the Old and New Testaments*, 95–207.

54. Ibid., 209–322.

55. Ibid., 349–716.

56. Brueggemann, *Theology of the Old Testament*, 117–44.

57. Ibid., 118.

58. Anderson, *Contours of Old Testament Theology*, 22–27.

59. Ibid., 138.

60. Ibid., 178.

61. Ibid., 179.

62. Paul D. Hanson, "A New Challenge to Biblical Theology," *JAAR* 67 (1999): 450.

63. On the interrelatedness of *Was* and *Wie* (the "what" and the "how"), see Gail R. O'Day, *The Word Disclosed: John's Story and Narrative Preaching* (St. Louis: Chalice, 1987), 11–15 and passim.

64. Barr, *The Concept of Biblical Theology*, 541–62.

65. "Walter Brueggemann's *Theology of the Old Testament: Testimony, Dispute, Advocacy*," in *SJT* 53 (2000): 228–38.

66. Brueggemann, *Theology of the Old Testament*, 40f.

67. Hanson, "A New Challenge to Biblical Theology," 459. If Hanson had read more carefully and not been so eager to caricature my work as "modern psychological," he would have noticed that my argument refers always to the matter dialectically, even as he himself insists.

68. Ibid., 459. Hanson appeals for "integrative moral and religious beliefs." But every such "integrative" belief is an act of imaginative construal that surely stands under the criticism of the text itself, especially the text in its abrasive counter voices.

69. See Walter Brueggemann, "Contemporary Old Testament Theology: A Contextual Prospectus," *Dialog* 38 (Spring 1999): 108–16; reprinted in this volume as chapter 8.

8. Contemporary Old Testament Theology: A Contextual Prospectus

1. Walther Eichrodt, *Theology of the Old Testament*, 2 vols., trans. J. A. Baker, OTL (Philadelphia: Westminster, 1961, 1967); Gerhard von Rad, *Old Testament Theology*, 2 vols., trans. D. M. G. Stalker (San Francisco: Harper & Brothers, 1962, 1965); G. Ernest Wright, *The Challenge of Israel's Faith* (Chicago: University of Chicago, 1944); *The Old Testament against Its Environment*, SBT 2 (London: SCM, 1950); *God Who Acts: Biblical Theology as Recital*, SBT 8 (London: SCM, 1952). See my summary review, Walter Brueggemann, *Theology of the Old Testament: Testimony, Dispute, Advocacy* (Minneapolis: Fortress Press, 1997), 15–38.

2. See my review of these developments, Walter Brueggemann, "The Loss and Recovery of 'Creation' in Old Testament Theology," *ThTo* 53 (1996): 177–90; reprinted in this volume as chapter 6.

3. Here I refer primarily to the *context* of text. But one must also attend to the *context* of the reader. The study of *social location* is an indispensable matter; attentiveness to social location, by way of social-scientific methods, greatly illuminates why we now have such widely variant readings of texts that eschew any claim of any hegemonic reading, either in the name of "critical objectivity" or in the name of "canon."

4. See a critical reflection on the work of William F. Albright, who championed such an approach, by Burke O. Long, *Planting and Reaping Albright: Politics, Ideology, and Interpreting the Bible* (University Park: Pennsylvania State University Press, 1997).

5. In any mode beyond sheer positivism, it is clear that "historical" is a rhetorical mediation of what is remembered. See especially Hayden White,

The Content of the Form: Narrative Discourse and Historical Representation (Baltimore: Johns Hopkins University Press, 1987).

6. It is telling that one of the most important books for new perspectives in interpretation, Norman K. Gottwald's *The Tribes of Yahweh: A Sociology of the Religion of Liberated Israel, 1250–1050 B.C.E.* (Maryknoll, N.Y.: Orbis, 1979), freely acknowledges that it was the matrix of the free-speech movement in Berkeley that was the immediate context for his groundbreaking study. This contextualization is a powerful example of the new awareness of connections between textual work and context.

7. See my review comments in *Theology of the Old Testament*, 42–60.

8. See Jon D. Levenson, "Why Jews Are Not Interested in Biblical Theology," in *The Hebrew Bible, the Old Testament, and Historical Criticism: Jews and Christians in Biblical Studies* (Louisville: Westminster John Knox, 1993), 33–61.

9. See the critical assessment of the classical tradition by R. Kendall Soulen, *The God of Israel and Christian Theology* (Minneapolis: Fortress Press, 1996).

10. Robert P. Carroll continues to produce an important corpus of scholarly material. What became his programmatic statement of the crisis of fideism is *Jeremiah*, OTL (Philadelphia: Westminster, 1986). His most frontal assertion of the issues is *Wolf in the Sheepfold: The Bible as a Problem for Christianity* (London: SPCK, 1991).

11. On the work of ideology critique, see David Penchansky, *The Betrayal of God: Ideological Conflict in Job*, Literary Currents in Biblical Interpretation (Louisville: Westminster John Knox, 1990). With more subtlety, see Regina M. Schwarz, *The Curse of Cain: The Violent Legacy of Monotheism* (Chicago: University of Chicago, 1997).

12. Clifford Geertz, "Ideology as a Cultural System," in *The Interpretation of Culture: Selected Essays* (New York: Basic, 1973), 193–233. See Paul Ricoeur, *Lectures on Ideology and Utopia*, ed. George H. Taylor (New York: Columbia University Press, 1986); and Michele Barrett, *The Politics of Truth: From Marx to Foucault* (Stanford, Calif.: Stanford University Press, 1991).

13. See, for example, John Van Seters, *The Life of Moses: The Yahwist as Historian in Exodus–Numbers* (Louisville: Westminster John Knox, 1994); *Prologue to History: The Yahwist as Historian in Genesis* (Louisville: Westminster John Knox, 1992); and Thomas L. Thompson, *The Mythic Past: Biblical Archaeology and the Myth of Israel* (New York: Basic, 1999). Attention should be paid to the work of Philip R. Davies, Niels Peter Lemche, and Keith W. Whitelam.

14. In using the term "modernism" I do so only as a convenient reference point and way of making contrasts: I intend no special content and certainly no notion of the periodization of intellectual history. I take "modernism" to mean the kind of intellectual revolution linked to Descartes against the hegemonic authority of church interpretation.

15. Brevard S. Childs, *Biblical Theology in Crisis* (Philadelphia: Westminster, 1970); *The Book of Exodus: A Critical, Theological Commentary*, OTL (Philadelphia: Westminster, 1974); *Introduction to the Old Testament as Scripture* (Philadelphia: Fortress Press, 1979); *Old Testament Theology in a Canonical Context* (Philadelphia: Fortress Press, 1985); *Biblical Theology of the Old and New Testaments: Theological Reflection on the Christian Bible* (Minneapolis: Fortress Press, 1993).

16. Childs has received powerful and compelling support from Jon D. Levenson, "The Eighth Principle of Judaism and the Literary Simultaneity of Scripture," in *The Hebrew Bible, The Old Testament, and Historical Criticism*, 62–81.

17. Childs articulates a notion of scripture as a more-or-less contained entity to itself that is in general reflected in the "Yale School." That enterprise has received serious and subtle critique from Kathryn Tanner, *Theologies of Culture: A New Agenda for Theology*, Guides to Theological Inquiry (Minneapolis: Fortress Press, 1997).

18. Childs, *Biblical Theology of the Old and New Testaments*, 67 and passim. The point has been strenuously elaborated upon in *Reclaiming the Bible for the Church*, ed. Carl E. Braaten and Robert W. Jenson (Grand Rapids: Eerdmans, 1995).

19. The thesis is pervasive in the book. See, for example, p. 91: "The specific characteristic of the canonical shaping of the two testaments into one Christian Bible lay in the preservation of two distinct witnesses to a common subject matter who is Jesus Christ."

20. On the use of the term "premodern," see n. 14, above.

21. Childs, *Biblical Theology of the Old and New Testaments*, 30–51.

22. Ibid., 95–207 (Old Testament), 209–322 (New Testament), 319–716 (theological reflection on the Christian Bible).

23. Especially Childs, *The Book of Exodus*. The entire matter of the relationship of theological interpretation to historical criticism is vexed and complex. Gerhard Ebeling, "The Significance of the Critical Historical Method for Church and Theology in Protestantism," in *Word and Faith* (Philadelphia: Fortress Press, 1963), has considered the matter and urges a radical historicality in our undertakings:

> Christianity, I say, is for all that not a phenomenon that abides always identical and unchanged, but it exists in history, i.e., it is subject to the march of time. It can never simply remain precisely the same as it was at the start, for then it would not exist in history at all. (37)

Childs, *Biblical Theology of the Old and New Testaments*, 6–9, makes a critical response to Ebeling but seems, in my judgment, to withdraw from Ebeling's radical historicality, seeking to find standing ground that is not so vulnerable to the pressures of the historical. But then that is the very point at issue.

24. Ebeling, "The Significance of the Critical Historical Method," 59, concludes:

> Systematic theology must therefore be required not only to respect the results of critical historical research—even on that point there is still much to be desired—but also to take up fully and completely into its own approach the outlook of the critical historical method.

Given Childs's approach, we are clearly not finished with these issues.

25. Francis Watson, *Text, Church, and World: Biblical Interpretation in Theological Perspective* (Grand Rapids: Eerdmans, 1994); *Text and Truth: Redefining Biblical Theology* (Grand Rapids: Eerdmans, 1997).

26. Watson, *Text and Truth*, 14.

27. Ibid., vii.

28. I use the term "postmodern" with the same diffidence as my earlier uses of "premodern" and "modern"; see nn. 14, 20.

29. Notice that the formidable final section of Watson, *Truth and Text*, 305–25, is headed, "Scripture in Dialogue: A Study in Early Christian Old Testament Interpretation."

30. In each case, one may move from the huge theological claim to a comment on the peculiar character of scripture. See Karl Barth, "The Strange New World within the Bible," in *The Word of God and the Word of Man*, trans. Douglas Horton (New York: Harper & Brothers, 1957 [1928]), 28–50; Martin Buber, "The Man of Today and the Jewish Bible," in *On the Bible: Eighteen Studies*, ed. Nahum N. Glatzer (New York: Schocken, 1968), 1–13. On these, see Walter Brueggemann, "Biblical Authority in the Post-Critical Period," in *The Anchor Bible Dictionary, Vol. 5, O–Sh*, ed. David Noel Freedman (New York: Doubleday, 1992), 1049–56; reprinted in this volume as chapter 1. In the magisterial study of Emmanuel Levinas, *Totality and Infinity: An Essay on Exteriority*, trans. Alphonso Lingis (Pittsburgh: Duquesne University Press, 1969), the linkage to the Bible is not as direct

and explicit, except that the principle of *alterity* is completely defining and certainly includes the unfamiliarity of the founding texts of Judaism.

31. Wesley A. Kort, *"Take, Read": Scripture, Textuality, and Cultural Practice* (University Park: Pennsylvania State University Press, 1996).

32. Ibid., 5.

33. Ibid., 28.

34. Ibid., 28–29.

35. John Calvin, *Institutes of the Christian Religion*, I.7.1, Library of Christian Classics 20 (Philadelphia: Westminster, 1960), 75.

36. Ibid., 74.

37. Kort, *"Take, Read,"* considers the strange, deconstructive voice of scripture under two modern rubrics: (1) chapter 2, "Modernity: Reading Other Texts as though They, and Not the Bible, Were Scripture" (Locke, Bacon, Paine "on nature"); (2) chapter 3, "Postmodernity: Not Reading Anything at All as though It Were Scripture" (Nietzsche, Fish).

38. Kort, *"Take, Read,"* 128. What Kort says here of the Bible is surely true of all great literature. It is surely the case of the Bible *versus scripture.*

39. Thomas Bridges, *The Culture of Citizenship: Inventing Post-modern Civic Culture* (Albany: SUNY Press, 1994), 121 and passim, suggests that even such a convinced modernist as John Rawls has found it necessary and compelling to move from "a hard metaphysical 'is'" to a "soft metaphorical 'is,'" perhaps a move not so remote from the *sicut* of John Calvin.

9. Biblical Theology Appropriately Postmodern

1. Horst Dietrich Preuss, *Old Testament Theology*, 2 vols., OTL (Louisville: Westminster John Knox, 1995, 1996), 1:1.

2. See my discussion of the problems and possibilities of a new interpretive context, *Texts under Negotiation: The Bible and Postmodern Imagination* (Minneapolis: Fortress Press, 1993).

3. Jon D. Levenson, "Theological Consensus or Historicist Evasion? Jews and Christians in Biblical Studies," in Roger Brooks and John J. Collins, eds., *Hebrew Bible or Old Testament? Studying the Bible in Judaism and Christianity*, Christianity and Judaism in Antiquity 5 (Notre Dame, Ind.: University of Notre Dame Press, 1990), 109–45.

4. See my comments in a review of Carl E. Braaten and Robert W. Jenson, eds., *Reclaiming the Bible for the Church* (Grand Rapids: Eerdmans, 1995), in *ThTo* 53 (1996): 349–53.

5. Jon D. Levenson, "Why Jews Are Not Interested in Biblical Theology," in *The Hebrew Bible, the Old Testament, and Historical Criticism:*

Jews and Christians in Biblical Studies (Louisville: Westminster John Knox, 1993), 33–61.

6. M. H. Goshen-Gottstein, "Tanakh Theology: The Religion of the Old Testament and the Place of Jewish Biblical Theology," in Patrick D. Miller Jr., Paul D. Hanson, and S. Dean McBride Jr., eds., *Ancient Israelite Religion: Essays in Honor of Frank Moore Cross* (Philadelphia: Fortress Press, 1987), 617–44.

7. Levenson's writings are impressive examples of biblical theology, albeit not in the conventional categories of the conventional Christian discipline. See *Sinai and Zion: An Entry into the Jewish Bible* (New York: Winston, 1985); *Creation and the Persistence of Evil: The Jewish Drama of Divine Omnipotence* (San Francisco: HarperCollins, 1988); and *The Death and Resurrection of the Beloved Son: The Transformation of Child Sacrifice in Judaism and Christianity* (New Haven: Yale University Press, 1993).

8. See Mark Coleridge, "Life in the Crypt, or Why Bother with Biblical Studies," *BibInt* 2 (1994): 139–51.

9. Leo G. Perdue, *The Collapse of History: Reconstructing Old Testament Theology*, Overtures to Biblical Theology (Minneapolis: Fortress Press, 1994).

10. On the decisive role of memory in a Jewish notion of history, see Yosef Hayim Yerushalmi, *Zakhor: Jewish History and Jewish Memory* (Seattle: University of Washington Press, 1982).

11. Jon D. Levenson, "The Eighth Principle of Judaism and the Literary Simultaneity of Scripture," in *The Hebrew Bible, the Old Testament, and Historical Criticism*, 62–81, has presented a study of Jewish modes of thematization that is closely paralleled to what Brevard Childs terms a "canonical" perspective.

12. David R. Blumenthal, *Facing the Abusing God: A Theology of Protest* (Louisville: Westminster John Knox, 1993), has most unambiguously offered an example of reading *seriatim,* an approach at the greatest remove from any "canonical" reading.

13. Gerhard von Rad, *Wisdom in Israel* (Nashville: Abingdon, 1972).

14. Walter Brueggemann, *Theology of the Old Testament: Testimony, Dispute, Advocacy* (Minneapolis: Fortress Press, 1997).

15. To speak of "interaction and dialogue," of course, is not far removed from classic notions of covenant, except that my terms mean to suggest a much more open and less structured I-Thou relation that is filled not only

with attentiveness of each partner to the other but also with abrasion and disjunction.

16. For a fine theological summary of the significance of covenant, see Ernest W. Nicholson, *God and His People: Covenant and Theology in the Old Testament* (Oxford: Clarendon, 1986).

17. On the cruciality of the Noah covenant for biblical theology, see Patrick D. Miller, "Creation and Covenant," in Steven J. Kraftchick et al., eds., *Biblical Theology: Problems and Perspectives: In Honor of J. Christiaan Beker* (Nashville: Abingdon, 1995), 155–68.

18. On doxology as data for biblical theology, see Walter Brueggemann, "Praise and the Psalms: A Politics of Glad Abandonment," in *The Psalms and the Life of Faith*, ed. Patrick D. Miller (Minneapolis: Fortress, 1995), 112–32.

19. On the judgment of Derrida, see John D. Caputo, *Demythologizing Heidegger*, Indiana Series in the Philosophy of Religion (Bloomington: Indiana University Press, 1993), 201–2.

20. See the discerning study of Patrick D. Miller, *They Cried to the Lord: The Form and Theology of Biblical Prayer* (Minneapolis: Fortress Press, 1994).

21. See Walter Brueggemann, "The Crisis and Promise of Presence in Israel," *HBT* 1 (1979): 47–86; reprinted in Brueggemann, *Old Testament Theology: Essays on Structure, Theme, and Text*, ed. Patrick D. Miller (Minneapolis: Fortress Press, 1992), 150–82; and Tryggve N. D. Mettinger, *The Dethronement of Sabbaoth: Studies in the Shem and Kabod Theologies*, ConBOT 18 (Lund: Gleerup, 1982).

22. Eberhard Jüngel, *God as the Mystery of the World: On The Foundation of the Crucified in the Dispute between Theism and Atheism* (Grand Rapids: Eerdmans, 1983).

23. Samuel Terrien, *The Elusive Presence: Toward a New Biblical Theology* (San Francisco: Harper & Row, 1978), 1.

24. On the verse, see Jack Miles, *God: A Biography* (New York: Knopf, 1995), 425 n. 324.

25. On the linkage of the Shoah and modernity, see Zygmunt Bauman, *Modernity and the Holocaust* (Ithaca, N.Y.: Cornell University Press, 1989).

26. On this dialectic in the character of God, see Blumenthal, *Facing the Abusing God.*

27. See the important study of R. Kendall Soulen, *The God of Israel and Christian Theology* (Minneapolis: Fortress Press, 1996).

28. See Brevard S. Childs, *Biblical Theology of the Old and New Testaments: Theological Reflection on the Christian Bible* (Minneapolis: Fortress Press, 1993), 25–26. See Levenson, "The Eighth Principle," 80 and passim, from where I understand him to be in essential agreement with Childs.

29. Quoted without citation by Elie Wiesel, *Memoirs: All Rivers Run to the Sea* (New York: Knopf, 1995), 354–55.

30. George Steiner, *Real Presences* (Chicago: University of Chicago Press, 1989), 231–32. The Friday-Saturday-Sunday sequence is decisive for the theology of Hans Urs von Balthasar, *Mysterium Paschale: The Mystery of Easter* (Edinburgh: T. & T. Clark, 1990). Von Balthasar characterizes the three days as (1) "Going to the Cross," (2) "Going to the Dead," and (3) "Going to the Father."

10. Theology of the Old Testament: A Prompt Retrospect

1. Gerhard von Rad, *Old Testament Theology*, 2 vols., trans. D. M. G. Stalker (New York: Harper & Brothers, 1962, 1965), 1:108.

2. Ibid., 1:302.

3. See Walter Brueggemann, *Abiding Astonishment: Psalms, Modernity, and the Making of History*, Literary Currents in Biblical Interpretation (Louisville: Westminster John Knox, 1991).

4. On the production of worlds, see Peter L. Berger and Thomas Luckman, *The Social Construction of Reality: A Treatise in the Sociology of Knowledge* (Garden City, N.Y.: Doubleday, 1967); and Amos N. Wilder, "Story and Story-World," *Int* 37 (1983): 353–64. More directly pertinent for us, see Wesley A. Kort, *"Take, Read": Scripture, Textuality, and Cultural Practice* (University Park: Pennsylvania State University Press, 1996), 9 and passim.

5. On the remarkable emergence of such interactionism in the twentieth century as a theological and philosophical perspective, see Hans Urs von Balthasar, *Theo-Drama: Theological Dramatic Theory*, 5 vols., trans. Graham Harrison (San Francisco: Ignatius, 1988), 1:626.

6. See the comprehensive perspective on "testimony" by Paul Ricoeur, *Essays on Biblical Interpretation*, ed. Lewis S. Mudge (Philadelphia: Fortress Press, 1980), 119–54.

7. See Claus Westermann, *Basic Forms of Prophetic Speech*, trans. Hugh Clayton White (Philadelphia: Westminster, 1967).

8. Emil Fackenheim, *To Mend the World: Foundations of Post-Holocaust Thought* (New York: Schocken, 1989), 11, refers to the Holocaust as "the most radical countertestimony to both Judaism and Christianity."

9. I refer to von Rad's rubric, "Israel before Jahweh (Israel's Answer)," as his title for the discussion of the wisdom traditions (*Old Testament Theology*, 1:355).

10. Jacques Derrida, "Force of Law: The 'Mystical Foundations of Authority,'" *Cardozo Law Review* 11 (July/August 1990): 945, has famously averred, "Justice in itself, if such a thing exists, outside or beyond the law, is not deconstructible. No more than deconstruction, if such a thing exists. Deconstruction is justice." Such a verdict seems to me to be quintessentially Jewish in its claim.

11. Rudolf Bultmann, "Prophecy and Fulfillment," in Claus Westermann, ed., *Essays on Old Testament Hermeneutics* (Richmond: John Knox, 1963), 75, has devastatingly expressed triumphalist Christian interpretation: "in the same way faith requires the backward glance into Old Testament history as a history of failure and so of promise, in order to know that the situation of the justified man arises only on the basis of this miscarriage."

12. On the prospect of role reversal, see Walter Brueggemann, "Prerequisites for Genuine Obedience (Theses and Conclusion)," *CTJ* 6, no. 1 (April 2001): 34–41.

13. It is important to recognize that the entire interpretive trajectory from Buber, given new voice by Levinas, is designed precisely to counter the Cartesian claim of autonomy. It is important that this counteroffer is *Jewish*, but it is equally important that it is a *public* claim not addressed simply to Jewish faith.

14. See the brief expression by John E. Thiel, *Nonfoundationalism*, Guides to Theological Inquiry (Minneapolis: Fortress Press, 1991).

15. This claim in the twentieth century was especially voiced by Karl Barth, "The Strange New World within the Bible," in *The Word of God and the Word of Man*, trans. Douglas Horton (New York: Harper & Brothers, 1957 [1928]), 28–50. See also Martin Buber, "The Man of Today and the Jewish Bible," in *On the Bible: Eighteen Studies*, ed. Nahum N. Glatzer (New York: Schocken, 1968), 1–13.

16. The phrase is from James C. Scott, *Weapons of the Weak: Everyday Forms of Peasant Resistance* (New Haven: Yale University Press, 1985).

17. See the analysis of R. Kendall Soulen, *The God of Israel and Christian Theology* (Minneapolis: Fortress Press, 1996).

18. This perspective has been powerfully advocated by Francis Watson, *Text, Church and World: Biblical Interpretation in Theological Perspective* (Grand Rapids: Eerdmans, 1994); and *Text and Truth: Redefining Biblical Theology* (Grand Rapids: Eerdmans, 1997).

19. See Jon D. Levenson, *The Hebrew Bible, the Old Testament, and Historical Criticism: Jews and Christians in Biblical Studies* (Louisville: Westminster John Knox, 1993), 76–81.

20. N. T. Wright, *The New Testament and the People of God*, Christian Origins and the Question of God 1 (Minneapolis: Fortress Press, 1992); and *Jesus and the Victory of God*, Christian Origins and the Question of God 2 (Minneapolis: Fortress Press, 1996). In a very different way and from a Jewish perspective, Jon D. Levenson, "The Universal Horizon of Biblical Particularism," in Mark G. Brett, ed., *Ethnicity and the Bible* (Leiden: Brill, 1996), 143–69, has offered a fresh scenario of the extent to which Jews and Christians may read together in a way that is seriously theological.

21. From this perspective, see also Peter Stuhlmacher, *How to Do Biblical Theology*, PTMS 38 (Allison Park, Pa.: Pickwick, 1995).

22. The issues are summarized in a quite conventional way by A. H. J. Gunneweg, *Understanding the Old Testament*, trans. John Bowden, OTL (Philadelphia: Westminster, 1978).

23. I take this, in a different voice, to be the point of William Stacy Johnson, *The Mystery of God: Karl Barth and the Postmodern Foundations of Theology* (Louisville: Westminster John Knox, 1997), an insistence that in Barth God's mystery is not finally reduced to theological control.

24. Brevard S. Childs, *Biblical Theology of the Old and New Testaments: Theological Reflection on the Christian Bible* (Minneapolis: Fortress Press, 1993), 67 and passim. A closely parallel argument is made by Stuhlmacher, *How to Do Biblical Theology*, 61 and passim.

25. Carl E. Braaten and Robert W. Jenson, eds., *Reclaiming the Bible for the Church* (Grand Rapids: Eerdmans, 1995).

26. Kort, *"Take, Read,"* 25–36 and passim.

27. Ibid., 124, 128.

28. Walter Brueggemann, *Theology of the Old Testament: Testimony, Dispute, and Advocacy* (Minneapolis: Fortress Press, 1997), 400–403.

29. George Steiner, *Real Presences* (Chicago: University of Chicago Press, 1989), 232.

11. Israel's Creation Faith: Response to J. Richard Middleton

1. J. Richard Middleton, "Is Creation Theology Inherently Conservative? A Dialogue with Walter Brueggemann," *HTR* 87 [1994]: 257–77.

2. Walter Brueggemann, *Israel's Praise: Doxology against Idolatry and Ideology* (Philadelphia: Fortress Press, 1988); *In Man We Trust: The Neglected Side of Biblical Faith* (Philadelphia: Westminster, 1983).

3. This theme runs through Ricoeur's work. See, for example, Paul Ricoeur, "The Model of the Text: Meaningful Action Considered as a Text," in *From Text to Action: Essays in Hermeneutics II*, trans. Kathleen Blaney and John B. Thompson (Evanston, Ill.: Northwestern University Press, 1991), 144–67.

4. Harvey Cox, *The Secular City: Secularization and Urbanization in Theological Perspective* (New York: Macmillan, 1990).

5. It is a great merit of Eberhard Busch, *Karl Barth: His Life from Letters and Autobiographical Texts*, trans. John Bowden (Philadelphia: Fortress Press, 1976), 212–14, 362–64, 392–95, and passim, that he reminds us and helps us to see how Barth's volumes were intensely contextual.

6. I refer especially to the work of Jacques Ellul, *The Technological Society*, trans. J. Wilkinson (New York: Random House, 1967), some of whose primary critiques have not been effectively answered. There is no doubt that Ellul is influential in my perception of our interpretive situation.

7. See the critique of this claim of distinctiveness by Thomas L. Thompson, *Early History of the Israelite People from the Written and Archaeological Sources* (Leiden: Brill, 1992), 27–34. Thompson's work critiques the program announced by Albrecht Alt, "The Origins of Israelite Law," in *Essays on Old Testament History and Religion*, trans. R. A. Wilson (Oxford: Blackwell, 1966), 79–132; Gerhard von Rad, "The Form-Critical Problem of the Hexateuch," in *The Problem of the Hexateuch and Other Essays* (New York: McGraw-Hill, 1966), 1–78; and G. Ernest Wright, *The Old Testament against Its Environment*, SBT 2 (London: SCM, 1950). The program of "distinctiveness" critiqued by Thompson insisted that in every way, but especially in confessional and ethical matters, Israel was in profound tension with "Canaanite" religion and culture.

8. Eric Voegelin, *Order and History, Volume 1: Israel and Revelation*, Collected Works of Eric Voegelin, vol. 14, ed. Maurice P. Hogan (Baton Rouge: Louisiana State University Press, 1956).

9. Gerhard von Rad, *Wisdom in Israel* (Nashville: Abingdon, 1972).

10. H. Martin Rumscheidt, *Revelation and Theology: An Analysis of the Barth-Harnack Correspondence of 1923* (Cambridge: Cambridge University Press, 1972), has carefully reviewed and documented the formation and significance of Barth's thought on this defining antithesis.

11. James Barr, *Biblical Faith and Natural Theology: The Gifford Lectures for 1991* (Oxford: Clarendon, 1993), offers a sustained critique of Barth's program. See especially pp. 111–17, on Barth's judgment concerning the gospel and National Socialism.

12. Some redress of the accent on distinctiveness, of course, has been to stress the commonalities Israel shared with ancient Near Eastern religion more generally. Norman K. Gottwald, *The Tribes of Yahweh: A Sociology of the Religion of Liberated Israel, 1250–1050 B.C.E.* (Maryknoll, N.Y.: Orbis, 1979), 667–91, has nicely organized the issue around the theme of "common" theology and "mutation." I believe that the accent on the common or the mutation is largely an interpretive judgment according to the predilection of the scholar. See also Patrick D. Miller, "Israelite Religion," in Douglas A. Knight and Gene M. Tucker, eds., *The Hebrew Bible and Its Modern Interpreters* (Philadelphia: Fortress Press, 1985), 201–37.

13. Walter Brueggemann, "Psalm 37: Conflict of Interpretation," in Heather A. McKay and David J. A. Clines, eds., *Of Prophets' Visions and the Wisdom of Sage: Essays in Honour of R. Norman Whybray on His Seventieth Birthday,* JSOTSup 162 (Sheffield: JSOT Press, 1993), 229–56; reprinted in Brueggemann, *The Psalms and the Life of Faith*, ed. Patrick D. Miller (Minneapolis: Fortress Press, 1995), 235–57.

14. See my discussion in "The Uninflected 'Therefore' of Hosea 4:1-3," in Fernando F. Segovia and Mary Ann Tolbert, eds., *Reading from This Place, Volume 1: Social Location and Biblical Interpretation in the United States* (Minneapolis: Fortress Press, 1995), 231–49.

15. Bernhard W. Anderson, ed., *Creation in the Old Testament*, Issues in Religion and Theology 6 (Philadelphia: Fortress Press, 1984); Anderson, *Creation versus Chaos: The Reinterpretation of Mythical Symbolism in the Bible* (Philadelphia: Fortress Press, 1987 [1967]); James Barr, *Biblical Faith and Natural Theology: The Gifford Lectures for 1991* (Oxford: Clarendon, 1993); James L. Crenshaw, *Old Testament Wisdom: An Introduction* (Atlanta: John Knox, 1981), and his earlier works, which he lists on p. 265; Terence E. Fretheim, *Exodus*, IBC (Louisville: Westminster John Knox, 1991); Fretheim, "The Plagues as Ecological Signs of Historical Disaster," *JBL* 110 (1991): 385–96; Rolf P. Knierim, "On the Task of Old Testament Theology," *HBT* 6 (1984): 91–128; Jon D. Levenson, *Creation and the Persistence of Evil: The Jewish Drama of Divine Omnipotence* (San Francisco: HarperCollins, 1988); Hans Heinrich Schmid, "Creation, Righteousness, and Salvation: 'Creation Theology' as the Broad Horizon of Biblical Theology," in Anderson, *Creation in the Old Testament*, 102–17; Schmid, *Gerechtigkeit als Weltordnung*, BHTh 40 (Tübingen: Mohr/Siebeck, 1968). An important exception to the scholarly momentum toward creation is Horst Dietrich Preuss, *Theologie des Alten Testaments 1: JHWHs erwählendes und*

verpflichtendes Handeln (Stuttgart: Kohlhammer, 1991), 259–74. Preuss continues to hold to the older position of von Rad that the core of Israel's faith is in the "historical traditions" and that "creation faith" is at the edge of Israel's confession.

16. See Middleton, "Is Creation Theology Inherently Conservative?" 271–74.

17. See Jon D. Levenson, "Why Jews Are Not Interested in Biblical Theology," in *The Hebrew Bible, the Old Testament, and Historical Criticism: Jews and Christians in Biblical Studies* (Louisville: Westminster John Knox, 1993), 33–61.

18. Brevard S. Childs, *Biblical Theology of the Old and New Testaments: Theological Reflection on the Christian Bible* (Minneapolis: Fortress Press, 1993).

19. Knierim, "On the Task of Old Testament Theology," 91–128.

20. Both Knierim (ibid.) and Schmid ("Creation, Righteousness, and Salvation," 102–17) use the term "horizon."

21. On Karl Barth, see Rumscheidt, *Revelation and Theology*; on von Rad, see n. 7 above.

22. See, for example, Jürgen Moltmann, *God in Creation: A New Theology of Creation and the Spirit of God* (Minneapolis: Fortress Press, 1993 [1985]).

23. See Schmid's accent on *Ordnung* ("Creation, Righteousness, and Salvation," 102–17). Schmid understands "creation" as having an "order" (ordering) decreed and guaranteed by God the creator. That "order" is not readily visible and is elusive, with a moral dimension. The divine ordering of creation is generative of blessing, but cannot be violated with impunity.

24. One's stance regarding commonality or distinctiveness matters enormously. An assumption of commonality or distinctiveness will generate very different interpretive methods and outcomes, so that the stance matters to one's entire enterprise as an interpreter. The issue of commonality/distinctiveness can be transposed into one of "universalism" and "particularism." On the modernist temptation to universalism, see Stephen Toulmin, *Cosmopolis: The Hidden Agenda of Modernity* (New York: Free Press, 1990).

25. For example, Fretheim (*Exodus*, 18–20) suggests that liberation in itself is not the primary point of the exodus narrative. See Walter Brueggemann, "Pharaoh as Vassal: A Study of a Political Metaphor," *CBQ* 57 (1995): 27–51, for a reflection on exodus and liberation.

26. I have no hard data, but I have come to believe that scholarly efforts do indeed reflect personal issues. Thus, for example, I believe that many scholars who engage in deconstruction of Israel's faith in the Hebrew Bible are in fact dealing with unresolved issues of a fundamentalist nature. I have already indicated how I believe a comparable matter operates in my work.

27. Terence E. Fretheim, "Book Notes," *ThTo* 45 (1989): 506.

28. See Middleton, "Is Creation Theology Inherently Conservative?" 277.

29. Ben C. Ollenburger, *Zion the City of the Great King: A Theological Symbol of the Jerusalem Cult*, JSOTSup 41 (Sheffield: JSOT Press, 1987), 161–62.

30. The rhetoric whereby Ollenburger makes "history" and "nature" points to be critiqued and "creation" the promissory note is not adequate, because what is claimed for "nature" can be—and has been—claimed for "creation." I like Ollenburger's relation of *"our vision of what is possible"* with creation. I believe, however, that Karl Barth (*Church Dogmatics* I/2.13, *The Doctrine of the Word of God* [Edinburgh: T. & T. Clark, 1956], 1–44) has more precisely correlated the "possible" and the "real" by referring to God as the "real." Thus Ollenburger might better contrast the *possible* and *God the creator*.

31. George Landes, "Creation and Liberation," in Anderson, *Creation in the Old Testament*, 143. The article was originally printed in *USQR* 33 (1978): 79–89.

32. See Middleton, "Is Creation Theology Inherently Conservative?" 276 n. 75.

33. Gerhard von Rad, *Old Testament Theology*, 2 vols., trans. D. M. G. Stalker (New York: Harper & Brothers, 1962, 1965), 1:136–39.

34. Schmid, *Gerechtigkeit als Weltordnung*, passim.

12. Against the Stream: Brevard Childs's Biblical Theology

1. Brevard S. Childs, *Biblical Theology of the Old and New Testaments: Theological Reflection on the Christian Bible* (Minneapolis: Fortress Press, 1993).

13. Walter Brueggemann's *Theology of the Old Testament: Testimony, Dispute, Advocacy*: A Review by Brevard Childs and a Response

1. Walter Brueggemann, *Theology of the Old Testament: Testimony, Dispute, Advocacy* (Minneapolis: Fortress Press, 1997).

2. Ibid., 711.

3. Hans Jonas, *The Gnostic Religion: The Message of the Alien God and the Beginnings of Christianity* (Boston: Houghton Mifflin, 1958), 141–43.

4. Cf. B. Hägglund, "Die Bedeutung der 'regula fidei' als Grundlage theologischer Aussagen," *StTh* 11 (1957): 1–44; Dietmar Wyrwa, "Regula fidei," in *EKL* 3:1524ff.

Index of Names

Index of Biblical References